RiDiNG THE MAGiC CARPET

a surfer's odyssey to find the perfect wave

tom anderson

summersdale

Summersdale Publishers Ltd
46 West Street
Chichester
West Sussex
PO19 1RP
UK

www.summersdale.com

Printed and bound in Great Britain

ISBN: 1-84024-502-6
ISBN 13: 978-1-84024-502-8

Maps by Breige Lawrence

Back cover photos by:

Alex Lewis
www.taith.com

Peter Britton
www.peterbrittonphotography.co.uk

Peter Price
A-Frame Photography

Translation of extract from Wang Wei's 'My Retreat at Mount Zhongnan' by Jonathan Clements

Contents

For Rob Middlehurst, Meic Stephens and Breige

'And should I meet an old man in the woods
We'd talk and laugh, and think not of going home'

Wang Wei, 'My Retreat at Mount Zhongnan'

'If they but knew it, almost all men in their degree, some time or other,
cherish very nearly the same feelings towards the ocean with me'

Herman Melville, *Moby-Dick*

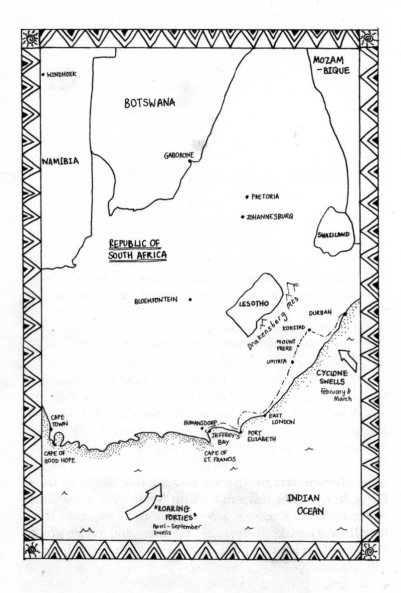

1.
Taking Off

A re we in Durban or Alcatraz, man?' asked the Kiwi standing next to me. 'Look at this place! What are we doing?'

'It's the beginning of something.'

'It's a prison, man.'

'No, it's a start.'

Although there were still over a thousand kilometres left to travel, J-Bay already felt close. Nine thousand down, one thousand to go. But before that, two crucial months of 'preparation' on the Golden Mile of Durban beach breaks that starts at South Beach and continues to the Snake Park. Here was where it would begin; 'Alcatraz', or was it some characterless backpacker hostel a few blocks in from Dairy Beach? You just can't tell in South Africa, the land of the reinforced door, window, gate, car – whatever it is, they'll easily make it burglar-, hijacker- and rapist-proof. Functional perhaps, but none too settling when you have to negotiate two perimeter fences just to arrive at the reception of the first place you plan to stay for the night. Were those the demented drawings of a 'lifer' surrounding the window bars above the pool table and being trespassed upon by an unfriendly cockroach? No, it was simply the usual cartoon drawings of 'The Big Five' that signalled one's arrival in the fragmented reality of the southern African backpacker circuit. Either way, it was only a start, and, I was hoping, a brief one at that. It was time to go for a walk, find the waves – oh, and an apartment too.

The Kiwi standing at the counter of 'Banana Backpackers' with me was Adam. Another fresh arrival in Durban and, given the accent and tightly clutched boardbag, proof I was in the right building. The main difference between us, though, was that Adam had already been to J-Bay. His attempt to surf the world's best right-hand point had already failed. He'd hired a car, driven up from Cape Town, missed the season, missed any rare off-season action too, missed the essence of J-Bay, and now he was counting out the last weeks until his flight back to 'home' and 'work' (words of serious consequence, judging from the way he mimed the inverted commas with his fingers).

'J-Bay was nothing like what I'd expected, man,' he rued. 'It was sunny, dead flat, boring. I was sitting there going, *Where the fuck does it break, man? I can't even tell. The point doesn't look very long, does it? Are you sure this is J-Bay?* But it was, and there was nothing I could do about it, man. I was sitting there, praying. Praying for a freak swell. But with all that calm, I just knew it was never gonna happen. Gutted. I'm spewing, man.'

Sunny, calm and flat? Not the J-Bay I'd read about, heard about, and hoped to find. The J-Bay I wanted to experience was a place where harsh elements combined to make one of the most spectacular forces of nature a surfer could ever dream of seeing in person. Jeffrey's Bay: the fantasy. The myth. The legend. The history.

Adam continued. 'I'm coming back, though. I'm gonna do it right – get the season, man. Like you are now. You bastard. Where are you from anyway? As long as you don't run out of money, or get killed, you're *definitely*, *one hundred per cent* gonna have surfed J-Bay by the time you leave. It kicks off around April, man. You bastard! Any natural-foot who doesn't dream of surfing there must be a sissy. Or at least in need of having his head seriously read, man.'

Phew! That meant I was free from the need for any appointments with a shrink for the time being. Yes, indeed; what natural-foot serious about surf travel wouldn't dream of making a pilgrimage to that little stretch of coastline just beyond Humansdorp? This trip for me had begun over ten years ago, with a decision. A promise. An *oath*. Thou shalt surf J-Bay once thou hast grown old enough to travel there and once thou surfest good enough to make it count. And how best to make it count? By going there early in the season, before the hungry masses, before the Association of Surfing Professionals brought its circus into town for June's Billabong Pro, and, most importantly of all, *not* after a winter of eating fish 'n' chips and drinking heavy beer back in Wales. So this was the start. The start of a meticulous plan. Two months in Durban training, then the final journey. This was going to be done properly.

'All I've got to look forward to is a fucken stint in this Alcatraz shit-hole,' my new acquaintance went on. 'Oh well, at least we might get some swell. Hey man, have you heard what Durban gets like in cyclone season? Fuck man, let's go check it. I think the breaks are down that road, that way. You up for it? Mind you, it's meant to be flat at the moment. Nothing out there. Worth looking, though, just in case…' Adam paused for a second, completing a thought pattern before making up his mind: 'Aw, fuck it. Come on then, man. Let's go and check the surf.' He seemed a highly-strung character, but at least he was keen to get in the water.

The Golden Mile was indeed about three blocks away, as the frantic New Zealander had predicted, although those three blocks hardly contained the kind of Manhattan-esque splendour that the term 'Golden Mile' may have implied. First impressions were of a grubby city, filled with old, poorly maintained buildings and a spirit-crushing humidity that was as far removed from beach life as you could ever hope to imagine. Faces showed the air of economic depression, as the once mighty South African rand dropped more and more in value. Fast-food buildings, shops and offices derelict, as if the heat had evaporated the finances and the tramps driven out all the businessmen. Compared to the bumper-to-bumper traffic of most major cities, the roads were depressingly quiet. The bubble had burst for this once wealthy port town, as was the case for most other post-European-colonisation ventures – a bully that had lost its clout.

The depression gave way, though, as we arrived at the beachfront and that familiar breeze kicked in – the beaches were the city's main hope for a brighter future. *More like it*, I thought. It looked little more than your average stretch of Indian Ocean-facing beach. Three piers, one jetty and a fifth groyne of rotten wooden pilings. But looks can be deceiving. This particular stretch is home to some of the most high-performance surfing on earth. Few spots are surfed as efficiently on a day-to-day basis as the peaks at Durban's New Pier and North Beach. Good surfing is in the air, the water, the food. You cannot avoid catching the virus. If they weren't so unfairly disadvantaged by the fiendishly low value of the rand, a fair proportion of these guys would probably be pro surfers, known well beyond the confines of this one province. And why not? It has the perfect incubation conditions for surf talent. A stifling city on the beach, warm water, consistent surf of all varieties – big and small, messy and clean. Add to that the crowded, competitive line-ups, right in the heart of a nation that lives for sport, and it's easy to see why Natal surfing is so revered.

'What a load of shit that looks like,' said Adam surveying the small peak inside of New Pier, known as the 'Dairy Bowl' to the schoolkids who were quietly using it to turn themselves into some of the hottest surfers on the planet. It was breaking at about waist-height, and trickling along a sandbar that was absolutely crammed with jostling surfers. 'I'd heard it's been flat for a while,' he went on. 'What a bummer.'

If you want to see flat, come and see South Wales in summer, I felt like saying, but kept schtum.

We watched it for about ten minutes. There weren't huge numbers of waves coming through, but the odd one looked rideable. Adam was unimpressed. Then a slightly bigger set came through, each wave being picked off and torn to shreds by youngsters in peak condition. 'This'll do fine,' I mumbled to myself. 'Just fine.'

★ ★ ★

The right-hand point at Jeffrey's Bay, about an hour south of Port Elizabeth on South Africa's east coast, is one of the surfing world's most exciting finds, and from about the age of twelve it had been my life's purpose to one day surf there.

I'd had a surf-free first decade on this planet, doing just what most other Welsh kids do at that age; following an often hopeless (but occasionally brilliant) national rugby team and a better English football club. Even then my desire to do something just that bit different from the others was emerging – not necessarily the best of ideas when you go to a private school that is located, believe it or not, directly in the rough epicentre of Ely, Cardiff; a place where a low profile is key to survival – especially if you're one of the kids from the 'posh' school. Everyone in my class would wear either a Manchester United or Liverpool shirt on the charity non-uniform days, while I'd turn up dressed either in a shameful Watford strip (my birthplace, alas), a rebellious Arsenal one, or that of some obscure country like Uruguay, or, in *soccer* terms at least, the USA. Naturally, it all led to some severe piss-taking from my classmates – until the day I wore an Ocean Pacific surf T-shirt.

Surfing, I suddenly realised, could be a way out of being crap at football, and from supporting odd teams. Sod *following* the football and rugby crowd, I realised. It was time to become the first surfer in the class.

To be perfectly honest, the main reason for starting was because I figured my chances of being good at it were higher than in any other sport. The logic behind this was simple: my father had been a top competitive surfer in his day, and he too was crap at football – so genetically the odds were in my favour. Unlike a lot of people who claim to remember their first ride as a key moment in their life, I don't. I just remember following the old man down the walkway to the nearest beach in Ogmore-by-Sea time after time, until one day it was proclaimed that I could surf. Being still a child and able to ride waves automatically made you fairly good then, by Welsh standards at least. Back then there were about ten kids my age on the whole coast who stand-up surfed. I later came fifth out of five in the under-14 division of my first National Championships.

As time went on the 'sport' grew, and after I incurred a harsh and seemingly motiveless kicking walking from school to the bus-stop one day, my family decided it was time for a change. A decision was made to move closer to the beach, and I was duly enrolled in a new middle-class state school, Porthcawl Comprehensive. Here I was no longer the only one to 'have the surfing bug', although most of the others my age practised what we 'stand-ups' believed to be the lesser art of bodyboarding.

So I wasn't unique any more, but by then the bug had taken a firm hold, and other ambitions were setting in. News was filtering slowly into the marine-minded town of Porthcawl of two major events, interlinked: for years apartheid had led the sporting world to boycott South Africa; something most high-profile surfers had also observed. However, when on the night of 2 February 1990 it was announced on the *Nine O'Clock News* that the South African President, F. W. de Klerk, had unveiled his plans to dismantle the regime, it became 'open season' on the biggest find in the history of surf travel. Just over a week later Nelson Mandela walked free from prison, and word was out that Tom Curren was going to Jeffrey's Bay. Tom Curren was *the* surfer of the time. The artistic but highly competitive son of the charismatic Pat Curren, who hailed from the perfect Californian point breaks at Santa Barbara, was in the process of winning three world titles and changing the way people rode waves forever.

I'll never forget sitting there, still only a boy, watching Curren's first ride at J-Bay on the big screen in the function room of a Porthcawl pub. All the best local guys had made it down there that night, to watch the wave of the decade. It'll stay with me forever, seeing some of the top surfers in my area (they surfed as well as I imagined it was ever possible to) just losing it as they watched the first under-the-lip fade, gasping as Curren emerged from tube number two, and then screaming and erupting into applause as he dropped out of sight and into the section they call 'Impossibles'. It was fantasy. As distant a reality as Bollywood stardom must appear to the average Indian citizen. Hard to imagine that this 'wave', this mass of water so suited to surfing, actually existed; that Tom Curren was a real human being who had gone there and taken off on it; that he had been so in tune with the swell that he had ridden it that well on his first attempt. The best surfer of the time had just proven once and for all that South Africa did indeed have the world's most perfect wave.

As of that moment, there wasn't a schoolbook I possessed that was spared a daydream doodle of me surfing at J-Bay. I'd made a promise to myself that night, one that took nigh-on a decade to fulfil, and one that has shaped the life I now lead. *Thou shalt one day go to J-Bay and surf it, and not only that, thou shalt go once thou art good enough and wise enough to really make the most of it and to MAKE IT COUNT.* That was the creed that started my journey to the day when Jeffrey's Bay would line up a trademark 'Roaring Forties' swell in front of my very eyes.

This ambition, rather conveniently, involved doing my best to become both a decent surfer and an experienced traveller, and all of my energies were now focused on realising those goals. As a young child, travel had meant little more to me than nauseating car and plane journeys, but now the combination of changing schools and seeing the Curren film had sent my imagination haywire. It would wind up teachers, perhaps because some of them secretly knew that the obnoxious surfers in their classes were hell-bent on getting more from life than pie-charts and quadratic factorisation were ever likely to give them.

Obviously when you're in your early teens there is only so much travelling you can do, but parents in Porthcawl were usually pretty supportive of surfing. Travelling and staying with family friends, older surfers and the Welsh Junior Team, my friends and I had seen most of the UK's and Europe's surf shores, along with the odd trip further afield, by the time we had to consider our sixth-form options.

Some were using this as a stepping-stone to becoming great competitive surfers, and others just for spontaneous hedonism (which gave way to booze and weed as the later teens set in). For me, though, it was always about progressing to the day when I could travel to Jeffrey's Bay and make a real go of it. I'm not sure what the full set of reasons for this infatuation were – perhaps it was simply an excuse to surf and travel as much as possible, while still having some higher purpose ready for citing if needed. There's also a wanderlust gene in each of my parents. My father left school at sixteen to hitch-hike to Morocco, and used to live in San Francisco; my mother now lives in Toronto; and my first trip abroad was to Brazil at the age of eight to adopt a brother and sister.

No doubt there's an element of all of the above in the decisions I reached as a kid, and later stuck to as a young adult, but perhaps most important of all was the idea of progression. Unlike some other sports where you turn up, play, and either win or lose, surfing is all about progression – a series of personal goals and motives.

Slowly, by way of plenty of learning, a lot of pointless pleasure and the odd hiccup, a life can be forged this way. The one simple truth throughout this life is obvious. After that first ride of Tom Curren at J-Bay was filmed, a whole series of videos called *The Search* came out. One clip in particular will always stay with me. A seventeen-year-old delinquent from eastern Australia sits on a boat somewhere in deepest darkest Indonesia marvelling at the effects that getting chosen for a *Search* film has had on his life.

'What do you think of surfing?' the man behind the camera asks him.

'Pretty good.'

'Where would you be if you didn't surf?'

'Uh, mowing lawns?' You can tell from the tone it's obvious he really means it. This isn't meant to be funny.

'What has surfing taught you?'

'A lot.'

'A lot?'

'Yeah. More than any school ever could.'

Like I said, it's obvious.

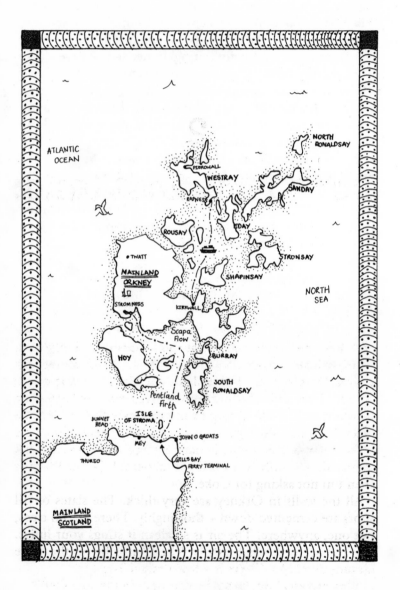

2.

Northern Scotland:

Searching the Stromas

Everyone always says that the Scottish drink like fish. Whisky, whisky, beer, Glenfiddich. What about Jack Daniels? 'Dan Jackiels! It's fur girls, is a soft drink, isn't it?' I like a bit of whisky too. It gives you a lovely feeling of warmth. The blood tingles and the body feels alive. The veins light up. No Jack Daniels, eh? Well, just chuck us a glass of that one there then, mate. Straight, with no ice. That seems like the only way to take it up here. If Jack is for girls then I'm not asking for Coke.

All the walls in Orkney are very thick. The slates on all roofs are cemented down – thoroughly. There are no trees, not one, anywhere. The air is so clean it stings your lungs. You can see orca whales daily. The islands lie on the same latitude as Alaska. There is a town called Twatt.

'Why are you boys trying to surf here in Orkney then?'

'Because the north and west coasts of these isles directly face and take the brunt of the furious North Atlantic. This place rivals Hawaii – except for the weather.'

'Oh aye? And what's wrong with our wee weather, my boy?'

We're at a bar, adjacent to which is a warm log-fire, surrounded by wrinkly, red-faced men lovingly caressing their own glasses of straight whisky. This is the only pub on the Isle of Westray, in the outer Orkneys, and I'm talking to the landlord (who seems to have a bit of a tavern-tan himself). At the bar is the policeman (based on the mainland), the postman, the builder and the haulier. These are the only people on the island who aren't either farmers or 'incomers'. It was the only place where we could find an evening meal.

★ ★ ★

The one thing that really stood out when I walked from my warm car towards the entrance of the Central Hotel, Thurso, late one September night about a week before this conversation was how very north we were. You always notice temperatures change on long drives, but never quite as much as when driving from late summertime South Wales to Caithness in just twelve hours.

A friend of mine, Joe, was waiting in the lobby. He was a good guy to go on trips with – always really stoked about everything. Early that morning he had woken me with a text message that read:

GENTLEMEN START YOUR ENGINES.

That was all. Four of us were travelling from different parts of the country, and in one case the globe, to meet up for this expedition (or, as some might call it, *surfari*). We had come to a place that, besides being conveniently close to home, was also one of our planet's genuinely unexplored places (for surfers, that is) – the Orkney Islands. Joe was working in the area for the surf company the Realm; a job that guaranteed great waves across most of Europe and occasionally elsewhere too (it is not difficult to organise corporate hospitality in the surf industry). His main love in life was tube-riding, be it at some of the lesser-known reef breaks of South Wales, the spitting sand pits of France or the tepid kegs of Indonesia.

And then there was Ed and Darrel. Ed had just been looking for waves off the south coast of India and was flying straight from a temperature of thirty degrees into something more like five. This was what Ed did for a living. He explored bizarre surf zones and then wrote articles on what he found for a plethora of magazines that ranged from *Surfer's Journal* to *National Geographic*. Cornish Darrel was more from my mould, taking whatever jobs necessary as and when he had to, but his main purpose was surf trips – that was when he really lived, and when all those long hours behind a bar, a production line or numerous other work stations suddenly made sense. What we had in common: everyone had chosen to live their lives largely around surfing. Joe and Ed were perhaps a little more settled career-wise, but logging as much water-time as anyone, if not more.

'It's good to see you,' Joe told me. 'Last time was in France, eh? At the Glissexpo – bit warmer then!'

'Yeah, can't be helped.' I do actually like the cold – but only when visiting it. Come November, when I know that there's no cheap escape, I usually sink into about four months of depression. Who doesn't? I didn't have to worry about that yet, though. The South would still be holding on to the summer when we got back. We were all looking forward to feeling snug in brand new five-millimetre wetsuits, and surfing some good waves. The cold was going to be a novelty.

'Orkney has to be stinking,' Ed had said when this trip was only in the planning stages a few weeks ago. 'Have you seen where it lies on a map? I've been looking on the Navy charts all summer and while Newquay and Hossegor were dead flat, Orkney was still getting hit by waves of six to eight foot! It gets *so* much swell it's unbelievable. All we need is to find some points or reefs to hold it, and I reckon it'll be easy.' The trip was his brainchild, and its mission simple: find some new waves. He was going to try to make a film this time, and we were essentially just along for the ride.

Wave hunting was something he'd had a fair bit of success with in the past – managing to find waves in places you'd never imagine surfers wanting to go to: Lebanon, Colombia, Pakistan, Yemen, Vietnam – political instability used to be the main factor in determining where to go. 'If it's unsafe, and exposed to swell, then it's probably got good surf,' he'd say. 'And more importantly, because most people don't like getting shot or blown up, any waves you do find will be previously unridden.' Now he had another fetish too: the cold.

'Nobody likes the cold,' was his new belief, 'so therefore any cold place with a big enough wave fetch must have good and, more importantly, *previously unridden* surf.' This trip to the Orkneys was meant to be a little tester before he moved into a new phase in his pursuit. If this one went well then more could follow. Norway, perhaps, or the Faroe Islands. Someone had beaten him to Russia, but he was damned if one of surfing's last uncharted realms – the more frigid waters of this planet – would be pioneered by anyone but himself.

The sensational developments in wetsuit design from recent years had meant that you could now feel comfortable in increasingly hostile temperatures, leading to new visions of just where people might actually be able to surf. Political danger was so last season to Ed now. This was where surf travel was at, as far as he was concerned – North Scotland.

I had lucked into the Orkneys expedition after visiting him in his southern French home a few weeks previously.

In it lay a plethora of maps and globes, doodles and scribbles everywhere, some more meaningful than others. A road trip somewhere new was just what I needed, having had a torrid summer of early exits in contests and very little in the way of good surf. Contest surfing is a nasty experience when things aren't going well. It can send your whole perception of the sport you live for up the creek. You become disillusioned with it all, seeing waves only in terms of what score they may yield from the judges. A good set of swell lines on the horizon becomes just another chance to try and impress. By the time I'd left for my annual late-August trip to France I had begun wondering what my reasons for surfing actually were – which is what made Ed's proposition seem so tempting.

'I'm going to India looking for waves next week, but after that me and Darrell are gonna head over to the Orkneys,' he had said. 'We're gonna take a few days in September, the best month for surf in that area, and go up there. There's fuckin' tons of swell that way all the time, and the jagged coast means we should find somewhere to surf in all conditions. Are you in?'

And that was that. A few weeks later it was on. There we were; sitting around a hotel suite about fifteen miles from John O'Groats twitching at the prospect of what we were about to find after tomorrow's boat ride north. I don't think anyone slept well that night – except the hideously jet-lagged Ed, who was out cold before I arrived and up before the rest of us had even nodded off. The smelly Scottish fry-up we woke to must have been a welcome change from the Indian rice meals he had been living on for the last ten days, causing him to do the unthinkable and eat the black pudding. The rest of us resigned ourselves to the motherly bollocking that all breakfast waitresses in Scotland give you if you leave anything on your plate. 'You dinnae want tae starve, now, do you? Black puddin's smashing. Dog's bollocks for the old constitution!'

'Yep. I'll take your word for it, thanks,' said Joe. 'I'm full, honestly. Now how do we get to the ferry port at Gills Bay? That's where the Orkney shuttle runs from, isn't it?'

The ferry port lay just the other side of Dunnet Head – officially the most northerly part of mainland Britain, as proudly advertised. At the end of the road to Dunnet stands a cliff hundreds of feet high. The lighthouse at the top is frequently bombarded with flying rocks, picked up and tossed by the monstrous swells that this part of the world is often exposed to. Across the water can be seen the Isle of Stroma, and on the distant horizon, the island of Hoy – the southernmost Orkney. 'Stroma' means current (as in deep-water current) in one of the ancient Scottish dialects. Something you always get from the Caithness coast is a feeling of total insignificance against the power of the sea, and the *stromas* were in full force as our ferry fled the tiny Gills Bay terminal, accompanied by a posse of seals and dolphins, and headed for that faint landmass in the back of beyond.

This was it. Thurso was considered the furthest north in the UK where any known bona fide surf spots existed. (The reef there is said to produce one of the best waves on earth when a proper winter storm spins off the Arctic Circle.) Once that ferry took off we had nothing to go by beyond a handful of unreliable tales and a map. Plus a classic little nugget Ed had turned up when researching Scottish surf travel: a crudely typewritten article from a home-pressed 1970s surfer-zine – written, in fact, by some friends of my father – which began as follows:

```
         SCOTTISH SURFARI AND BEER
         SAMPLING EXPEDITION '73
       by Bernard (The Red Baron) Davies

  Someone shouted 'Let's go to Scotland' -
  - - - - the reply was half way between a
```

```
groan and deep laughter, but eventually
we gathered together all the interested
persons, and the necessary green drinking
vouchers prised out of very deep pockets.
Dai Cornelias's father very kindly loaned
us his Transit van and after much buying of
fodder and loading of boards and equipment
we got together one Friday night (after
watching Kung Fu on the tele) and started
on the long trek up to McScotland.
```

Alas, 'The Red Baron' and co had only got as far as the Western Isles, where they seemed to find the pubs more interesting than the beaches, returning penniless and wave-starved. I finished the article quickly and slid it into my bag in the hope Ed wouldn't notice. He'd probably pilfered it from someone else anyway.

All anyone could think about was swell. Only an unsettled crossing would make us happy. I made my way to the top of the boat to sit at the ship's bow and feel the sea-rhythms. Large climb; smaller, gentler drop; long intervals between waves – there was a good swell running. The other three were all thinking exactly the same thing, of that I was sure. Just as our combined anticipation was starting to build to a blood-boiling crescendo, the swell lines disappeared from underneath us, intercepted by the coastline of approaching islands to our north.

'North swell,' reasoned Ed. 'It must be hitting the other side of the island full pelt. There is nothing but really, really deep ocean between those north shores of the Orkneys and the Arctic. The storms that spin off the polar ridges up there are sick! We're gonna be surfing *big* waves in an hour or so.'

It was at this point that Ed challenged me to spot a tree before we arrived back on the mainland. Buildings have trouble fighting off the storms that batter this place, so trees would stand no hope. At the moment, however, there was no wind at all. This suited us all fine, the surface of the ocean looking like sheet-glass as our boat bored its way north. Nothing but those big, powerful 'corduroy' swell lines behind us, and the subsequent butterflies in my stomach.

Disembarking was a simple affair, and as soon as the boat docked we were all crammed into Joe's van and on our way to a bay, the location of which Ed swore us to secrecy over. One of the Thurso locals claimed to have surfed a big left-hander there, which made it the obvious place to start. He'd obviously had more luck than us, a taunting wind coming up just minutes after we docked, as it can in the small islands of the North Atlantic. As a result, all we found there was a load of messy wind-chop – no use to anyone except a pack of horny seals who stared hard enough to dissuade us from crashing their party.

Not put off at all, Ed pulled out a tattered Ordnance Survey map of the area that was covered in scribbles and wrinkled in a way that could only have been done by tropical air – the humidity causing the paper to warp. This guy had been sitting on the idyllic coasts near Madras fantasising about the freezing Orkney Isles. He and Joe had a look at it and decided to try another part of the island.

Sure enough we found a couple of waves there – a long point playing host to what could, on a less windy day, have been a string of good left-handers. Could *be*. There was swell, but not enough swell for the point to 'connect up'; the waves were shutting down unpleasantly all the way along. It wasn't rideable. It took us about half an hour (the time it takes to drive around the whole of Orkney) to conclude that there weren't any other decent waves breaking that day either. There had been something going on at a west-facing beach, but it wasn't what we'd come for – two foot and devoid of any real shape; the sort of stuff you'd surf at home just to keep fit. So Ed decided that it was time to head for the outer islands, and straight away.

'No point fooling around here,' he said. 'We know there aren't any waves on this island today, so why not try another one?' The alternative was wasting the day staring at waves that, however hard we tried to visualise it, were basically rubbish. That kind of time-wasting would inevitably lead to mutinous attitudes towards Ed, upon whom we were all relying to score some virgin Scottish perfection. Fortunately, he was more than willing to take charge of the situation. Out came the maps.

'These four islands all look all right for the possibility of having a wave in a north swell. It's just a case of taking our pick.'

It sounded easy enough and the dice landed on the Isle of Westray. Two hours and another ferry ride later, we were there.

Nothing could come close to the actual first-hand feeling of standing on one of those outer islands. I stood still, took a deep breath and tried to absorb every detail of the surroundings.

Right, now look around, here you are. Westray [breathe]. It's so beautiful. Look around [breathe], take it in, feel this moment, 'cause you'll be gone soon.

I like to think certain moments can be made to last forever. Philosophers ask if the past still exists. Is memory a reliable form of record? These questions seem particularly relevant to travellers, who don't just act *for* the moment but to *savour* the moment. Most spend their lives collecting fragments – be they photographs or ticket-stubs or just plain and simple memories. These fragments are part of the objective.

There is a phrase, frequently used by surf photographers: 'Documentation is the destination.' While the act of wave-riding is itself pretty damn enjoyable, it seems that while travelling surf must be shot, or filmed (as Ed planned to do), or at least discussed at ridiculous lengths upon return (as the rest of us planned to do). Going 800 miles across the UK just to *ride* waves alone is insufficient. We were like hunters, our job being to travel to Westray, find, capture and bring home for exhibition.

Genuinely interesting news is a rare commodity in the far northern reaches of the Scottish archipelagos and the crew of surfers on Westray was headline news. Various farmers and fishermen were climbing over each other to tell us of spots around the island that they thought would be good for us.

Despite all the help and support from locals, the only source of entertainment we'd found so far that day was an enormous beached and bloated elephant seal. Its head had been bitten clean off, which is no mean feat considering the ferocity and size of these beasts. ('It's more like tae be the work of one of your *Orcinus orca* than the white shark,' our beetroot-cheeked bar friend had told us later that night. 'Nah, your white shark likes swimmin' aboot the Hebrides rather than aboot these watters. Only an orca would give a meal like that a miss after killin'. The buggers'd bite the heid off for jollies. The white shark kills for food, enda story. White shark wouldnae left bugger all.') Now it was the turn of the smaller sea life to feed. Death bringing life; it's no wonder so many poets go to remote Scottish isles to seek inspiration. Joe and Darrel satisfied their own appetites for a cheap laugh by seeing who dared stand downwind of the corpse for the longest. Darrel, vomiting but victorious, managed to place himself just two yards downwind for three minutes.

'It's starting,' noted Ed. 'That delirium that comes from being here too long without enough waves. And it's only taken two days!' On our way back to the car he then spotted and harvested a batch of magic mushrooms. 'If it stays flat for too long don't worry about me,' he could be heard saying. 'I know where I'll be going.'

There is only so much someone can do on a tiny island so, after we had visited the shop and the pub (the *only* shop and *only* pub), we'd come full circle. It was time to go for another surf-check. Success was imperative this time in order to prevent Ed from turning himself into a psychedelic mess. He persuaded Joe to drive us over to the other side of the island, where the wind was blowing from the wrong direction for us to really expect any well-shaped waves. His grounds? 'Just a hunch – something to keep us busy.'

With hindsight we were beginning to realise that we had broken one of the golden rules of a surf trip: never leave one surf for the possibility of a better one – you'll always get skunked. We had done so on mainland Orkney, letting expectation drive us on, past what would have at least been a surf of some sorts. True, that little beach break hadn't looked anything special, but it would have been a chance to wash the journey off – a starting point for better things.

You always seem to remember surfs more fondly when they took place on a trip anyway. Had we given it a go, perhaps our memories of the session missed could have matured with age into a classic surf. It'd happened before. I think it's because you tend only to savour the good parts. So what was actually two freezing hours waiting for a decent wave to come can turn into the simple memory of a good ride a month later. Even if the waves don't look too exciting at the time, there's always the chance that you may end up doing one single turn that felt good, or getting some other sort of personal enjoyment from the session.

The same theory goes into overdrive when the surf is actually good. While most other fantasies are no longer quite so fantastical when finally realised, surf fantasies grow better and better *after* having come true.

That's probably why I seem to remember weeks upon weeks of back-to-back great surf at home as a kid – something that rarely happened any more. You hear that often: 'The surf was always much better when we were younger.' All the older guys say it. The myth is that weather patterns such as

El Niño and global warming have altered surf, making good days fewer and farther between. The reality, though: waves simply get better through memory. The surf was, and is, as good as it's always been. As Salman Rushdie once wrote, 'Sometimes legends make reality, and become more useful than the facts.'

This can work against you on a surf trip – and on most other trips too for that matter. To find a session that can rank up there with sessions past that have been steadily fermenting into wonderful history is almost impossible... Unless the bubble has already burst, expectations have already been dashed upon kelp-covered rocks by uninspiring onshore surf, and you've resigned yourself to not scoring. It is at times like that when you are left open – exposed to the possibility.

'Look at *that*!'

'No way!' Now on Westray, that is the sound of Joe and Ed spotting a perfect reef set-up, just when they least expect to. Around the headland, sweet head-high waves are folding over a small shelf of slate and tubing for around fifty yards before draining into deep blue water. Perfect surf, in the outer Orkneys, with no one but seals to hear us scream.

Again I'm trying instantly to log this moment. Ed is hurriedly taking a load of stills of the line-up, while Joe and Darrel are getting into their wetsuits not quickly enough for their liking. There cannot be more than half an hour's light left, but the thought of spending that time watching perfect waves instead of devouring them is ridiculous. As the three of us reach the water's edge and find a jump-off spot, the sinking sun comes into view beyond the cliffs to the south. We surf for about twenty minutes in the trippy lighting conditions before that sun turns deep pink and slides beneath the small, mushroom-covered hill.

Half an hour's light can always be pushed to three quarters of an hour when the waves are good and by the time we paddle in, it's pitch black. Darrel keeps a little trick up his sleeve for a paranoid Ed. As he takes a wave in, leaving Ed alone in the dark vastness of what is almost the Arctic Ocean, he screams out 'Orca!' Ed knows it's a joke, but shits himself anyway and we now have yet another component of a good surf trip – a prank that everyone finds funny, except for the victim, who is really not in the mood. Ed partly deserved it anyway – after all, he was supposed to be filming.

It was after dark when that Scottish cold began to set in; an embracing cold that fills you with energy. It was a refreshing experience being on a surf trip that actually involved going *to* the cold, as opposed to running from it. Normally this kind of weather would make getting out of your wetsuit an ordeal, but somehow it now felt rewarding. Nothing was done in a hurry. The layers of clothes were going on at a slightly slower pace than they would have after just another boring go-out at home. Again, it was almost as if we were trying to draw the session out just a little longer.

That same cold also serves another function: it draws you to the pub.

As I said, Westray only had one village, and that village only had one pub, so the choice was easy. On the other side of the hill was Pierowall, the sleepy urban sprawl that was the island's capital hamlet. Our little discovery had got in the way of any plans to buy food before the island's only shopkeeper locked his doors and went to said pub, making this the only place on the island where we could have found anything to eat that night. Thankfully, they were able to knock up some bar food.

Walking in, we came face to face with old Beetroot Cheeks about ten seconds after going through the door. He was one of those rare landlords who couldn't bear to be beaten to the task of welcoming the new boys. From that moment

Ed decided that his goal for the evening was going to be getting a tale out of him, and it didn't take long. There was a photograph on the wall of a lighthouse that had been built in the middle of the sea, quite some distance west of the Orkneys. Apparently two guys living in it had been stuck there for three months, as the storms didn't let up enough for anyone to take a boat out to visit them. It ended up that one had died before the authorities were able to make contact, and everyone in the islands believed he had been murdered by the other.

'What did they do?' I asked.

'Who?'

'The police.'

'Not much.'

'Why, no evidence?'

'No proof, other than the fact that they were locked up there for yonks.'

'So it's just a rumour then?' I can be boringly rational about things like this.

'Uch, dinnae know aboot that; he was a wee bit funny after they brought him back, apparently. Said the other guy had just died one night, of natural causes. "Natural causes", is always a wee bit suss, if you ask me.'

'But he may have been telling the truth.'

'Aye, but no dogs would go near him after he got back. Dogs can suss what humans can't.' This was starting to sound like a load of bollocks, but entertaining bollocks nonetheless.

'So where's the guy now?'

'Oh dead, dead. He would've died a long time ago. This happened in the nineteen-twenties. Would never happen now. Lighthouse ain't manned any more. It never breaks down. Disnae need anyone. We're slowly winning against the storms.'

We asked him about the ferocity of some of these tempests, and he showed us a few more pictures. One showed Pierowall getting bombarded by torrents of seawater that had blown clean over the hill without losing any of its density. I hadn't realised how battered that place got in mid-winter, being essentially just a little chunk of rock and grass in the middle of one of the roughest seas on the planet.

There was another photo on the wall too. A faded one of an old man, with the look of a hard-core seafarer about him. He was sitting on a tiny upside-down fishing boat. One hand was proudly holding up a lobster, and the other nothing, since he only appeared to have one finger.

'Who's that?' Ed asked.

'It's just one of the old guys who used tae have a drink here,' Beetroot Cheeks replied. 'Aw, he passed away, was it, aboot, oh...' And then, turning to a man on his right, 'Hey, how long ago did Ark pass away?'

The other bloke paused for a minute, before returning his answer. 'Around nineteen, er... eighty-three?'

'Aye, one year short of a hundred he was... Wife died three days later.'

'Three days?'

'Aye. Just three days.'

Ed looked back at the photo. 'What happened to his fingers?'

'Always like that. Must have been when he was a bairn. Oh, he was a character all right.'

Something about this guy's voice just made you want to listen to him for hours. Which is exactly what we did, getting the low-down on all the important issues of life on the outer Orkneys. None of us spoke more than a few words at a time, and then it would only be to guide old Beetroot Cheeks onwards to more stories. We learned how 'incomers' are looked down upon by the born-and-raised Orcadians, how most of the kids get bored by the lack of entertainment on Westray, and end up leaving for the mainland – mainland Orkney, that is. We heard all about the wildlife, and sea life.

We heard about those *Orcinus orcas* and *Carcharodon carcharias* (great white sharks). We were told tales of storms, and of waves so big they would blacken out the horizon. And above all, we learned how well whisky can go down in a proper, remote Scottish tavern.

After a while he asked us where we were going to stay. 'Probably in the back of Joe's van out there,' I told him, pointing to the 'car park' outside. The whisky-warmth would surely see us through the night with nothing but sweet dreams of perfect Orkney reef breaks.

'Don't be silly,' was his reply. 'I'll give my son a ring. He can sort out a couple of rooms for you.'

'Nah, we'll be fine, honest.'

'It's nae hassle at all. I swear.'

We started looking at each other.

'How much will he want?' Joe asked.

'Auch, not much! I'll call him now.' There wasn't a prayer of this guy backing down, and a room sounded pretty good anyway, so off he went to phone.

Beetroot Cheeks turned out to be right about one thing, and wrong about another. He was bang-on about the not much. His son, living about twenty yards along the road, said he'd stick us in a pair of double rooms for a fiver a head – including 'whatever we wanted from the kitchen' for breakfast. Bargain. However, he couldn't have been more mistaken about the nae hassle. Those 'double rooms' turned out to be the kids' bedrooms. Two bunk-beds in each, and piles of toys around the floor, while the evicted tenants had to huddle up inside a large living room, where the air was, er, fresh to say the least. There was something about these people, though, that made you feel that saying 'No thanks – this is great but we can't let you do this' was going to be even ruder than accepting their bizarre offer.

But it didn't seem to bother Ed's conscience too much. 'I hope they won't mind us fucking off early for a dawnie tomorrow,' he said. 'That left is going to be steaming in the morning. I can tell.'

On second thoughts, 'steaming' wasn't really the best word for it. We'd woken up at first light to find the stillest weather conditions you could hope for, and, more importantly, a slight increase in the swell. Apart from the sea, Westray looked like a model, absolutely motionless. Not a breath of wind anywhere, clear skies, silky water, juicy, head-high waves and not another surfer in sight. Joe kept pinching himself in order to make a point, but it did little to alter the situation he found himself in.

The tide was also slightly lower than it had been the night before, which made the wave longer. Instead of running fat and deep at the end, it was now rolling onto another ledge of forgiving slate rock, before still providing that same easy get-out, albeit another twenty yards down the line. The previous day there had also been a tricky second section, as the deep water around the wave sent small bits of backwash running through the shoulder, causing me to catch edges turning off the bottom of the wave. This time though, the second section was sucking right out, sometimes even throwing the lip right over. Darrel managed to get some cheeky tubes on a few, which was driving the rest of us mad, since we weren't getting his luck.

Everyone surfed for hours, until Nature called time on our little party, by making the wind come up and blowing it to shreds. Such is life.

The most important thing for Ed was that he'd finally managed to get some filming done. It must have seemed like a pretty thankless job, as we'd only complain later when he broke it to us that he'd missed most of the best rides. That always happens with filming. Since most of the guys who've chosen to make surf films surf, they soon find themselves caught up in the catch-22 to end all catch-22s.

Having taken up filming as a means of doing less 'real' work, they promptly find themselves missing just as much surf as if they'd chosen the office or factory routes. However, they still get to watch the waves, which is even more frustrating.

Ed never seemed to be missing out on the surfing side of things too much, though, and still always returned from trips with plenty of footage. That said, Sod's Law always means that the best rides take place off film, often because of silly factors like the angle of the sun casting the wrong light for the cameraman. It was disheartening to think how much good surfing guys like Kelly Slater, Taj Burrow or Andy Irons must have done on those media boat trips when the cameras weren't rolling – the extensive collection of deep tubes and airs that we got to see were usually just the best bits of what would have been left on the cutting room floor. It had probably been the same with that trip Tom Curren took to J-Bay – who knows what else he did that swell that was even more amazing.

More sadly for Ed, though, he would have to make do with a trio of half-wits, and then hope the wave turned into the real star of his film. We took a brief walk around the cliff corner, finding at least another three similar set-ups to the one just surfed. It was impossible to tell if any of them would be any good, because the wind was now blowing too hard, making the sea just a mass of white-caps, but you had to wonder at the possibilities. 'Real potential,' Ed told me. 'Real potential.'

Real potential maybe, but late last night Joe had stuck his laptop into our hosts' phone line to find out that the Navy's wave charts were predicting a *very* big swell – uncharacteristic for the time of year, and big enough to try surfing that legendary Thurso reef – back on the Scottish mainland; this was a wave we'd all heard about before, but never seen in action. This had put us in a tricky situation. A case could now be made for declaring Westray a success, going back to thank our hosts, catching a couple of ferries, and then making our way back to Thurso. If it did break, we couldn't miss it for the world.

The prospect of scoring Thurso East was a particularly inviting one for me, since I was the only 'natural-foot' on the trip – meaning I stand with my left foot forward. Joe and Darrel were both 'goofy-foots', standing the other way round, and Ed was a bodyboarder (about which he has endured a lifetime of stick, 'sponger' being the gentlest of the nicknames – a reference to the fact his boards were made of sponge instead of fibreglass). Although it's not the end of the world if unavailable, natural-foots will generally prefer right-hand breaking waves, because they can face it as they ride it. The opposite applies to goofys, while bodyboarders don't really have an issue with either, since they ride lying down – or 'on their guts', as stand-ups tend to put it. Surfers are a selfish bunch, and the one thing that was starting to become a bone of contention (or actually a bit of a joke for the others) was the fact that all the waves we had seen on the Orkneys so far, and all the possible set-ups, were left-handers – 'backhand' for me. This was a goofy-footer's heaven, but I was gagging to score some rights.

'Right-handers', or 'rights', are waves usually more suited to natural-footers like me. It can be a little confusing because as you look out to sea, a right will actually break to your left. The reason it's called a right is because the surfer will have to turn right to go along the wave. With your left foot forward as a natural-foot, you will be riding face to face with a right-hander, while a left-hander will require having your back to the wave – known as surfing backhand, or backside. The repertoire of turns you can pull backside are completely different to those available on a frontside wave, and often more limited. It's also much harder to ride the tube backside than frontside.

But, as I mentioned, the others were all frontside here, and didn't care about my plight at all.

'If we see any rights,' Ed had kept saying, 'we're going to just drive past 'em! You were the one who chose to come on a trip with two goofy-foots and a sponger.'

They wouldn't be able to pass up a chance to surf Thurso so easily, though.

'No debate,' I told them on the way to pay up and give these poor kids back their beds. 'Thurso. It's meant to be one of the best waves on earth. We'd all be idiots to turn down a chance like this.' They knew what the right thing to do was. But none of them were going to admit that yet.

'Let's get some food before we do anything,' Ed grinned.

Over an early lunch of biscuits and crisps, the oldest topic in the world came up – maybe triggered by the prospect of a Thurso swell. What is the best wave on earth? Everyone had their own ideas.

'G-Land,' said Joe, without any pause at all. G-Land referred to a long left-hander in the Javanese fishing village of Grajagan. By far Joe's favourite wave to date.

'Mundaka.' The Spanish-Basque rivermouth was Ed's obvious choice, being as he lived only two hours' drive from it.

'Thurso…' I had to keep making the point.

Ed, ever the academic in these matters, had a means of classification for waves; 'A1', 'A2', 'B', 'C', 'D' and so on. 'Anything with an "A" is world class,' he said. 'But I'd only reserve A1 status for the handful of waves that really can claim to be the best waves on earth. Waves that have no equal. G-Land and Mundaka for sure. Along with Jeffrey's Bay, Pipeline, Teahupoo, Cloudbreak, Kirra and, er… that's about it.'

'And Thurso?' I suggested, again meaning to drop a big hint. 'What rating would you give Thurso?' I'd normally have championed J-Bay right off the bat in a conversation like this, but I didn't want to deflect attention from my main aim of getting us back on the Caithness ferry.

'A2. From what I've heard, Thurso's definitely world-class, but there are a thousand and one places like it. Indo is riddled with waves like that. As very well may this place be with the right conditions.'

'Yeah, but the water is too cold to surf as much here as you can in Indo,' Joe suggested.

'Of course it is. And then there's the wind.' Ed was assuming the position of know-it-all as usual. 'The wind is too unpredictable here.'

He was right. There was no real pattern to these winds. In the tropics, and at J-Bay, there were often definite wind patterns that suited the waves. Most of the waves mentioned in the laborious 'A-B-C' diatribe were usually subjected to an offshore wind every morning – if, in fact, there was any wind at all.

'Those places have such predictable winds 'cause of the temperatures of the land and sea,' Professor Ed continued. 'If a storm does come along to mess the waves up, it won't last long. Tropical storms never do.'

'But here a storm can last for days.'

'Exactly. Even weeks.'

'Which is great for swell…' I began.

'Yeah,' Ed agreed. 'But most of it is probably proper victory-at-sea type stuff. You want to try and come up here when there's no wind – which is where you need a bit of luck.'

'And that isn't going to be any time when you're talking,' Joe noted through a mouthful of food.

Too much wind can make the surf poor, by messing up the shape of the waves. In Britain, wind is usually the first thing a surfer will look at before going to the beach. If the trees outside your window are moving, then there's probably too much wind for a good surf, but if they're still it means putting down everything and racing to get your board. It wouldn't work in the Orkneys, though – no trees.

'Bet it would be really frustrating living here and being a surfer,' I commented.

'Probably,' said Ed thoughtfully. 'Bitter-sweet though.'

'Who gives a fuck anyway?' Joe cut in, having finished his sandwich in about two mouthfuls. 'We scored, and that's all that matters.' He really knew how to wrap up conversations.

Our hosts had been unusually trusting. We'd buggered off with all our gear that morning and not paid them a penny, so it was time to call back at the house, which was when we found out that Westray was also home to a rock star. A *Christian* rock star. Some woman, who bore the look of one terrified of that final day of judgement, had told us so outside the shop. There was actually a pretty strong religious movement on the islands – a very strict form of Christianity, far more extreme than the more enlightened church scene on mainland Orkney. (It was the only way they could cope, according to Ed. 'And besides, it stops inbreeding too, or at least until they're married anyway.') What we hadn't realised was that we had already met this musical messenger of the Lord. It was the barman's son – our host! Beetroot Cheeks Junior!

'No fucking wonder they didn't mind persecuting themselves to give us a bed,' exclaimed Ed when he found out we had been sleeping in the presence of a saint. It also seemed as if he had decided subconsciously to up his swear count, perhaps as a means of fending off any unwanted holiness.

'And that's why the surf's been cranking the last day or so, too! We've been blessed,' he continued.

We'd all been wondering what was in the huge boxes we'd sat on for our morning toast. CDs was the answer. Hundreds of copies of Keith Spencer's new album *All Glory, Honour and Praise*. I couldn't decide if this discovery was a let-down or not – we'd been hoping to find out that Beetroot Junior, or

Keith as it turned out, behind the guise of an exceptionally polite and innocent looking family man was actually a drugs baron, hiding an enormous cache of designer cocaine. Ah, maybe Christian rock star wasn't that bad a substitute.

Keith didn't appear to have come back yet, so Joe just placed our money, along with a little extra for the Internet use and a note of thanks, on the table underneath the copy of Keith's previous album, *His Name is Blessed* – a CD we hadn't noticed that morning in our rush to go and check the surf.

When we'd met him the night before, it hadn't occurred to us that the guy was a Christian – but perhaps that was the impression he wanted to make. The man we'd met looked nothing like the white-dressed, Stetson hat-wearing liturgical maestro now staring out at us from the sleeves of the CDs lying around in the kitchen. Darrel even put a few tracks on for us. 'Relaxing music,' he said. 'Or, well, it *would* be if the words weren't so freaky.'

'Turn it off, you idiot,' ordered Ed, clearly uncomfortable. 'Just get your stuff together.'

And then we were on our way. The evening ferry back to the metropolis of Kirkwall, capital of mainland Orkney.

After boarding the rusty boat that lay harnessed to the small quay like a rodeo bull raring to go, we all headed below deck for a cuppa, finding the captain, a sleepy-looking seafarer, necking a strong coffee before taking our lives into his mucky hands.

'Surfin' be fooked! You'll be doin' a lot of that in the next day or so. There's a hell of a storm comin'!' (It's amazing how many people still confuse surfing with *wind*surfing.)

As if Saint Keith had sensed Ed's insolence, the storm that ruined the lefts on Westray was now set to ruin Thurso East as well. Joe hadn't reckoned on the fact that the Navy swell charts only show wave heights, and not wind speeds. The increase in wave heights that he had decided was a swell was actually one great big fuck-off storm that was heading straight for us. A taster of Baltic rage that had cropped up a little earlier than usual, yinging away the yangs of flatness that had plagued the summer we'd just put behind us. The Atlantic was on its way from one extreme to another.

The mood deflated almost instantly.

'Well, that's that, then,' said Ed. 'When the captain of a boat tells you the wind is coming up, it really means the wind is coming up.'

'Bye bye Thurso,' said Joe. 'I know another spot nearby that can still be ridden in a storm. Maybe we can still go somewhere for a wave or two.'

A wave or two at 'another spot nearby' wasn't nearly going to make up for missing out on a session at Thurso East, and Joe knew it. After the surf we'd had yesterday, riding some sort of dribbly, wind-proof contingency wave was probably going to be worse than not surfing at all.

'I'm not here to surf the sort of shite waves I could see a million and one times at home,' Ed said. 'I vote we fuck surfing off until the storm's gone and have a pint in Stromness instead. It's not going to hurt to spend a night on Orkney, especially if we're not missing any surf. Let's follow in the spirit of The Red Baron and co!' I thought about the old magazine extract hiding away in the bottom of my bag. Ed hadn't noticed it missing yet.

Not much resistance to that plan, and so it was settled. A pint in Stromness.

Stromness was one of those towns that really wanted to be dubbed a capital, but knew deep down it never would. It had its own Tourist Information Centre, which only told you about what was going on in Stromness, a website which did the same, and a wide range of books about its history. Some of the residents even claimed it was the capital.

But it was all wishful thinking. Comprising little more than a cobbled central road and a couple of streets, Stromness's size did little to help it live up to the large-black-dot status it had been awarded by most maps. It could never be Orkney's capital anyway, since Kirkwall had forever claimed that title (and proudly enjoyed even-larger-black-*square* status as a result). However, despite such setbacks, Stromness tried very hard to entertain the considerable population of tourists that were now visiting annually.

Having just come back from a far smaller island, we found the taverns on the Stromness 'strip' positively cosmopolitan. They served a wealth of bar meals that could only be described as gourmet in comparison to the fish 'n' chips or curry that Beetroot Senior had put on for us the night before. Ed was delighted to find steak 'n' ale pie on the menu in the first place we checked, and forced the rest of us to sit down and order. He ate it up as if he hadn't seen any food for a week, while the rest of us bored our way into a bizarre mixture of spare ribs and chicken fajitas. A small live band dressed in tuxedos played some easy-listening music in the background, sticking to some well-worn numbers in a way that was both cringeworthy and relaxing at the same time.

As the Chariots of Fire theme tune merged into the plodding score of 'Amazing Grace' I began to notice that the Scottish accents were actually outnumbered. A group of Irish rig-workers were bingeing themselves into oblivion on one table, while three middle-aged English couples looked on sourly from another. The barman was French, though the waitresses were local. You could still make out what they were saying quite clearly, however, despite the noise being made by the musicians and the rowdy clientele. Their accents were much softer, and the grand height of the room was allowing background noise to rise safely into the rafters, like it might in a large church. The music and chatter was never too loud.

We could have easily stayed in there all night, but our recent pub-going experiences had made us all start wanting something a little more intimate.

'Where do the locals drink?' Ed asked the barman, frowning back towards the melee behind.

'You should try going to ze little bar opposite ze harbour,' he replied, nodding as if he was letting us in on some sort of secret. 'Ze little yellow house next to the video shop. Side door.' It sounded exciting.

'We're on it,' Ed replied, and drank up, nodding to us to do the same. Once he hatches a plan, he likes to get straight on with it.

The harbour was filled with small private trawlers and, just like the last time we'd passed through, no signs of any activity at all. I remembered Beetroot Cheeks telling us that most fishermen were away at sea for at least a week at a time, and that they usually tried to avoid storms. Speaking of which, the wind was now really blowing a gale.

'Looks like that storm is starting,' I thought aloud.

'No shit,' said Ed. 'Let's go and have a pint in the locals' pub. Harbours are boring at the best of times.'

We'd probably have missed it if we hadn't been told where to look as it barely resembled a pub at all from the street and didn't appear to have a name on the outside. We timidly pushed open the door, and headed inside.

There was no mistake once you'd walked in. A crowd of less than ten were actively cackling and guffawing away to the taste of some vile northern lagers.

Making my way straight to the toilet, I opted against going shoulder to shoulder with the scruffy drunk that was pissing freely everywhere but the urinal. The dirty but graffiti-free cubicle looked the better option – and it even had a lock.

Moments before opening the door again, I heard someone the other side shout loudly at the guy who, as far as I knew, was still peeing away without a care in the world. It didn't sound like a fight – just as if one of his mates had crept up on him for a laugh. Then after half a second I recognised the voice. Joe! Oh no!

'Oh, fuck. Sorry buddy. I thought you were someone else. Oh shit, man. I didn't mean to…' I was sure he was about to get his head kicked in. 'I saw my mate go in here a moment ago, so I thought I'd creep up on him,' he went on.

Shut up, Joe, I thought.

But the pisshead was far too gone even to realise what had happened. I waited until I knew Joe was alone again and came out of the cubicle.

'Shit!' Joe laughed. 'I just pushed that guy into the wall thinking he was you. He pissed all over himself!'

Quite how a ten-foot-tall sailor could have looked anything like me was a mystery.

'At least you just tested the water with the locals for us,' I told him.

'They seem OK,' Joe laughed.

We headed out to the 'lounge'; a small room with one table in the far corner, and every other seat right against the bar. The centre of attention was the pool table, a sorry looking article that wore a shameful turquoise cloth covered in all sorts of stains. A corridor led away at the back of the room, but had been equipped with neither lights, seats nor tables. There were no doors there either, just a wall. It was dark at the far end so I couldn't really distinguish between shadows and dirt. I counted six others in the bar besides us and the frowning landlady, who didn't speak other than to take drink orders.

Ed had made friends already, touting Darrel's pool skills about, despite the latter's pleading with him to shut up. Even though he hated to admit it, Darrel was pretty dangerous on a pool table, always an ice-breaker in cliquey pub situations. As always, he rose to the challenge as soon as one of the locals racked up, and at that point we'd as good as lost him for the night.

Understanding most of the locals was a complete guessing game. Someone would bombard you with a pile of incomprehensible babble, usually the product of both drink and unfamiliar dialect, and you'd have to guess how to reply. The rising intonation of the first diatribe made it pretty clear what the desired response should be, and I could make out the words 'are you one of', 'who didn't' and 'yesterday never'.

'Yeah!' I replied.

'Ah, ha, ha, ha, ha,' came the response – and a pat on the shoulder to boot.

Phew, I thought. Got the first one right, anyway. That's always the most important one. If you fuck up now you'll definitely be given a second chance to tell them you hadn't understood.

Another lengthy waffle. This one was a little harder, but the hints were still there that the best reply was going to be affirmative again. I was sure he'd said something about having 'flipped over', and he definitely said 'twat' – although that could have been a reference to the place name.

'Yeah, yeah.' I acted as if I was really starting to find stuff in common with him now. It was the correct response again, and sent him into another hail of laughter.

His third one was the hardest, and the way he had ever-so-slightly cocked his head back hinted that this time I should be answering differently. The only word I could make out was 'storm', repeated several times. This game reminded me of playing 'Hi-Low' on a fruit machine – the percentage game where you have to guess whether the next number will be higher or lower. Feeling pretty sure of myself, I went for it.

'No. Nor me.'

A brief pause…

… and then:

'WEH-HEY!' It had worked. The game was a success. My new friend seized my hand and shook it to death, before turning back to the bar to get a refill on his pint of neon-orange local lager.

This could get interesting, I thought, before turning to the surly landlady and placing my order. 'I'll have one of those too, please.'

Several more of 'those too, please' went down before we reached that stage of the evening where everyone was perched at the bar having deep conversations with whoever hadn't left yet, or wasn't asleep in the pub somewhere.

A few of these fine pub-goers were actually from Manchester, which was a relief because it meant we could understand them. Nobody bothered exchanging names, but we did discover two of them were a father and son duo, come to Orkney to work on the fishing boats. You'd never have guessed, since the son looked older than the dad.

'We work our bollocks off,' the father had said as Darrel thrashed his apparent junior at pool, 'and then we drink our bollocks back on!'

The other guys worked on fishing boats too and, although they were all Scottish, only one of them was actually from Orkney. He was called Julian, and he also claimed to have known the 'character' we'd seen a photo of on Westray.

'Oh, Ark was a right proper one. Every time you went to Westray, he'd be there smiling like there wasn't a care in the world – which, now you think of it, there wasn't.'

Julian kept reminding us how Orcadians prided themselves on not getting too weighed down by the troubles and sorrows of the rest of the world.

'No crime, no political trouble, no noise or pollution,' he said. 'Why bother going over to the mainland?'

'Don't forget to add great waves to your list,' Ed interjected. 'Yeah, why do we bother going home? I don't fucking know!' Most times we mentioned to locals that the Orkneys had good waves, they'd respond by saying that they already knew. This could have been a bluff, but it could also mean that others had been before us and left the same feedback.

People on Westray and mainland Orkney had very different attitudes to the thought of more people moving there, too. On the mainland you were given the impression you'd be welcome as a resident, but on Westray 'incomers' were despised, and holiday homes or visitors much less encouraged.

My eyes had been drifting towards a television that was playing without any volume, in a corner above the bar. It was showing BBC News 24.

'Now why'd you want to be bothering yourself with the poxy news?' Julian said to me. 'Let me tell you something about life here on Orkney. We make a point of not worrying about silly things like the news. Keep up to date by all means, but don't bother yourself with it like you seem to be.' He was right. I had been watching it for ages now, although that was more a product of sleepiness than interest.

'Here in Orkney,' he told me, dramatically rotating on his bar stool to look me in the eye as if an important sound bite was about to be delivered, 'we have a *duty* to ignore what is going on in the rest of the world if it doesn't concern us directly.'

'And nothing ever does concern us directly,' said the landlady, suddenly breaking her evening-long silence, perhaps because she wanted this conversation wrapped up so that we could all bugger off and let her close up.

'So if you have this "duty", then,' Ed asked him, 'why is the feckin' news on in the pub?'

Julian's eyes lit up. This was exactly the question he'd been waiting for, and he now relished delivering the well-rehearsed answer: 'So that we can ignore it!'

That night we slept like logs in the back of Joe's van. Unusually, we'd managed to bully Ed into sleeping up front.

He's a light sleeper, and his tossing and turning wasn't welcome with the rest of us.

The gutting thing about the front seat was that you got woken up by first light (which was way before 6 a.m. this far north, since it was only early September). When there are waves to catch it's not such an issue because you could then wake everyone else and not miss a session by sleeping in – but after a wind-induced piss-up, as Ed rightly protested, it was. Despite his complaints and our delicate state, however, it turned out that putting someone on dawn patrol was the best move we'd made all trip.

'Boys! The fucking wind has dropped completely! Look beyond the harbour. It's sheet-glass out there. Wake up – Thurso is going to be absolutely *fucking cranking*!'

It seemed Ed's theory about Beetroot Junior blessing the trip could have been right after all. Not only had the wind indeed dropped, but Ed's restless vigilance up front (no doubt also a by-product of the uncomfortable head left him by nasty Scottish booze) had now meant that we were awake in time to catch the early morning ferry back to Caithness.

One thing about a good storm: it can be computer-forecasted by the best meteorologists around, and still do nothing like what is predicted. Weather charts had set us in for three days of wind, but right now that proved to be completely overturned. Sometimes wind drops when you're right in the eye of a storm (which was probably now the case), and sometimes they blow over more quickly than expected, but either way, we were not going to stay put.

Whether or not one of us was fit to drive was another issue. But nobody was going to refuse the task of negotiating the van along some of the mellowest roads on earth simply because of a nasty hangover. Darrel had had the least, it was decided, having just played pool all night, and was therefore pushed into the cockpit of the van and handed a map, while everyone else got more shut-eye in the back.

'Get us there by six-thirty or you're a fucking dead man,' said Ed, moving firmly back into his leadership role.

Again, here we were – sailing that same ferry back towards Gills Bay, rocked by swell, mesmerised by glassy conditions. This time, though, it was a bigger swell. Huge climbs, huge drops, eerily long intervals between waves. It was impossible not to feel a little nervous imagining what all that power was going to do when it finally arrived at the slate reef of Thurso East, and pitched forward with board-breaking ferocity.

All hangovers had disappeared by the time we docked. They had to. It wasn't the first time any of us had ended up getting pissed thinking the surf wasn't happening, only to get cruelly taken by surprise the next morning, and we all knew what to do. A few bottles of water and a blood-stream full of adrenaline can do a lot when it needs to. Everyone was suddenly safe to drive, and this time, last night's beers long forgotten, the choice was going to be made on who could get us there quickly.

The task of getting the van from Gills to Thurso fell on Joe (partly as it was his van, and he was therefore most likely to drive it fast without crashing it). Delighted that his surfing destiny was now in his own hands, he did not fail to deliver. Dunnet Head flew by, with only enough time for one quick pun ('Been there, Dunnet'). The knock-on effect of this was that everyone began trying to arrange the other silly-sounding Scottish town names from the rest of the trip into pointless sentences. Look on a map if you don't believe me, but besides Twatt and Dunnet, Caithness is also home to towns called 'Tongue', 'Brawl' and 'Mey' – plenty of entertainment for a restless group of surfers on their way to the water.

'Tongue Mey Twatt, you've really Dunnet now!' Hardly the conversation of geniuses, but addictive nonetheless. Yes, surf-stoke can do funny things to you.

After a five-minute drive that had seemed like fifty, we finally pulled into the little lane behind Thurso Castle. Everyone was jostling in the back of the van to get the first view, which was always going to go to Joe in the driver's seat anyway.

'*Fuck! Bollocks!*'

My heart stopped. 'What's wrong?'

'*Nightmare!*' Joe went on.

'What is it? What's wrong?' Still none of us could get a clear view of the line-up.

'Now that is a Twatt!' shouted Joe, holding back for just a second longer. 'It's crowded! There's two people in the water! What a fucker!'

You could feel the change in air-pressure, as everyone breathed a sigh of relief. Yes, Joe had been joking. World-class waves and only two people in the line-up is something you won't find often these days. Although, that said, Joe had made a point. It could just as easily have been no one.

Within about twenty seconds of Joe letting us out, a set of waves came through to show us what we were dealing with. Three double-overhead right-handers poured across the reef, tubing flawlessly all the way. There then followed a brief interlude, allowing the water over the reef just enough time to settle before another wave lined up. Again the lip pitched forward, rolling perfectly for a moment before a puff of spray flew out of the tube. When hollow waves gather too much pressure they can tend to do that. It looks a bit like a volcano going off, only it's water. That was all it took to send us into a selfish frenzy; every man for himself.

'Where's my wax?'

'Who cares!'

'I can't find my fucking wetsuit – move your board!'

'You move it!'

'Fuck! Look at that one!'

'Sod looking at it, get in there!'

'D'you reckon it's OK if I leave the keys in the van?'

'Do whatever you like!'

Entry into the water at Thurso East was incredibly easy. You just had to jump off a slab of slate into calm, deep water and then paddle sideways. It was actually possible to take off on your first wave with your hair still dry. For me, as for many others, such factors contribute no end to the suitability of a surf spot – without the hassle of duck-diving walls of whitewater you could just concentrate on wave-riding, conserving all your energy towards catching as many as possible.

And speaking of suitability, these waves were right up there with the sort of stuff I used to doodle on the inside cover of schoolbooks while teachers bore on about the periodic table, photosynthesis or anything else that didn't seem as important as designing my perfect wave. And now here it was. No longer a doodle or a bit of pub-talk. Easy entry to the line-up, big, hollow (meaning tubing) surf but easy enough to ride, relatively low-consequence wipe-outs (due to the thick wetsuits and smooth surface of the reef) and virtually nobody in the line-up.

'Those guys are gonna be gutted when we arrive out there,' laughed Joe as we prepared for the launch off Jump Rock. But the two guys in the water were absolutely delighted to see some new faces. They introduced themselves straight away as Chris and Scott. This, we learned, was essentially the entire Thurso surfing community. Chris actually surfed bloody good too – which isn't surprising given the fact that he got to surf waves like this on a semi-regular basis. He was keen to watch other people surfing live, though, explaining that he only usually got to watch surf videos to see someone other than Scott riding waves.

Chris ended up being a real source of inspiration to us, threading his way through some of the longest tubes I've ever seen with an astonishing calm and style. This was more the sort of surfing you'd expect of a good Hawaiian or Australian, as opposed to a low-profile Scotsman who had chosen for a hair-style the practical and quick-drying crew cut as opposed to any of the many variations of blond locks you'd usually expect from someone who lived only for the tube.

Scott was pretty ballsy too, refusing to get put off taking any big drop, especially given the fact that he now had visitors to impress. Unlike Chris, he did have long hair, although it was dark red, not blond. Scott was a goofy-foot, therefore having to take on the thunderous Thurso lip from the tougher backhand stance. This didn't phase him at all though.

The duo complemented each other perfectly. One small, one tall; one loud, one quiet. Chris the natural-foot, Scott the goofy.

Besides being heavy, the wave at Thurso was frighteningly mechanical. The take-off was easy, no sudden hair-raising changes in shape as you dropped in, no water getting into wrong parts of the reef and buggering waves up. Everything ran with symmetrical order: the rip taking you back to the take-off spot, the booming peak, the fast inside section and that shot of spray that fired out of the tube, signalling eviction time for any surfer still inside. Getting a little extra nitro-boost from that spit as you exit the barrel is something most surfers dream of their whole lives – and yet almost every wave was doing it now. We each lost count of the amount of times we felt that cool rush of air and water as we flew into the channel.

By mid-afternoon delirium had begun setting in.

'Too many tubes – I feel dizzy,' Ed was going. 'That's it. If I have to look down any more perfect barrels I'm going to lose it altogether. It's been a gruelling twenty-four hours!' He mentioned going in, citing fatigue and cold as his reasons, but then another thirty-minute barrage of breathing Thurso pits came through, and that idea was sidelined. We eventually headed back to the van after almost four hours of continuous surfing. This was going to be the last surf of the trip. It had to be. Shoulders were seizing, cramps setting in, but, more importantly, smiles were stuck to our faces.

'Now this is what surfing is all about,' Ed joked. 'Thick winter wetsuits as early as September. Instead of palm-trees we've got this castle and silage barn, and the waves are as good as anything we're ever likely to see again. Bollocks to chasing the sun. We've come here for waves and waves alone, and it's paid off. I could stay here forever. I don't care if I never see France again.'

'Er, that's a pretty bold statement Ed,' Joe warned him. 'If you never saw France again, that would also mean never seeing French *femmes* again.'

'At this point, that'd suit me fuckin' fine! Who needs anything else when you've got this?'

Before we headed back south to go our separate ways again, Scott and Chris insisted on inviting us to their home for a round of teas. It made us respect them even more. These guys lived for the wave at Thurso. They had a rundown little cottage behind the point, which you could tell was theirs a mile off. The garden sported a range of rotting wetsuits and broken surfboards, along with the odd roadside item that had obviously been pilfered during drunken nights when the waves weren't on. The inside of the building was basic, heated only by a small, portable gas fire that was never to be turned off ('because you canae turn the fucker back on,' according to Chris). No two doors were to be opened at once because of drafts, and the smell of damp was everywhere. Besides their life-saving fire, they had about another ten surfboards lying around in the living room and bedrooms (three of them broken in two), a simple video recorder and a library of surfing films, both old and new. 'This is all we need,' Scott told us, 'along with my guitar.'

But above all that, their most valuable possession among all the big-wave boards and stained teacups turned out to be an unmarked video cassette. 'This is what Thurso really should look like,' Chris grinned, before sliding it into their ancient light-grey VCR, initiating a whirring process that was over a minute long. Eventually their giant, wood-veneer television fizzed to life, and before us rolled a succession of huge, frigid right-handers at Thurso East.

'New Year's Day last year,' Scott explained.

'Aye, watch Scott take the drop now!' Chris leapt to life at the sight of the first empty wave rolling down the slate stones. A wave this perfect would never slip through unridden in most of the world's more known surfing destinations. The waves were absolutely firing, and this pair had had it to themselves. No wonder they were so content with these virtually sub-human living conditions. These two knew they'd found their wave, and had no problems admitting that for them this was the end of the road.

'It's never gonna be any different either,' said Ed. 'It's fuggin' freezing here, it's miles from anywhere, and for most UK surfers it takes the same amount of time to get here as it does France. Now, given only two weeks of holiday, where would you rather go, and be honest with yourselves. Bearing in mind what it's like to only get a few weeks off a year like normal people do – not being like one of us lot, wasting our lives on surf trips. Where would you go? Here or France?'

'France,' answered Darrel.

I agreed with him.

Then Joe had to be awkward. 'I'd go to neither. I'd go to the Canaries.'

'Yeah, well that still makes the same point,' Ed persisted. 'You wouldn't come here because it's cold, *ergo*, it's never going to get crowded, is it?'

As we pulled away from Chris and Scott's place, watching them wave us into the distance as might a rarely-visited grandparent, I couldn't help thinking about what would happen if this part of the world ever did catch on in a surfing sense – a dilemma that often faced surfers going to some of the world's lesser surfed places. You want to tell everyone about what you found, but at the same time there is an even more pressing need to keep the details of a spot close to your chest. People are always talking about how surf spots can be 'ruined' by overexposure. 'That place is fucked now,' you might hear. 'It's so crowded.'

Everyone has equal rights to surf wherever they want, but we're a selfish tribe, and hate the prospect of wave sharing – having to jostle and compete with others in order to snag a good one – which is what you will invariably end up doing at a popular spot. Some may also start to believe that the 'soul' or essence of a place is lost once it becomes too mainstream, too 'on the beaten track'. I lost count of the number of times older surfers have grumbled to me about how they used to have a spot to themselves, 'but now all these kids have turned up, and think they can have any wave they want…'

So could this, would this, ever happen to Thurso, to Orkney and that spot on Westray? Could big hotels, surf hostels and hire shops ever spring up on the hills by Beetroot's pub, solely as a result of the waves? It had happened before, at spots where the waves were of far lower quality.

The most likely scenario, however, was that nothing would change. The left-hander on Westray may never be surfed again (unless we went back). Thurso had already been in various magazines over the years and even hosted the odd contest (for which it usually stubbornly refused to produce waves like those we saw there), but it was yet to have any trouble with line-up congestion. Nobody went there, because it was Scotland, and it was cold.

'Ahh, the cold,' Scott had said with affection. 'It gets into yer bones, but it keeps the pussies away, and anyone who does come here deserves every wave they get – just for making the trek.'

We had to hand it to Ed in this instance, since the whole trip had been his idea. He was the one who'd persuaded us all to spend 'a France-trip's worth of cash and time' to come to this hinterland of cold and, as it had fortunately turned out, waves. We all owed him a debt, but it fell on Joe to pay it, by giving him a lift to Edinburgh Airport, where he would duly fly off to his next uncharted destination somewhere along the Sahara Desert's Atlantic coast. In a car park on the outskirts of Thurso we said our goodbyes, and Darrel and I jumped back into the car we had left there for the past few days. Already the Orkneys seemed hard to recall with any lucidity.

As we drove back towards the cities, hangovers and fatigue kicking back in, the details of what we'd done in the past few days began to sharpen.

'How good was that left on Westray really?' I asked Darrel.

'Brilliant,' he replied. 'And there could be fifty more like it back there.'

A long night of alternating driving shifts lay ahead. 'How good will it be by the time we arrive in Bristol?' I went on.

'Even better. And by then there could be a hundred more like it!'

By the following afternoon we were staring at a messy Devonshire beach break, and a crowd of about fifty desperate but slightly warmer surfers. Neither of us had the slightest bit of desire to go in.

'I'll tell you the maddest thing,' Darrel said. 'He's right, Ed. If you offered any of those guys out there that choice right now, they'd go south, wouldn't they?'

'Probably.'

'Well,' he said, a gluttonous grin appearing on his face. 'I say let them. God speed to them. We'll keep Scotland for ourselves.'

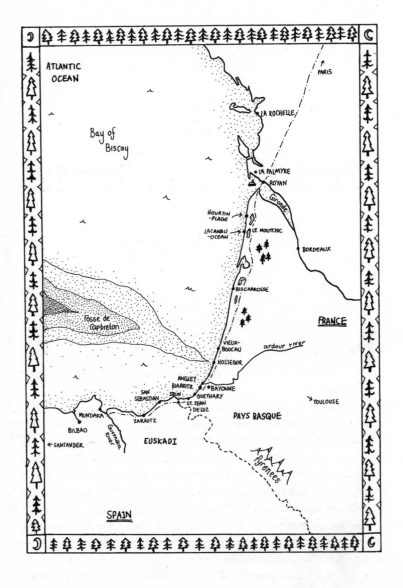

3.

France and Spain

(Part I): Crossing the Wastelands and Surviving the Circus

Naturally, we weren't fooling anyone, and while promises were made to return to Scotland, it was only a matter of time before we'd each end up back in France.

After all, France is a place you can't ignore for long, excellent for cutting your teeth, getting used to heavier surf, or for just playing around and soaking up the essence of surf culture. *Le sud-ouest* has sandbars known worldwide for their perfection, where during my teens I'd found invaluable experience. Like the best British beaches, but on steroids. And who do we have to thank for it? Napoleon!

I'm not joking – he was a clever bastard. Besides seizing power off the back of a revolution, winning wars, building heaps of fantastic stuff and ruling for years, he also created one of surfing's most prized phenomena: French beach breaks. Before Napoleon the entire south-west coast of France – Le Gironde, as it's known – was nothing but useless, boggy marshland. Hundreds of miles of it. Frustrated by the sight of all this almost-land, Napoleon embarked upon an insanely ambitious drainage programme. Insane maybe, but it is widely agreed that France was built, developed and is currently run by the insane.

Napoleon decided that he'd plant the world's greatest pine forest in the marshland, hundreds of miles square, with a view to increasing the French land mass. Ambitious, perhaps, but it worked! The pine tree absorbs ridiculous amounts of water, and the several million that were planted in this case sucked the marshes dry, creating the regions of Aquitaine and Les Landes.

The Ardour river , which had been responsible for creating the marshes, was then diverted south, giving birth to my favourite city, Bayonne. Ardour's vast channel of consistently flowing water provided the vital element for a much-needed port. Without this diversion, Bayonne would have been just a small village cowering at the foot of the Pyrenees.

Napoleon then ordered that the site of the river's original *rencontre* with the Bay of Biscay be turned into the lake and beachside town of Hossegor. The section of the estuary immediately inland was isolated, creating the lake, with the mouth of the river dried up by the thirsty pine trees and tons of sand.

What nobody realised at the time was that Ardour's volumes of water had already provided something much more important than a port (to us anyway). For the river had spent centuries pouring trillions of tons of water over the sea bed, and had left a scar deeper than the Grand Canyon. The *Fosse de Capbreton* is a deep-water trench that runs into the Bay of Biscay from the central Atlantic ridge in the shape of a finger. You can see it on most physical maps. The two-mile tip of this finger ends just a few hundred yards before the shoreline at Hossegor beachfront, and allows waves to travel at open-ocean speeds until just seconds before they eventually break. Without the usual steady decrease in ocean depth to slow them down, the waves that come through the *Fosse de Capbreton* pitch forward perfectly for tube riding. After the Mexican semi-close-out of Puerto Escondido, Hossegor is probably *the* most powerful beach break on the planet – now known as Surf City Europe. As if this wasn't good enough, the sand that graces the beaches of Les Landes is perfectly formed, bending the waves into shapes of such variety that almost every world-class surf spot on earth is likely to be in some way mimicked along this two-hundred-mile stretch. And to think we owe it all to Napoleon and a martyred river...

The landscape is unchanging, comprising dunes, pine forest and an endless beach – and I mean endless. Besides the odd groyne, the only man-made objects are a handful of decaying bunkers used by the Germans during the war, covered in sun- and salt-faded graffiti, which are now being absorbed into the dunes; a symbol of nature's power over human megalomania that calls to mind the 'colossal wreck' of Shelley's 'Ozymandias'. Anywhere along the *côte Atlantique* both ends of the horizon will still reveal that same stretch of sand. As the summer sun batters down, these horizons form a golden glow that looks as if the outskirts to some Celestial City lie just beyond what the eye can see; a trick of sunlight and sand that brings the transcendentalists among us a step closer to divinity.

Besides that, the water is warm, and the complete absence of rocks means wipe-outs seldom hurt. Paradise. By midsummer the beaches have turned into a writhing mass of young, suntanned, semi-naked bodies, in what becomes a glorious tribute to youth and health. I go back every year.

For me, France is a home away from home. My grandfather on my mother's side is a French speaker, having taught it along with Russian for most of his working days, and he used to talk to me in these languages from a very early age. The Russian never stuck, but I soon took advantage of a head start in school French classes. Yet the love affair with France began when my parents started sending me there every school holiday as a teenager from the age of thirteen. I'd stay with family friends, and basically live a second life there – having two sets of mates, in Wales and France. This meant I learned to speak French fluently by my mid teens, as well as becoming a little more independent travelling there and back regularly.

I suppose that however hard I try to gloss it over, though, what I am essentially talking about here is the dreaded French exchange known to so many British teenagers. The Lacroix family whom I had stayed with for two summers at the Lacanau lakeside town of Le Moutchic were great – they had a bit of money as the father worked in Parisian banks, and enrolled me each year in the academy at Surf Sans Frontières (at the time one of Lacanau's major surf clubs) along with their sons. But one year, when I was fifteen, they weren't around, and I was sent to other friends of my parents in St-Jean-de-Luz. That was when I truly began to identify with other schoolmates who moaned about their upcoming French or German exchanges.

To start with, St-Jean-de-Luz had no surf. The family claimed it did, but it didn't. A few weeks before going I remember the father sending a letter with a magazine shot of someone surfing a twenty-foot bomb near the harbour. He thought it to be proof St-Jean-de-Luz had waves, but for me it was simply proof they hadn't a clue about anything. Surf only broke there during the severest of winter storms, so Easter and summer trips were going to be a complete waste of time – especially once I learned that their sons were bodyboarders!

My parents were deaf to my pleas, though, and I was sent anyway.

It was every bit as bad as I expected. The French kids that were supposed to become my friends overnight were snooty and toad-like, more interested in table tennis than surfing, and their friends were no better. They weren't willing to head to Biarritz until day three, and even then wouldn't listen to my advice that the tide and wind were going to ruin the waves if we didn't move early. And I was right. We arrived on the beach at about one o'clock in the afternoon, just as all the real surfers were going home grinning. The onshore wind was up, and high tide had put too much water over the sandbars to stand any chance of surfing.

The father placed his picnic box in the sand with a contented smile on his face, and took out his tobacco rolling machine. He saw no reason why this wasn't an ideal surfing situation.

'*Et voilà! La plage.*' He drew out the 'e' of 'plage' into a pompous monotone. I was ready to scream. We spent the afternoon sunbathing (boring), and swimming (frustrating when you can't surf), and then, just as things looked set to improve with the wind dropping for the evening and the tide receding, it was time to go home. The mother of the family started putting her reddening breasts away again, and the rolling machine went back into Jacques's pocket. Back to St-Jean-de-Luz and the flat, flat Bay of Doom.

After another four days without riding a wave, I could stand it no more. Each morning they looked out of the window at the flat ocean and said, 'Sorry, no surf today.' That meant a two-hour breakfast, a smoke, a coffee, and then a trip somewhere pointless – often to a *petit village à la montagne*. I tried explaining that no moving water in the bay at St-Jean-de-Luz didn't mean the whole coast was flat, that we could look elsewhere at better times of day, but they refused to understand. So I ran away.

I left at five in the morning. Jacques was snoring as I slid my boardbag out into the hall. It took me about half an hour to walk to the train station, throughout which I was constantly looking over my shoulder, shitting it that they would come running after me. I saw them by now as ogres whose whole motivation in life was to stop me from being able to surf. Fortunately they never appeared. I boarded the train to Bordeaux safely, even going for a walk along the carriages once it departed to make sure I hadn't been followed.

At the other end I called the Lacroix family's grandfather and he came as quickly as possible to pick me up. I had to think of a story before he came, otherwise he'd tell my parents and send me home – or even worse back to St-Jean-de-Luz. I told him I was going to meet a friend from Wales who was in a contest at Lacanau. How he believed it, I'll never know. He asked no questions and simply dropped me off at Surf Sans Frontières, where I planned to spend the next few weeks. Not so. By the end of the day my parents had found out where I was and reserved all the necessary rail and bus tickets, with changeovers planned perfectly to ensure my arrival home by the following afternoon. Still, as a fifteen-year-old it was a good experience. I rode across France and then under the English Channel into the London Underground system, where I naively irritated commuters by sticking my surfboard out into the fast lane of the escalators. The only thing that went wrong, which those irked commuters will say served me right, was the bus driver from National Express refusing to take the beloved 6'3" on the coach.

'I don't give a fuck how old you are, or how much space there is, and how far you have to go. You can either get on now without it, or stay here and I'll leave without you,' he barked.

The board was old and next to valueless anyway, so I left it in the street – something you could probably get arrested for today. Not to say I wasn't gutted to lose it; it had been my first ever custom-made shape. I'd saved up the £270 to buy it by doing 27 weeks of a milk round with Porthcawl Point legend Gerry McKay. That board was like a part of me. I thought about how Gez had paid me a tenner per round, waking me at midnight to place freezing bottles on even more freezing doorsteps. 'Being a milkman's ideal for surfing,' he used to explain. 'I never miss the Point when it's good.' (He has since joined the police, which he claims is even more friendly on one's water time.)

Perhaps it was a sign. Leaving that magic 6'3" behind, its fluorescent orange and green spray job, a hideous clash of colour that only a teenager who didn't know any better could have asked for, now lying undignified on the curb of a London bus station, and with it a bit of innocence lost. I arrived back home tired but excited, feeling that another level of travel was now within my capabilities. The J-Bay dream was taking shape. I'd travelled from Lacanau to my home doorstep alone, with only the loss of an old board as a casualty. How much harder could it be to get to South Africa? The sense of accomplishment told me that J-Bay was a very real goal, but that I would also require a lot more experience in order to travel there and make a real go of the place. I couldn't just hop out of the playground and onto a plane to South Africa. There would need to be other places first, a few dress rehearsals. But where? France numerous more times, of course, but eventually further afield – even further outside my comfort zone.

Was this the first time surfing had taught me something?

Possibly, but I surely had France to thank as well.

Undoubtedly the main benefits of my early French experiences lay in surfing, though. However hard you work at it, improvement in Wales is a slow process. The waves are infuriatingly fickle for starters. While most of the more open-ocean places in this world get great surf when a swell is running, and something innocuous but rideable the rest of the time, we tend to get great surf once in a blue moon, something innocuous but rideable in a swell, and absolute mill-pond flatness the rest of the time. Then you need to account for half the year being too cold to surf more than once a day, or to stay in the water for any long periods of time. I used to try to calculate just how advantaged kids in Hawaii, California, Florida, South Africa, Brazil or Australia were over us poor hopefuls – and it wasn't fun. Those kids could go in and of out the water all day in light wetsuits (if they even needed one at all), surfing great waves the majority of the time without having to worry about massive Bristol Channel tides, nasty North Atlantic wind patterns, numb fingers and ice cream headaches, the sun going down at half four in winter or any of the other factors that held back their underprivileged Welsh counterparts.

Perhaps the worst of these factors was the fact that at the time we were practising a non-mainstream sport that nobody gave a shit about. Despite being geographically one of the best situated schools in the country for grooming surf talent, Porthcawl Comprehensive had a headmaster who I was convinced had not come into this world to help make it a better place. His spite was a sinister one that can only be practised by those with some degree of power and influence. He systematically refused to accept that surfing was something his pupils loved, benefited from, and were becoming good at – not even when we won the British Schools Championships for half a decade on the trot. He'd forbid teachers from announcing our successes in assembly and, worst of all, surfing was not allowed to be mentioned on the honours board. It didn't matter that Mark Schofield had won the European Junior Championships, or that four kids from my form class alone had all made it into the Welsh team – one of them being me. The lack of vindication or support hurt badly. We'd come back from summer breaks dying to tell tales of free trips to Portugal or Spain, only to find out that the football captain had had a trial for Crystal Palace – whoop-dee-doo! Two hours down the road with Mum and Dad just to kick a football in front of a couple of Second Division has-beens and this guy was a hero. But us going to Lisbon for ten days and helping Wales Juniors beat Ireland for the first time in yonks? No big deal, apparently. Surfing was *not* under any circumstances to be associated with the school.

Eventually one of my good friends, Paul Lovell, landed the strongest case ever for getting on the honours board: after the school ignored his multiple British junior titles, Paul actually won the borough's Young Sportsperson of the Year award – beating ball-sports and athletics candidates from all over. Even our draconian head couldn't get around that one, and Paul finally made the honours board – the only kid to do so from three generations of talented surfers – but his sport was left off. 'Paul Lovell: Ogwr Young Sportsperson of the Year,' it read – but at what? Croquet? Trampolining? Gurning?

Ours was a school of Oxbridge candidates, swimmers, rugby and football players, future doctors and dentists and, most importantly, drama students. The adverts for Porthcawl Comprehensive's success were the stars of the annual school show, or those going on to study theatre at uni. Besides Mr Crystal Palace, quarterly newsletters drew our attention to the ex-student who had now reached the dizzy heights of picking up the phone in a television advert for Direct Line Insurance. Never the lazy surfers – who, for the record, were usually out of the house by seven most weekends checking the waves, while the drama lot made forays into the world of underage drinking and teen pregnancy.

Most of the ground-level teachers, to be fair, loved us. One of them moved on to another school that year, and in his last ever lesson walked up to the surfers at the back of the room and stated that ours was a 'noble cause', but it was just a shame we were 'up against a regime worse than the Nazis'. That teacher naturally took his place in folklore, but the situation remained the same. The view from the top was that surfing was an activity for druggies and drop-outs, while the drama students were immaculate, model pupils. And if you'll believe that, then you'll believe that Porthcawl Point breaks as often as Malibu.

But France? Well, that was like the Promised Land.

Compared to us, French surfers were spoiled, and I'd spend every possible minute in the ocean on trips there, taking full advantage of the warm water and powerful waves. Their schools loved what surfers were doing, the national newspapers covered the competitive scene and, best of all, the waves pumped. France was, for much of my schooldays, a beautiful land of escape. A place where I was infinitely closer to doing what I wanted with life. I used to arrive filled with an excitement that still lingers to this day. France helps me to relive 'grommethood'.

A 'grommet' or 'grom' is a nickname given to a youngster who surfs. The grom is a particular breed of child. A grom is often obnoxious, usually facetious, skinny, tanned, almost always blond, covered in freckles and neckline wetsuit rashes. Groms are an enlightened bunch, stoked that they're onto something special. Groms tend to do silly things like getting wave sizes embarrassingly wrong, or wearing boxer shorts under their wetsuits. Groms get picked on badly by older surfers, a rite of passage they usually accept willingly; slaps on sunburnt backs, wedgies, dead arms, noogies and endless errands to fetch and carry things. In return, older guys allow the groms a few waves at the local reef break (and then laugh at the youngsters shitting themselves when they take off on the wrong one and get worked), take them on trips (if there's room in the boot) and look out for them when bullies come knocking. And, like all good times, grommethood is usually behind you before you realise how bloody good it is.

It's hardly surprising that everyone has their own ways of remembering their grommethoods. Why wouldn't they? Some talk about it, some just wait until they have their own groms, but one of my ways of rekindling the grommet spirit has been by going to France.

As a result, my memories gathered in France stand out more than those from all other surf trips put together and this is something that will hopefully never change. And not just because of the waves either. Over the formative years I spent there, the country itself came to represent a cosmopolitan outlook, its surfing areas filled with travelling Americans, Aussies and others, all looking for ways to make a living from something related to surfing. As a grom, southwest France used to inspire me; the hub of the European surf industry, a place where a career around surfing and its culture was always a very real possibility.

But despite the international feel to Hossegor, you will still never forget you're in France. Besides the pompousness of a stubborn country that has in most respects resisted globalisation, there is an element of light-heartedness that is good for the soul. Potentially dominant British, American and Australian cultures have been allowed in here and there, but only in a very French way. In what other country on earth could you hear 'The Shoop Shoop Song' by Cher followed by Lauryn Hill's 'Doo Wop That Thing', Aqua's 'Barbie Girl' and then Dire Straits's 'The Sultans of Swing' in succession on the same radio station, I ask?

Then there's the obvious: food and drink, especially cheese, strong coffee and, of course, wine. Bordeaux rouge. Bollocks to nectar, *this* is the drink of the gods.

Today the French surfing experience is a quintessential part of anyone's global itinerary. It is a journey through several aspects of surf culture, which must be properly done from north to south, starting in August and ending in mid-October. This voyage has the makings of a Tolkien- or C. S. Lewis-esque epic, laced with fantastical characters and pit stops. There's the cheesy tourist towns, the pro-tour circus, then the magnificent autumn swells, the grandeur of the Basque land and a quick jaunt to Northern Spain to catch one of surfing's most incredible sights – the rivermouth wave at Mundaka.

Before that, though, you have to get that drive out of the way...

★ ★ ★

'Pardon, monsieur, est-ce que vous savez qui a gagné le foot ce matin?'

As I disembarked at Le Havre on a drizzly, sleep-deprived morning, it seemed as if the whole of France was preoccupied by one thing alone – international football. It was the summer of the Japan and South Korea World Cup, so matches were being beamed into European front rooms and bars at unusual times – the latest of them being midday. France were the reigning champions, and most people believed they were going to mount a good defence.

The French have a fine sporting tradition, and the success of their athletes, including surfers, towards the end of the nineties was testament to a government policy of increasing sports funding as a platform for national well-being. Where had I heard that before? Anyway, it was working. Along with rugby, international football seemed to be as capable of grinding the country to a halt as any dissatisfied truckers. Ed, that bossy friend of mine who organised the Orkneys trip, has been living in France for years, and during the last World Cup he claimed cities had been turning to ghost towns and perfect waves going unridden, as everyone made for the nearest TV – yes, even the surfers seemed incapable of turning their backs on a good international. All radio stations that morning were re-iterating one important phrase: '*Allez les Bleus!*'

Ahead of me lay the Wastelands – the non-surfable inland country that I usually try to cross as quickly and as painlessly as possible. It is a long, lonely and eventually sweaty drive, throwing up little in the way of comforts for someone who is suffering serious ocean-withdrawal symptoms. With a good five-gear car at your disposal the journey isn't too bad, but in an ageing Nissan Micra that can't go faster than 50 mph and drinks as much oil as it does petrol, it's a different story.

To make things worse, my radio was only powerful enough to pick up the roadside channel – the name of which I don't think anybody knows, or wants to know. It is a dirge of depressing drive-time music paid for by the grumbling motorists who choose to take the *péage* – worse than silence in most cars, except that I needed something to drown out the otherwise alarming sound of my car's clanging piston-rings. I had hoped to listen to coverage of Les Bleus beginning their title defence, but the slimy DJ was making no mention of any of it. Could that be because the station was pre-recorded? Hmmn… It was probably just as well, as I soon realised things weren't going to plan for the eleven heroes running around in a distant continent, upon whom national well-being now relied.

At my first petrol-cum-oil stop I saw a middle-aged beret-capped trucker being consoled by a florid woman in her forties. I've no idea what relation to him she was, but they had both just come out of a bar together. The way she only dared rub his back tentatively suggested they weren't lovers (yet, anyway). The man sat down on a step next to his juggernaut cabin and began shaking his head disbelievingly, his face sinking into the palm of his hands. It was clear Les Bleus had lost. This was indeed confirmed by a brief stop in a nameless town just outside of Tours, where one look inside another bar was enough to cover the whole story. The disgruntled barflies were hanging their heads slightly lower than usual, and appeared quite ready to tell me all about it, explaining how they had got used to not getting their own way lately. Their teams had stopped winning, and society had stopped listening (or at least that was how retirement age had made them see things).

You could have had the same conversation inside any bar in the country that lunchtime. These men were the midday drinkers in anyone's hometown. Ex-civil servants of varying rank, disgusted that National Service had been abolished and that the youth of the day had things so easy, while the evils of the EU they had fought to protect us from had come back – and *they* were the only ones who could see it. On this occasion they had even more cause for outcry, as the nation that had just sent their world-beating footie team reeling was none other than Senegal – an old colony! (Not much more than a week later France lost again, getting eliminated at the earliest possible stage – a shambles for a team filled with players who earned in a week what most people would in a year.)

It was always great to hear the French moan, nonetheless, and the quick lunchtime *demi* was an excellent excuse for me to get out of the air-conditionless rust bucket that seemed to be my regular French travel accessory, and into some shade. That close inland summer heat had come out to play, as I had anticipated earlier, judging from the way the roadside thermometers had been showing 30 °C before my car had even arrived in Conteville. (Everyone takes a photo of the signpost here – mine lies on my living room wall right next to Twatt from the Orkneys trip, and Phokmi in Thailand.)

Heat made the next three or four hours of driving feel like ten, and it seemed an age until I eventually guided my noisy motor as best I could through the tacky tourist-market hell-hole of La Palmyre, arriving just in time to board the last ferry of the day across the Gironde estuary. Unfortunately, any chance of reaching the beach in time to wash the drive off with an evening surf had by now evaporated, along with my last drop of engine oil. That ferry was just too damn slow.

The ride down towards Hossegor is infinitely more bearable once you're south of the Gironde. The pine trees start appearing at the roadside, making you feel as if you're on the home strait, and if you take the ferry route from Royan, as I had just done, you'll be able to surf within a few miles – provided there's enough daylight left. On this occasion I'd blown it – paying a heavy price for that lunchtime *demi*.

The first beach I normally stopped at was Hourtin or Lacanau. Hourtin is less crowded, it's a little nearer to the ferry and there's a good Welsh contingent there – so you can always have a relaxed surf, which helps after a long drive. But if I can be bothered to stay in the car an extra twenty minutes, then Lacanau tends to be where I'll have my first few waves.

It would have been amazing to take a quick half-hour before sunset in the playful beach front peaks there, but with sunset imminent, I'd known there was no chance of that before the boat even left. Pissed off, I opted to drive on all the way down to Hossegor then and there. Hossegor was my ultimate destination anyway – it was where several friends were staying for the summer, and therefore the best place to hopefully blag a bit of work if I got skint (absolute last resort).

Within an hour of dusk my car had gone from sauna to fridge, which brought the growling air-heaters out to play. It wasn't far off midnight when I eventually made it down to the campsites at Vieux-Boucau, where a couple of crooked holiday reps were doing a great sideline in fitting their mates into accommodation they had told their bosses was full of paying customers. With the first and hardest part of the trip behind me, the voyage across the Wasteland complete, the next thing to wait for would be the glorious contest season.

The ASP (Association of Surfing Professionals) usually arrives at the beginning of August. Surfing promptly becomes *the* coolest sport on earth for four short weeks in the lives of mainland Europe's inner-city holidaymakers, hell-bent on reinventing themselves for the summer before they slink back into their respective colleges and offices for another eleven months. The Scandinavians, French, Germans and Dutch watch on as south-west France becomes a proving ground, the host of three consecutive, mega-buck World Tour qualifying contests. A must-do for anyone who ever wants to be anybody in the sport.

These events are total bloodbaths and never fail to separate the men from the boys, or, in other words, the athletes from the party-goers. For over two decades, France has hosted three or more major annual events, almost always in the month of August. Things have changed over the years, but the three contests will always be there, regardless of whether they carry championship points or merely qualifying points.

When I was a grommet, the World Championship Tour itself used to stop in Lacanau, Hossegor and Biarritz consecutively, often having a huge bearing on the outcome of the World Title race. I used to meet French people in places nowhere near the coast who had obtained Kelly Slater's autograph without even knowing who he was. 'I saw him when I was on holiday,' they'd say.

It was at these contests as a grommet that I first saw most of the pros surf. In the week before the Lacanau Pro, I and a group of friends from the surrounding area would all have a go at the Pro Junior event, just to get the wristbands that would allow you into the VIP area. Then, once we'd done our bit, and the Pro Junior had been won (always by someone other than us), it was time to sit back and watch the freak show. It used to blow me away. I'd look at heat sheets and schedule my own surfs carefully: Kelly Slater Vs Damien Hardman – a big one, not worth missing just for a few waves; and Rob Machado Vs Vetea David, another hot potato. Better leave going surfing until Todd Prestage Vs Victor Ribas, but even then only a quick one, because Ross Williams's heat is next...

When I was a grommet, these ASP events would be a chance to get bowled over by how good someone could actually be at the sport of surfing. Watching them was truly inspirational. OK, I wasn't witnessing any events as momentous as that ride of Tom Curren's at J-Bay – the ride that was slowly shaping my whole purpose as a surfer – but I got to see, and remember, some pretty cool stuff nonetheless. Sometimes it would be little titbits of impressive surfing, like Shea Lopez squeaking through the tightest backhand barrel ever at a two-foot low-tide sandbank, Rob Machado taking off hopelessly late on a semi-close-out and driving straight back up six-feet of whitewater, or Shane Beschen tearing into big onshore right-handers at Lacanau Central. Such moments would remain with me forever as examples of the freakish talent these guys could display.

But above all that, I got to see Kelly Slater's rise to dominance. He'd been billed as Tom Curren's successor, and it was in the mid nineties that he began fulfilling that promise. For that golden decade of pro surfing, France was a grandstand. And I was often somewhere on the sand taking in every possible wave.

All year long we'd see and read about these guys ripping it up all over the world; Indonesia, Australia, Hawaii, South Africa and elsewhere. And then, simple as you like, they were in the water next to you, surfing the same peaks, buying ham and cheese baguettes from the same shop as you, standing on the same stretch of sand, enjoying the same midsummer heat, the same evening glass-offs, and on occasion the same nightlife.

And in return, France loved them. By finals day you wouldn't be able to move, as seemingly all of the Gironde turned out to watch someone get declared event winner. Immediately the final was over, I'd paddle straight out and surf the very waves in which it had just taken place. Imagine being able to do that at other sports venues! And at the end of the year, when the ASP World Surfing Champion (usually Slater) was crowned, I could feel content that their title probably wouldn't have been possible without the ratings points they'd gained under my watch in southern France.

This all changed a bit at the end of the nineties, though. Slater took a several-year sabbatical, and the Tour needed something injected into it, something to make people want to watch it again. The decision was made to move all the events to their best wave windows – which for France is late autumn. The pros were stoked, but it meant spectators slipped down the priority list, as TV rights and web feeds became the new way to watch the 'Top 44' surfers eligible to win the World Title. The three French August events were downgraded to World Qualifying Series status (known as WQS, or 'QS' for short).

But the WQS events still have cut-throat excitement to them – sometimes even more. The QS guys are often literally surfing to eat, meaning that there's always a subtext when you see a no-name from the Brazilian slumlands beating an eighteen-year-old Californian megastar-to-be. The QS is all about hunger. The surfing isn't always pretty, and it can be a real stumbling-block to up-and-coming riders from the wealthier nations – kids who are already on a good wage just for getting their photo taken, but who won't get taken seriously until they 'make it' by securing a WCT berth.

And besides hunger, the QS is often about Brazil: a great surfing nation whose riders have a unique outlook on the sport – fiercely competitive, and sticking together through thick and thin. They annoy a lot of people, often getting accused of lacking in soul, or missing the point of it all, but like it or not, in the French qualifying contests they are a force to be reckoned with.

This summer the Brazilians were more invigorated than ever. With the footballing flops Les Bleus out the way, Brazil had inevitably claimed back what was theirs, beating another team from Old Europe, Germany, in the World Cup final. August was only a month into their new four-year reign as the best soccer nation on earth, and the party spirit was in full flow. Wherever you went, there were smug Brazilians with more energy than you, be it bars, supermarkets or even secret surf spots.

Seasoned veterans liken the French leg of the tour to Jesus' forty days of temptation. If rookies can survive the lure of forest parties until ten in the morning and the desire to waste money eating out, then they will probably beat the guy next to them just by being healthier and more relaxed. By event two, the streets are lined with tragic young pros trying to sell their surfboards and clothes (and sometimes even their bodies), because they've spent all of their winnings from the last event on cheap red wine, or at Hossegor's infamous Rock Food bar, and then failed to win any more cash as a direct result of said wine.

Rock Food is the devil's den. Crazy DJs, who don't have to get up in the morning, spend the whole night trying to persuade healthy young people to abuse themselves to the point of near death, spending the last euros their parents have desperately wired them in case of hard times. And at whatever hour the various watering holes choose to close, the fallout is probably worse than the French Revolution. Hundreds of E-jacked campers from mainland Europe and city-dwelling 'pro-hos' run for the beaches, forests and car parks looking for somewhere to continue the party. A vicious circle of headaches and sunburn develops – each becoming the remedy for the other – until the season ends and the victims wash home, brittle shells of the virulent youths they were back in July. While most of them are having the time of their lives, this scene is something the pros have to stay away from if they are to survive.

Careers are made and lost. While some surfers hit rock-bottom, others use the ego-boosting media circus to embark on competitive surges, grinding out the results that will invariably mean that they won't need to work that winter. Surf travel is the prize. Endless surf travel, with someone else footing the bill. Making a successful pro career is a ticket to some of the world's best waves. Rip it up in a big French QS contest and you could soon be on your way to Indo on a luxury yacht, or to Central America with *Surfer Magazine*. Not to mention the itinerary that would await anyone who actually won enough points to get promoted to the Championship Tour – the summer party scene and onshore winds would then give way to the raw juice of autumn Hossegor perfection. A spot on the CT would also send you to Australia, Tahiti, Fiji, Japan, J-Bay, California, France, Brazil and Hawaii in one year – at a minimum. But to get there, these guys first need to survive a French August.

Winners and losers are not the only thing made in that August mayhem either. A quick look inside one of the many warehouses in the forest behind Hossegor reveals billions of euros worth of clothing and equipment which is sent off to various parts of the continent from these distribution buildings, and the names that are most in demand are the ones being worn by the contest winners. Whoever is flavour of the month is worth their weight in gold. Prize money is peanuts compared to the sponsorships that a surfer can command if the French holidaymakers incline to like him. The companies with the biggest warehouses, like Quiksilver and Billabong, have never underestimated the knock-on effect that signing the right teamrider can have on a label's reputation. All the most successful brands have a major star that helped make them: Quiksilver rose largely off the back of Kelly Slater's success, Rip Curl from Tom Curren, and Billabong owe a big debt of thanks to Mark Occhilupo. And all of those guys had to come and make a name for themselves in France at some point. Hossegor is the scene of Slater's first ever WCT win – it was in the same postal zone as those very warehouses that he beat the Aussie veteran Gary Elkerton to officially begin his march on the record books, and the arrival of pro surfing as business.

But then, as quickly as a blurry night in Rock Food, the masses disappear, most gone home to forget about surfing until next year. By the beginning of September the Parisian schoolchildren are writing 'what I did this summer' essays about surf stars, while back in Les Landes, supermarkets begin selling their stocks at half price. This particular season there are thousands of unsold soft-drink cans with the losing French football team's autographed mug-shots on them left to clear before it's time to shut for the winter. By mid-September another car passing by has become a rare sight, on a road that had been gridlocked day in, day out for the last eight weeks. Most of the bars are back to looking like that sleepy establishment near Tours, where I had gone the day it all started going wrong for Les Bleus. Once Hossegor looks like this, I end up with two decisions: go home to find work, officially declaring an end to the summer, or head into the Basque land where an entirely new consciousness awaits.

Wherever possible, I choose the latter. For years I used to bemoan the end of summer, trudging back to school, just longing for the year when I could finally stay away into September. Eventually it came, and within a few years I found it hard to imagine anything different to the routine, hard to remember how anyone ever coped with going home too early to experience those cooling, offshore autumn mornings. The Basque land feels like the afterlife that French surf culture goes to post-August.

So once World Cup fever had subsided, and the circus moved on, I was looking forward to making my way further south. Anyway, this time I had unfinished business to accomplish before I could continue to destinations further afield: the world-famous Spanish left-hander Mundaka had been evading me for years, and this time it wasn't going to get away.

Yes, besides a fascinating and strong people, the Spanish Basque land is also home to Europe's best wave. Situated just in the mouth of the Guernika river, Mundaka is a small village with a big secret. Concealed below the watermark there lies a tongue of seabed that tickles and tricks any swells malleable enough into rolling down it for half a mile, spitting and dredging sand in and out of a frothing cavernous tube the whole way. But go there on the wrong day and it will be totally flat, hidden from view.

Mundaka is a fickle bastard of a spot, to say the least. It takes dedication and careful oceanic understanding to score good waves there. Swell conditions must be massive, strong and coming from the north-west; the wind must be southerly, or south-westerly; you need a low tide which is preferably in the afternoon in order to get the most daylight surfing hours; good, recent rain patterns to make the river optimum for shaping the estuary bed; and then a dose of luck. Since these elements come together rarely at the best of times, Mundaka succeeds in becoming a myth to most.

At some point I needed to make a concentrated effort to turn that myth into reality. Previous attempts to catch the place working had been to no avail, but now I was going to add patience to my arsenal. This time Mundaka would happen for me.

When it did break, Mundaka was said to be a spectacle that drew audiences from all walks of life. Young Aussie scoundrels could draw gasps from the same air as Catholic families in Sunday dress. And, as if the perfection of the waves wasn't enough, the backdrop was a gargantuan thirteenth-century church that towered over the take-off zone like a stern teacher supervising a playground scuffle. That alone made it a favourite among visitors.

Mundaka now had a place in my plans. I was determined to make it my first experience of what Ed called the 'A1 world-class waves'. Getting to surf at this mythical left-hander was becoming a vital part of the bigger picture, and would also include the collateral benefit of hanging around one of my favourite parts of the world for a while longer.

And so, one September morning the mobile home lent to me by the crooked rep crew was emptied of my essential belongings, and the keys turned in. It was time to move on, the plan being for Ed to put me up (although he was going to be the last to find out about it). Three quarters of an hour later, the outskirts of the Pays Basque were in view. A moment was spared for the French France getting left behind, the summer of great, playful surf. Then crossing the bridge into Bayonne, thoughts turned on towards the autumn, to the prospect of some more serious swells – and a chance to wax up the big-wave board. On towards Euskadi and the Basques. And Mundaka.

(Part II):
Pays Basque/Euskadi

Having crossed that bridge, the changes are at first subtle, growing on you the more time you spend in Pays Basque, and the deeper you travel inside the border.

At the centre of French Basque culture is Bayonne. Nowhere on earth can so much eccentricity, so much character be found in stone. Parallels with the Celestial City are easy to find. That heroic river Ardour guards the border back into French France, like a moat, breached only by the bridge that has carried the pilgrim over into the land beyond. The first sight of Bayonne revolves around the twin spires of a gothic cathedral, one slightly lighter in colour than the other (this is because it's newer, rebuilt after heavy bombing during WW2). Surrounding the cathedral is a network of ancient streets barely wide enough to fit small cars. A canopy of tall buildings blocks out the sun, keeping the air cool and giving each street a feeling of intimacy and nobility. Napoleon's tracks; Old Europe. As some of the world's cities become more and more homogenous, this is a place that will hold its character for a long time yet.

Bayonne is a bustling student city, crammed with riverfront cafés and bars that hum with intelligent debate. The female half of this populace is undoubtedly what had attracted Ed to move here of all places – although he would claim his reasons to be food and culture. I knew him better, but there may still have been some truth in his excuse. The food is, as can be expected of any key French cultural-historical city, bloody great as standard. After a feed of garlic mussels, salad, steak and spicy red wine, the taste of a lemon-flavoured gâteau Basque is one of my most indulgent guilty pleasures.

In the lee of the city is Anglet, where we would surf while I waited for a Mundaka swell; a quaint beachside town with a reputation for fostering great surfers. No surprise, given the collection of world-class beach breaks that lie within a few hundred yards of each other – yet another Napoleon Bonaparte Production, as they are again a by-product of the Ardour's diverted magic. Anglet was the adopted home of three-times world champion Tom Curren for years, and he still returned from time to time. 'Nobody rides it like Curren,' most local surfers claimed. From there, the beachside road runs quickly into the grandeur of Biarritz. It is in Biarritz that European surfing was born in the fifties, brought over from California by a crew of pioneering hedonists that included a Hollywood filmmaker who had come to the town to make a screen adaptation of Hemingway's *The Sun Also Rises*. The area's profile soon grew, and it quickly became a summertime haunt of some of the big stars of the era, such as the late Malibu legend Miki Dora.

Part of France's notoriety back then was due to a sandbar a few miles north, dubbed simply 'La Barre'. La Barre was a perfect spitting left-hand tube that quickly got compared to Pipeline in Hawaii. Soon all the top surfers of the age were coming over to try and take it on, but it didn't last. A jetty extension at the mouth of the Ardour river killed the wave, moving the sandbanks away by disrupting whatever coastal drifts had caused La Barre to happen. It was a sad day, but not enough to prevent the bug from catching on in Europe.

Just beyond Biarritz is a succession of quieter Basque villages, and more good surf breaks, particularly Guethary, one of the first big-wave spots in the Atlantic Ocean – a mammoth winter peak that has been compared to Hawaii's Sunset Beach. In decades past Guethary could have been the 'A1' I was looking for, as its big shoulder would have once deemed it the perfect spot to ride huge surf. But now, with modernised equipment, surfers considered Mundaka's pitching tubes to be a better ideal of the perfect wave.

The other reason I wasn't so drawn to Guethary was that I'd already surfed it in previous years. At the time it had been scary, but I knew it was nowhere near the quality of a wave like Mundaka, or J-Bay – waves that stood up to you at speed.

Beyond Guethary there are one or two more reefs and points, before the bay of St-Jean-de-Luz opens before you; the wave-starved town where I was tortured as a grommet, a place I had little desire to go back to – until it became necessary to pass through on my way to Mundaka.

The waves had been small since the day I turned up at Ed's place in Bayonne, and impatience was setting in. There had been rumours for some time that a swell was due, but nothing had been showing at all on the beaches. Rumours are always rife in flat spells, but in the past few days some of the more reliable forecasts had begun agreeing that the Atlantic would soon come to life. The US Navy's wave-buoy chart, the modern forecasting tool used by any surfer with access to the web, was indicating the right conditions for Mundaka to break, and so it appeared time to move again. The tired Micra, which had been enjoying some temporary rest while I made Ed drive to the beach every day, was duly loaded with essentials, and reluctantly fired up for a hopeful Spanish road trip. Stopping for a quick evening surf at Anglet in the building swell, I got back in the car, making headway towards St-Jean-de-Luz and the border.

After the Spanish border begins Euskadi, the Spanish Basque land. General Franco refused to grant the Basques a homeland, which led them to claim provinces of both France and Spain. Euskadi begins at the French border, includes some of the Pyrenees (as does Pays Basque on the other side of the border), and ends about halfway between Santander and Bilbao, where the slightly less rebellious province of Cantabria takes over.

Travelling to Mundaka from France was like going to Narnia, Wonderland or Middle Earth. Just like every other time I'd done it, the drive through the Pyrenees became a battle with a moody gatekeeper, as the sky dropped everything it had on me; hail, sleet, stone, rainwater. The storms that live in those hills only seem to have one goal: to disorientate the traveller. Just as you think the rain is going to shatter you to kingdom come, the lightning starts, making you wonder if you've taken a wrong turn and ended up in a war-zone. By the time it clears, the transition has been made. Flat, pine-irrigated France has turned into the dramatic landscape of Northern Spain. Glacier-formed valleys abound, with high ground often dropping straight into the sea. Everybody here has a good sense of their own insignificance in the face of nature. Even the cars seem to have wise and weathered facial features.

I arrived in the middle of the night after a particularly violent storm had turned a ninety-kilometre journey into a six-hour endurance voyage. The rain on the car window was so thick it was hard to make out much of the town, but the thin cobbled roads and a familiar glade of trees were evidence enough that this was the village of Mundaka. Somewhere in that darkness, not more than a hundred yards away for all I knew, the wave could have been firing then and there, perfect tube after perfect tube going unridden in the stormy night. Hopelessly late for finding hotels, and scared of getting soaked to the skin, I parked in the first space I could find, and decided to lock myself inside the car until morning.

As always happens in the lap of a world-class surf spot, I was woken by two surfers trying to creep unnoticed into the water's edge just before dawn. Recognisable accents... Australian.

Mundaka was breaking. You could tell from the mood. A still autumn morning with a light mist, no evidence of the storm any more, and a steady flow of pedestrians in the direction of the churchyard from where people watch the wave. I followed, wanting to overlook the line-up from this eerie vantage point.

As the mist cleared it all came into view; a pulsating swell charging into the Guernika rivermouth. Lots of moving water. I turned and ran back to my car to suit-up, returning minutes later to the harbour from which people were paddling out.

It is an incredibly intimidating place to surf. The huge valley dwarfs the huge river estuary, which dwarfs the huge waves, which dwarf the surfer. Anyone who jumps into that harbour without butterflies in their stomach has not properly taken in their surroundings. From there, the next step is to ease yourself out of the entrance and into a deep-water river current. The rip was alarmingly fast, but it carried me into the dense crowd of aggressive local surfers and selfish visitors with barely the need to paddle at all.

Within a few moments, I was going to be up and riding on one of the most famous left-handers in the world.

Different accents and dialects drifted through the heavy air, but one stood out above all others: Basque. Mundaka has always had a sternly enforced local hierarchy. The regulars knew exactly what they were doing, and went about it with no time for any bullshit. They commanded a respect for their homeland, and rode the wave with awesome abandon, taking off deeper and steeper than anyone else. Visiting surfers sometimes meet a hostile attitude in Spain, not just Euskadi. It is a place where waves are guarded jealously. Not many Spanish surfers travel, and those who do stand out in any crowd because of their sympathetic and informed attitude to other travellers.

Several seasons previously, I had been attacked in a Spanish line-up for 'catching too many waves', and it taught me all kinds of lessons. Hot-headed territorial behaviour towards visiting surfers is known in surfing as 'localism', and most countries are plagued by it in one way or another. Localism usually tends to develop in certain spots more than others, for a variety of reasons, its effects varying from a dirty look and a waxed windscreen to criminal assault and expensive car vandalism. Lunada Bay in California has often been described as one of the most localised spots around, along with some of Hawaii's lesser-known breaks. I met an Australian professor once who claimed that localism occurs most in underprivileged urban areas, but I'm sure it's unlikely to be the only cause.

However you see it, localism was to blame for the black eye landed on me one 'quiet' September afternoon. It was my first summer after finishing school for good, and I had naively travelled to an exposed beach break near Santander with two friends, after having yet again been fooled hook, line and sinker by rumours of a Mundaka swell. We were revelling in the fact that for the first time in our lives there was no need to return home in September, and in the event of failing to surf our original target wave in Mundaka, were simply keen to surf anything, as long as it was in Spain. It was a reasonably pleasant day, although in the rapidly weakening sun you could feel the summer's power receding as we pulled up at the inconspicuous beachside car park. Some twenty surfers were scrapping over a waist-high peak. I fancied a few waves before dark, and paddled out.

On arriving in the line-up it was obvious the crowd wasn't very friendly but, undeterred, I proceeded to hassle my way into three set waves almost straight away. Sadly, I was known for this. Friends always regretted sitting next to me when a good wave came through, since I'd never been good at wave sharing.

At my fourth consecutive attempt to steal the peak a man in his thirties dropped in on me, and started shouting. He jumped off his board and tried to tackle me. When we surfaced he began to scream.

'*Lo siento, no hablo Español,*' I pleaded, guessing this may not be the time to try practising any of my other more shaky Spanish phrases.

He had, however, obviously rehearsed this situation before. 'OUT, OUT, OUT!' He pointed to the beach. 'GET OUT!'

Getting ordered out of the water is not uncommon in certain places, and is usually just a warning to you to simmer down and leave some waves for the locals. Rarely is such a command to be taken seriously. I decided to play dumb at first.

'You what?'

'OUT!'

Actually, he did look kind of serious. Having no time for localism, though, I decided to make myself known in no uncertain terms. 'Fuck off!' It wasn't rude, just defensive, and maybe slightly scornful. Then came the punch, and about four or five other surfers turned and started paddling towards me. I shit myself straight away, any attempts to play the hard man vanishing instantly. Instead, I paddled for dear life, scraping my way back up the rocky slope to our car.

When I arrived in the car park my friends were laughing their heads off. Another rule of surfing: never have too much sympathy over your mate's misfortune – especially when deep down inside you feel he is a deserving recipient.

It later emerged that this particular spot has always been notorious for localism – the reason most savvy travelling surfers tended to stay away.

My trips to Spain had often ended in this kind of frustration, as either the waves decided not to come up, or something else went wrong. And even though I was now finally getting to surf my first A1 world-class surf spot, at long last catching an elusive Mundaka swell in action, this occasion was still no exception.

I'd made it into the line-up without anything going wrong, and after taking a few minutes to watch and gather my bearings, stroked into a couple of waves. Eventually I grew less tentative and started to get into some really good ones. So far so good. I saw a few broken boards, and one guy twist his knee about forty degrees the wrong way, but misfortune seemed at this point destined to avoid me. After a couple of hours in, which just about everything went to plan, I decided it was time to catch one in – a light lunch was in order if the afternoon's low tide was to be taken full advantage of. It was an idea to choose waves wisely at Mundaka, since the first few sections were really tricky and hard to make. The wave would begin by pounding its way over a sandbar that looked to have the consistency of concrete, and my successful session had been based around calculated risk. I hadn't been fooled by the locals making it look easy, remembering that taking the wrong wave usually carried quite a stiff penalty – at least a chance to get up close and personal with that concrete-like sand.

But now, feeling dangerously invincible, I saw one that looked good (and, perhaps more importantly, unridden) and swung round to take off. Just as everything was looking hunky-dory, the wave's bottom seemed to drop away leaving a long, airborne drop onto the uncovered sandbar. The time had obviously come to resolve myself to a beating, and to take a deep breath. Water rapids ran off the sand in front as Mundaka cruelly drained any water cushion from under my feet. The beating wasn't as bad as expected, but when I came up, my only board was broken in two.

Gutted – but at least it wasn't a body part. Nobody in their right mind would lend someone a board at Mundaka, so the only way to surf again would be to buy another one. There were supposedly a couple of shops selling a good range of boards in a place called Zarrautz, about half an hour back towards the French border, so I set off straight away.

(Part III):
Franzia: 31km

The road that hugs the Basque coast of Spain is quite impressive, threading its way in and out of small headland tunnels and cliffs. The drive is quiet, punctuated only by the odd near-death experience as suicidal maniacs fly by on the other side of the road. Bollocks to terrorism and disease; foreign roads are the most dangerous thing a British traveller will ever encounter.

Intense scenery occasionally gives way to depressing towns of high-rise flats and thick pollution. The Monte Carlo-esque highway rounds one last piece of headland, dipping briefly into a tunnel before squaring up to another set of high apartments overlooking a lengthy beach break, which is rarely worth surfing, however desperate you are. But it didn't take long to find a surfboard shop.

Everything could have all run to plan if, in a blinding moment of ignorance, I hadn't forgotten about an aspect of southern European culture that has been the downfall of many surfers, usually hungry ones: the *siesta*. While Britain was built around cups of tea, Spain was built around siestas. And if you need anything that involves retail, be it a sandwich or a surfboard, during this time, then your luck is certainly out. A sign on the shop door read:

HORAS:
SABADO: 11.00–13.30 & 16.00–20.00
SEMANA: 11.00–13.00 & 16.30–20.00

It was 13.35.

Contrary to my French, my Spanish is poor at best, so although I had my suspicions it was hard to be totally confident which of these referred to the weekend, and I wouldn't know for sure until 16.00 when the shop would either open or stay shut for another half-hour. Meanwhile, I was well aware that low-tide Mundaka was probably going off the perfection scale in my absence.

All the other shops were shut too, so to kill time I went for a stroll along the beach. The surf actually looked OK, which was frustrating given my current surfboard predicament. Instead of torturing myself further, I retreated to the promenade to drink a few strong coffees and eat a particularly rancid burger, while watching a football match in one of the bars. The Spanish season was now in full swing, and a Real Madrid team, full of excited and newly signed Brazilian World Cup heroes, was annihilating some poor cannon-fodder side in front of a capacity crowd. Each time they scored the whole bar would leap to the roof screaming – even at 5–0. It wasn't even their team playing, but that meant nothing. Football was football.

I looked at my watch and set off back to the shop – which, I had managed to gauge from one of the friendlier locals, was the only surf shop that had any chance of reopening at all that day. At 16.00 nobody came. At 16.06 it started raining heavily. At 16.30 nobody. At 16.47 the rain stopped.

The shop eventually opened at 17.00. A small man with wet hair came running down the road clutching a salad roll.

He'd obviously been surfing through the siesta and decided it was too good to get out just to sell a surfboard to a grumpy Welshman. And who can blame him?

As I sat impatiently waiting for the guy to unlock the door, a terrible mistake dawned on me: by making my desperation visible I was sure to have weakened myself in his commission-hungry eyes.

'How much are your boards?' I asked urgently.

'Four hundred and thirty euros,' was the casual response.

'No they're not. My friend bought one here this morning for three hundred and seventy!'

'Which board?'

'A six-two with FCS,' I bluffed. He looked at me hard.

'Why you need new board fast?'

I made a snapping gesture and said, 'Mundaka'. That seemed to break the ice a bit.

'Four hundred,' was the new and improved offer.

'Four hundred with FCS and leash?' I replied. In most of Europe and America, you can often strike a deal over boards in a good surf shop – as long as you ask properly.

'OK. Which board?'

I started to look around. Two sticks caught my eye; a 6'2" and a 6'3", both made by different visiting Aussie shapers. 'Which of these do you prefer?' I asked him. He didn't know which one I was thinking of, and didn't want to risk further undermining my already low trust of him by trying to sell me the wrong board. After about thirty seconds he settled on the 6'2" – not the one I'd been thinking of.

'I prefer the six-three",' I explained. He instantly backpeddled and agreed with me. I paid and ran straight to the car park to wax the thing up. It was too late to go back to Mundaka now, as the rising tide would have certainly put too much water over the sandbar for it to continue breaking properly. It was frustrating, but the last few hours had made me decide to cut my losses. At least I'd finally surfed it, and the session up until the broken board had been a good one. It was definitely time to leave Spain and get back to Pays Basque. Not before a quick surf out front, though.

Surfing on a brand new board sucks, put simply. You're scared to turn it too hard in case it hasn't properly cured yet. New boards generally need two or three weeks of curing time before the fibreglass reaches optimum strength – during which time they should be rested in a warm, dry room, admired in their virgin waxlessness, stroked, fondled and lovingly bonded with. Anything less than a fortnight and a board can be brittle.

All this was in my mind walking onto the sand to choose where exactly among the shifting peaks I was going to surf. The paddle turned out to be an absolute mission, no friendly rips to help you sneak around the sandbars, and no let-ups in the swell either – just mountains of whitewater, pounding me back to shore. By the time I got out the back, I was wondering why I'd bothered. The waves were a lot heavier than they'd looked from the beach, and hardly ideal conditions to try out a new board. My hesitant attitude soon got me into trouble. Paddling for a thick lump of a wave, I didn't commit properly to it. My strokes were slow and reluctant, failing to get me over the ledge properly, and promptly leading to an exact replica of the position I'd been in at Mundaka that morning: suspended in mid-air and falling fast. That wasn't where the parallels ended either. My new 6'3" had obviously not spent three weeks in storage before going onto the shop floor, because it broke easily, the nose half washing into the beach with the remaining whitewater.

I was furious, especially when, marching into the shop holding the two halves, I came across the portly salesman catching up on some surf-stolen siesta time.

'The board was cure for six weeks,' he told me.

'You're a crap liar.'

'What you want me do?'

'Give me that six-two,' I told him. He let out a forced laugh, trying to act taken aback, as if this was the first time he'd ever heard of such a demand. Legally, it was not his problem, but good surfboard manufacturers will usually replace a brand new board if you can convince them it broke in an innocuous situation. Maybe it was pity at having seen me break two boards in one day, or maybe he simply realised the chances of this one giving in were slim; either way, he began reluctantly fitting the FCS fins onto the fresh board. I left him looking frosty and aggrieved, and headed for the toll road back to Bayonne. It was annoying to let a silly beach break get the better of me – in most other circumstances it would have been necessary to have another surf – but there was no way I'd risk breaking a third stick in one day. It felt as if this was a losing streak that would only end once back in France.

While Bayonne is my favourite city on earth, I fear that San Sebastian (*Donostia*, in Basque) is my worst. On paper it should be a reasonable enough place to visit, with its Rio de Janeiro-style Christ statue, promenade and designer shops all highly proclaimed by the local tourist board. But my reality of it is that traffic slows to a Central London halt, tempers flare in the heat and unpleasant smells waft through the windows, many of them including vehicle emissions. And then there's the constant bleating of car horns too. I always go to Euskadi with one rule in mind: avoid San Sebastian, and this I was able to do now.

It started raining hard as I passed the junction labelled Donostia, and the traffic began to slow at an alarming rate. The Pyrenees were throwing their best at us again. The inside of the car was misting up and my rain-soaked clothes were itching. *Mundaka is a fickle bastard of a wave*, I reminded myself.

As the traffic crawled along, bombarded by more water than you'd ever have imagined a sky being able to hold, I began remembering all the times I had taken trips to Mundaka, hopeful of world-class surf and intrigued by Euskadi, only to return to France annoyed and tired.

Maybe that's what the Spanish Basques want, I thought. After all, most people immediately associated Basque with the acronym 'E.T.A.'; a terror group whose cause was to shake off the label of French and Spanish nationality. Not many advocated violence, but a lot of people in Euskadi were passionate about a dream of independence – leaving all sorts of slogans by the roadsides. Maybe my constant bad luck with going there was somehow part of the campaign. Perhaps the Spanish Basques wanted to make the experience so wretched that anyone sympathetic to the French oppressors wouldn't ever want to come back. I started to think about the divides that existed in the region, and its bitter history of localism and separatism, wondering if a day would ever come when French, Spanish, French-Basque and Spanish-Basque would all cast aside their differences and unite. Maybe surfing was going to be the catalyst for it all. Then, seeing that it would be the smaller country Euskadi making the most compromises, I began to realise why they might resist it so forcefully.

As the border town of Irun drifted by to the west, a road sign was supposed to read, 'Franzia: 1km'. The bridge over Ardour and into 'France proper' was thirty kilometres further on from this border, and someone had used that fact to make clear their views of nationality. A big black '3' had been graffitied in front of the '1'.

Franzia: 31km.

Basque territory until then.

I wondered where Ed would have been surfing that day, and whether he'd have any food when I got in.

Mundaka hadn't quite got the better of me, I decided. It had shaken me up, toyed with my comfort zone a bit, but surely that was a good thing. I was going to recharge my energies and move on. The ambition was growing.

And I had other important questions to think about too. Like where was I going to go for a winter trip this year?

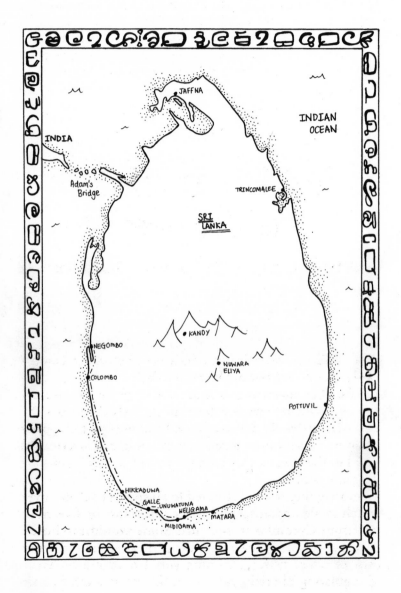

4.

Hell for Half
a Rupee:

Getting Closer on Sri Lanka's Galle Road

A kalanka was a pretty safe driver. One of Sri Lanka's finest, and boy did he need to be.

The first thing to strike anyone about the country formerly named Ceylon is how ridiculously dangerous the traffic is. *Statistically*, it could be said that the first thing most likely to strike you is actually a speeding and overloaded bus, but then again, that'd only be another way of making the same point.

Before going there, I listened to all sorts of debates over which mode of transport was the safest for the five-hour run from Colombo to the surf. Some would say buses, because they're biggest, while others favoured your own personal driver, claiming you'd have more chance of regulating his risk-taking – in theory, at least. I chose

Akalanka; the giggly, hard-working, safe-driving son-in-law of two of southern Sri Lanka's original surfer-hosts, Jai and Sumana – who are known to wave-seekers worldwide for their cooking and kindness.

Several nerve-jangling journeys later, I knew it was a wise choice.

'Look, look. Ack-see-dent,' he squealed gaily, pointing to the side. Varied responses erupted from the back of the van, but the loudest was Johan, a normally reserved and articulate Swede: *'JESUS CHRIST!'* he yelled. A black Lexus had flown off the road, missing a turning and sailing twenty yards into the jungle, the result of which was that the crumpled car now resembled little more than a metal bin-bag. On the scale of horrendous Sri Lankan car crashes this one would have to lie close to the top, which was why scores of locals milled excitedly around it. Some were holding T-shirts over their noses to fend off the smell of decay that already hung in the fertile tropical air, while others just stared in fascination. It was an event, and good or bad, events will always entertain.

'No ambulance yet,' Johan noted, quickly reverting to his usual, controlled self.

'No, no ambulance yet,' I agreed. But then again, what use would an ambulance's sirens be in a country where every car drives like one? Yes, south-west Sri Lanka's mighty Galle Road is nothing short of a rollercoaster ride leading to an early grave. New cars gather dents as fast as mileage, smog fills the air, and the presiding sound is a cacophony of overused horns (far worse than in San Sebastian, and many of which have been customised to play all sorts of outdated Western jingles). Their message is simple: *'Get out of the way right now or I'm going to run you off this road!'*

Despite all the chaos, there is still an implicit hierarchy, and it goes like this: the biggest vehicle has right of way. Simple; and pretty effective too if you happen to be towards the top of the traffic food-chain – a position that is staunchly defended by the buses. These steel-bodied highway dictators are closely followed by their equally fearless counterpart, the 'AC Bus' (air-conditioned). ACs are faster and ruder, thinking they own the road simply because they ferry a slightly richer clientele. While the ordinary buses are often so overflowing with sweating and terrified passengers that they can barely take a bend without going onto two wheels, the AC's limit themselves to seating room only. They will also get you there quicker (if at all), and cost more to ride, although if you think any of the above makes them safer, prepare to be sorely mistaken – AC drivers are the craziest of all, the dangerous blend of vehicle weight and manoeuvrability too much for them to resist.

Further down the pile are cars and tuk-tuks. They know they'll come off worse out of a head-on with a bus or lorry, and take fewer liberties as a result (but still won't be shy of giving a pedestrian or dog a nasty scare). Living alongside this free-for-all are cattle, and then bicycles, which often swerve alarmingly under the weight of two or more people, making them frighteningly prone to a lethal bus attack at any time.

Akalanka was used to this mayhem, though, knowing when to go for the overtake, and when not to. And if ever he did have a close scrape, he'd just turn round to face you with an *oops!*-expression, and giggle it off, usually forgetting about it in the very same breath. He loved the road.

'Wanting puttin' in music?' he asked, and then inserted a cassette into the machine. Before long his minibus's enormous speakers were thumping along to the sound of his favourite tape: *Golden Hits* of the legendary Boney M, including such tracks as 'Brown Girl in the Ring', 'Ra-Ra-Rasputin', 'Hooray! Hooray!', and, of course, 'Daddy Cool'. In Britain, this band had long ago resigned itself to doing the circuit of university balls, and to being admired for their kitsch. Here, though, Boney M was the latest in-thing, along with the perennially cool trio of Michael Jackson, Bob Marley and Elton John.

While this worked wonders in calming Akalanka down, it failed to provide much comfort to any of his Western passengers. No amount of rousing boogie music was going to disguise what was still going on outside. A glance ahead showed that the car in front had a sticker across its back window that carried a simple message to would-be overtakers: 'Don't go; it's my life.' Like most other signs along Galle Road, it was little use written in English, as we soon found out. A tenacious petrol-tanker decided to pull off the move of the morning, riding wide into the oncoming lane as we headed into a blind bend. As usual, it turned out an AC bus was coming straight for him, which caused Akalanka to ram on the brakes and let the maniacs past. The tanker whipped back in line just in time, with shocking manoeuvrability for its size and weight. As this potential Weapon of Mass Destruction screeched off terrifyingly into the distance, a thick, black chemical smog ripped from its behind, destroying all visibility and causing us to slow down even more. I did manage to make out one feature of the speeding tanker's rear as it passed: another English sign which read: 'How's my driving? Call 11-5784367.'

Welcome back to Galle Road, I thought.

This was my second time in the country, and a good stretch into the trip. It was to Sri Lanka that I had headed that first winter out of school – just after the Autumn of the Black Eye.

It was my 'Asian Travel 101' class – an important part of the bigger picture if I was one day to have the savvy to make a go of some of the world's more cut-throat surf destinations like Indonesia, and eventually Jeffrey's Bay.

Sri Lanka became like a rite of passage. Three close friends and I waved goodbye to the European surfing communities we'd known so far, and set off on our first long-term cross-continental expedition. And, of course, the Galle Road was the first thing we saw the other end.

Perhaps that's why roads have ever since, in my mind at least, been the best scene-setter for a fresh destination. It's no doubt the same for many other people – and surely that's the way it should be. After all, what better a symbol could there be for the Journey than a road? When you arrive somewhere it's almost always the traffic and the passers-by that give you your first glimpse of the way a place runs, be it a barren dirt track, the complete single-lane serenity of the outer Scottish isles, a manic Asian free-for-all or the uber-tame regimentation of the British motorway system.

That first Lankan odyssey helped make us the people we are today. Once the culture shock had sunk in, and we'd become accustomed to the smells, the noises, the millipedes, mosquitoes, scorpions, cockroaches, electricity shortages, the sweating and the itching, we knew the conditions would be perfect for the sense of adventure – the travel bug – to grow in each of us.

It was on that initial trip to Sri Lanka that I first began to understand the real nature of the exotic. Before going there, the exotic had always simply meant palm trees, blue water and perfect line-ups. Our European travelling experiences to date had been relatively shallow in nature as, being still so close to home, we only really took in the superficial elements of the trip; food, waves, drink, waves, sun, waves. It was in Sri Lanka that I realised *exotic* simply meant the excitement of that which was new and different – and that it could come in almost any form. It was a word that began to mean the noises of the smelly market place, or the whining chords of Sinhalese sitar music as much as it did your bog-standard palm trees and blue water. Exotic, I realised, was all about variety, and adventure.

Before that trip I had seen Sri Lanka merely as a good place to go for getting better at surfing and gaining some travel experience, with the sole purpose of progressing to Indonesia – a place where I could learn to ride the kind of waves you'd see in J-Bay – as soon as I got back and saved up enough money. But *after* the trip, things looked very different. Sure, Indo followed by J-Bay was still the plan – but why get it over and done with straight away? Why not draw things out a bit first?

I started making excuses to myself, some legitimate, some not. The best one was that I wasn't ready. As I'd always said, my trip to J-Bay had to be a success at the first attempt – that was part of the goal. I wanted Jeffrey's to be a place where my every hope and expectation could be fulfilled, and before that could happen I needed to make sure every aspect of the trip there was within my capability.

When you come from Britain, chances to ride truly powerful waves are limited to one or two times a year, or to times when you go abroad. As a British surfer, I had a lot to learn before being ready to tackle the juice and pace of a wave like J-Bay – a period of training, and studying the art of surfing. Indonesia would be a good place to get proficient in heavy surf, but that itself was a big step up from Porthcawl, and one I hoped Sri Lanka would bridge.

That was when I realised that travel also had its own learning curve, its own levels of experience. Besides getting used to sketchy reef breaks and the punchy Indian Ocean swells that hit them, we learned about insect bites, infections, touts and con artists. We learned to feel familiar amongst the smells, sights and sounds of Asia, a world which bore almost no resemblance to that in which we'd been raised. Even electricity wasn't a certainty in south-west Sri Lanka, and we loved it.

Besides that, the surf was constantly good, and we had just about every spot on the coast to ourselves the majority of the time. While most of my friends back home shivered the winter away, surfing sporadically in awful conditions, we immersed ourselves in the waves, the food, the Buddhism and the freedom of life in the Sinhalese beachside village of Midigama. Before we left, Jai and Akalanka took us to visit relatives in the inland towns of Embilipitiya and Kataragama – places where travellers hardly ever went, and that was when I realised surfing was beginning to lead to an education that far superseded that possible in school.

By the time I got back from that first Sri Lankan trip and wandered, skinny and shivering, into the now surreal cinema complex of a Western retail park for the first time in months, a new bug had bitten, every bit as gripping as the surfing one. But satisfying it would require patience.

For better or for worse, my parents went their separate ways, my dad moving to San Francisco just before I began an English course at the nearby University of Glamorgan. Student loans weren't quite enough to get myself on another several-month sojourn (not to mention the small matter of trying to single out and attend important lectures), so next up was a shorter trip – under two weeks – to California and Baja Mexico, travelling down by road with my father. Compared to other trips, it seemed like no time at all, and the emphasis on spending time with Dad took over from the thrill of travel and the need to take in my surroundings. After that came a few other small trips, often to do contests in places like the Channel Islands, and Scotland several times, and then another summer and autumn in mainland Europe, with that little mini-goal of finally catching Mundaka in action written in to the itinerary.

It began to occur to me that, within reason, I could go on like this as long as I wanted before declaring myself ready for J-Bay. And so, after this latest French stay, I returned to Sri Lanka for another winter, but this time with my girlfriend Breige.

We'd met not long after I got back from my first trip there, and she took up surfing almost straight away, immediately emerging as pretty bloody good at it. Before meeting me (in the basement of a seedy nightclub, of course), she claims not to have known Porthcawl was a surf town. She had seen people bodyboarding and swimming during the summer, but remained unaware of how serious some of the local populace were about swell-chasing. Being several school years younger than me, she had grown up during a period marked by a drought of groms. None of her peers had seriously taken up the sport, and the older surfers were wondering where a new generation would come from (the Demon Headmaster was still firmly in place). That said, when I met her, the fact Breige had never formed any associations between Porthcawl and wave-riding was something I found baffling and slightly annoying. Surfing was all I knew, and the idea someone could have existed in the same town for all those years without knowing about it was, to me, both absurd and offensive. So the very next sunny day with waves, I took her to the beach to watch us do our thing.

She seemed to enjoy the experience, so upon returning to my place we watched a surf film (Jack McCoy's *Nine Lives*), during which I left the room to make a cup of tea. When I came back in, she was wearing one of my wetsuits. 'Let's go back to the beach, then,' she said. 'I want to try it.'

'OK,' I replied without really assessing the implications of what could happen. 'I'll put a board in the car.'

It was early summer, and daylight hours were already long, but the evenings cold. As it got dark, I pushed her into the one-foot wind-swell, at freezing low-tide Rest Bay. Fortunately, the dismal conditions meant none of my friends were around to see me in what, at the time, I would have considered an embarrassing situation. Girls didn't surf, or not in South Wales anyway. The frigid, brown water and pitiful swell should have been enough to put her off for good, but when we got out she told me it had been real fun.

'Do the waves often get this big?' she asked.

Obviously there was a lot for her to learn, but we went again, and again. Within a few weeks, she'd bought a beginner's board and a wetsuit of her own. I thought the board was disgusting, but, like all true novices, she decided the garish yellow and pink floral colour scheme was amazing. It was designed to be super buoyant, picking up any little ripple and remaining stable however much you lost your balance. The only trouble was she couldn't carry it properly if the wind rose above a light breeze.

If taking my girlfriend for a surf in crap low-tide Rest Bay was potentially embarrassing, then walking down to the water on a good day with her girly-coloured board under my arm was a total social no-go. As damaging to my masculinity as being seen outside the changing rooms of Top Shop holding a handbag. But by now I didn't care. Breige had the bug.

By the end of the summer she could surf properly, riding across the faces of waves both backhand and forehand, bottom turning and trimming. More importantly, she had changed to an all-white board that was small enough for her to carry in all winds. We travelled to a few places together, none of them too adventurous – France, the Canary Islands – before deciding to go to Sri Lanka, a place she'd never been. As with all good trips, we didn't really know what the purpose of the exercise was, just planning to go with whatever happened. And for me, it was like arriving in a new country altogether.

In just a few seasons Sri Lanka had changed, and so had the nature of its surf trip. In days past, overstaying was the done thing. Only geeks went all the way back to Colombo to get permission to remain in the country for more than thirty days – it just wasn't done by any surfer in the know. In fact, the average overstay on the passports of any given group would have probably been at least two months. It was never an issue at the airport, as the sensible placing of a 1,000 rupee note (about £7) inside the relevant passport page was usually more than enough to ensure that the correct embarkation stamp was hammered down. That corrupt seal of approval; the product of a country brought to its knees by civil war and desperate to attract visitors at all costs.

It was a different ball game now. Tales of stoned surfers who would sit hundreds of miles from the visa office, laughing as they made and stamped their own extensions out of clever forgeries, bought for next to nothing in the marketplaces of southern India, were being replaced by those of itchy nights in a Colombo jail cell. Yes, Sri Lanka had changed all right. No longer that feral, unknown surf zone, filled with secret waves and ridden only by the privileged few who bothered going. The south-west was now only a few steps away from burgeoning into another Indian Ocean surfing hotspot. The water temperatures, and waves that look like a safer, toy version of Indonesia's fabled reef passes, were making towns like Midigama and Hikkaduwa rise up peoples' hit lists rapidly.

This had had its ups and downs. The ups were the decreasing levels of poverty, improving communications and standards of living, increased availability of Western commodities and a general buzz about the beach that said things were finally on track. The main down was an increased number of surfers in the water, which had led to some discontent – particularly among the few who seemed to think the fact they came first meant they owned the waves.

Despite the horror stories about the Tamil Tigers and a concerted campaign of terrorism, the south-west coast of Sri Lanka had never actually been that dangerous for foreigners in the first place. There was plenty of political unrest, but any violence had mostly been isolated either in the north of the country, or in certain obvious political targets around the capital. This had always been the case, and a handful of surfers actually managed to keep it a virtual secret for years, enjoying season upon season of uncrowded waves as a result.

Things pretty much stayed like this for decades, until something much more severe happened to burst the bubble of this little Eden – a negotiated cease-fire that, in Sri Lankan terms at least, looked set to stay. As a result, the country was finally able to devolve some energies towards enforcing legislation, and that glorious visa scam was the first casualty. Anyone who now wished to retreat to the idyllic southern surf breaks for anything more than thirty days had eventually to go to Colombo – a city for which the word 'hectic' would appear as the softest of euphemisms.

And, after four weeks of surfing on the south coast, nobody was relishing that prospect.

In Colombo, anything that could be wrong was wrong. It was dirty, it was loud, it was disorganised and it was dangerous (if a rogue element of the Tigers wasn't waiting to pounce then some other political radical probably was), and it was hot – too hot. By the time we made our way through the ululating masses of local emigration-hopefuls and up to the second floor of the Ministry of Defence building that dealt with visa applications, I was beginning to question whether or not this was actually just some nightmare. Surely I was about to wake up and go surfing instead.

Sadly, though, it was all true, and as my body adjusted to the pitiful attempt at air conditioning that poorly serviced that plain and basic building, I realised that things were only getting worse.

It was mayhem in there. Rather than a vital government department, the scene that confronted us was more that of a cut-throat, Third-World market, or a very busy bookmaker's. Like any sort of gathering in Sri Lanka, it was noisy, and everyone seemed to know where they were going except us.

Unlike in banks, the Sinhalese authorities had made no attempt to keep Westerners apart from the rabble of con-artists that hid the odd genuinely lucky Sri Lankan who *was* actually there preparing to travel somewhere. And just in case this crowd wasn't unsettling enough, guards with AK47s wandered around outside, their bodies inebriated with power.

Deserted by Akalanka, our little party gingerly stepped into the sweaty office: myself, Breige, Johan and a crazy young man from 'the bailiwick of Jersey' called Chips (he wouldn't give his actual name out to anyone unless he really, really had to). Having first met back at Jai and Sumana's in Midigama, this group had been pulled together by the simultaneous need to extend visas.

The next stage was equally unnerving – handing our passports to a bored woman who didn't speak a word of English, and whose eyes made it clear that she couldn't give a shit if we ever got the little magic books back. In fact, the only communication anyone made with us was through hand gestures. After you responded correctly to the *gimme that passport now, I haven't got long, come on, hurry up* gesture, you were instantly ushered on. *Over there; take this ticket; that way*. The ticket shoved into my hand read, 'Room 3'.

Inside Room 3 was, to quote George Orwell, a 'small beetle-like man', who had institution written all over him, and looked diametrically opposed in world view to myself, or any of the other three back in the queue.

'Sit down, please,' he said, in polished English.

His glasses drifted ever so slightly down his nose as he took a breath and began reading the pages of my passport, which had somehow made it into the room ahead of me. He was looking at the stamps, and I waited uncomfortably for him to notice my overstay in the same country from a few years previously. Miraculously, he didn't flinch on that page, and handed it back to me with another ticket and yet further instructions.

'Desk 5.'

'I'm sorry?'

'Other room.' He pointed back to the free-for-all I'd just come from. On the way down the corridor I passed Johan and Breige. They'd started the process ahead of me, but were only now heading for the seemingly pointless visit to Room 3, 101, or whatever number their own tickets were sporting.

My passport was again rudely taken from me back in 'same room', and there was still no mention of a fee – which is usually bad news in Sri Lanka. Chips was still sweating in line, waiting for his own appointment with bureaucracy.

If any of this was supposed to make things tighter or more official, I thought, then it wasn't working. The bloke who'd just relieved me of my passport was writing everyone's names into a book, but his failure to recognise a word of any other language but Sinhala was fundamentally undermining the whole operation. He entered me as 'A. Thomas' – getting my forename and surname back to front. Watching him for a while, it became clear that this was an often repeated confusion. I was rejoined by my three travelling companions before getting any further in the process.

First to be called for the next stage was Breige, who returned looking pissed off. She'd finally found out the price: 4,950 rupees (over $50US), five times more than we'd been otherwise told and, as she was only planning to overstay by four days, an absolute rip-off. It may not sound much but you do get kind of tight-fisted after a long time in Sri Lanka.

And by now we had become totally accustomed to seeing money in such miserly terms. This had been the case last time I went too. After a whole winter of expecting to get overcharged for everything, I went into my local pub within hours of being back in the UK, ordered a drink and plunged into a real moment of culture shock. As I pulled a ten-pound note out of my pocket, I panicked for a split second. *Now he's seen how much money you've got, the price will automatically be the full tenner*, I almost told myself. Back in Lazy Lanka, that's how you have to think in order to preserve your funds to stay in the country for months on end.

Chips came back similarly dismayed. His budget just wasn't big enough for unexpected losses that equated to what he'd otherwise spend in a fortnight. 'If that compensation money I'm owed back home for whiplash doesn't come through in the next few weeks, I'm gonna be on an early plane, eh?' he lamented.

We weren't the only ones a bit taken aback by the charges. As Johan moved up to the counter to face his own Swedish fate, the man in front lost it.

'How much? You must be fuckin' jokin',' the portly, fake-gold-watch-wearing fellow exclaimed in a British southern-geezer accent. 'Gimme my fuckin' passport back. I'm not giving you idiots that sort of money for fuck-all. I'll go to the fuckin' Maldives and back before 4,950 roops leave me pocket in a place like this!'

Johan began to smirk. He'd just learned that Swedes only had to pay 500 – his reward for hailing from a country with a more lenient immigration policy. He brought a copy of the price-list back to the seats, and we all marvelled at what other countries it would pay to belong to right now. Further bad news for Breige, who could have brought her Irish passport, but hadn't. If she had then Johan wouldn't have been smirking quite so much. The Irish tariff was only 300 – less than $5 US.

'Lucky we're not Yanks, eh,' said Chips. 'Look, they've gotta pay over a hundred quid! Just for a friggin' visa to this shit-hole!'

The home country of choice, perhaps for the first time ever, would have been Pakistan, at only 70 rupees, closely followed by 'Halty' at 140.

'Halty? Where's that?' asked Johan.

'It's *Haiti*,' Chips replied. 'It's spelt Lankan-style.' With that, he leaned back and prepared to wait, as did the rest of us. We weren't free to head back yet.

Back in the safety of Midigama, meanwhile, Yannick Poirier was enjoying a peaceful, late-morning solo session in a balmy ocean.

The wave known as 'Lazy Left' was doing what it did best; running sweetly off a soft bed of dead coral into a deep turquoise sand lagoon. The morning crew had all headed in for some food and a smoke, leaving him alone with his thoughts and the rainbow-coloured parrot fish. A set stood up, and the Frenchman began to paddle. Enjoying the luxury of being able to pick his wave, he let the first two run by. The third one was different, swinging deeper behind the point than the others, and Yannick knew it was going to be a good one. He took it on, made the drop smoothly and began to wind his way into the bay, the longest ride of the morning eventually brought to an end by a stream of backwash that tossed him into the air like an unlucky matador. No drama, though, since he knew to avoid landing on his board, plunging harmlessly in the thin, tepid water. *One more*, he thought to himself, *one more*, before turning round and pulling his tired body back towards the line-up.

Although the waves were good, the backwash was new. Once confined only to the inside section during big tides, it was now moving further and further along the wave. The Lazy Left was changing.

After picking off another two waves that failed to live up to his recent ride, Yannick prepared to head in. It had been a great surf – just what he needed, and now it was time for a chilli-riddled local rice 'n' curry. A small wave came through, perfect for heading in on because it would hug the point and run far into the bay, as long as the backwash didn't rear its head. It didn't, so Yannick climbed off his board as the wave petered out, and began to paddle across the twenty or so yards of deep water between the end of the wave and the soft, lapping shore break.

As he took a quick breather, though, his mood began to change. Next to a giant floating inner tube, a series of bubbles turned into snorkel blow-outs, as three Sinhalese divers broke the surface. Coral thieves.

''Allo sir. *Whearugoing?*' The only English-language greeting most Lankans knew.

Immediately a heated argument broke out, comprising three-quarters Yannick's broken Sinhala and one-quarter the bandits' even worse English. The coral thieves had no concept of the fact that a wave needs something to break over, and that one of the reasons Midigama could claim to be a 'rich neighbourhood' was because of cash injections from surfers, who came to the village because of the reefs that moulded the Lazy Left and the nearby 'Ram's Right' – the very same reefs that these *carriahs* were turning into lime, day after day.

'Zis backwash – it's made by *you!*' the Frenchman exclaimed. 'No reef at the end of ze wave – deep water.' But he knew he was wasting his time. The wave's days were numbered, and although it could still take years, even decades, it was an inevitability that the precious reef would one day become disfigured enough to send Lazy Left up to the big wave park in the sky. It wasn't going to be the first time this kind of thing had happened to a surf spot, and, as Yannick often said, the destructive aspects of human nature meant it probably wouldn't be the last. Would this wave go the same way as his homeland's La Barre – once deemed the best sand-bottom wave on earth before they built *that groyne*? Would this be a story similar to California's legendary point once known as 'Killer Dana' – the dreamy right-hander used in the film *Big Wednesday* which was snuffed out by harbour developments. Or could Yannick still get on top of this situation, making the Lazy Left's plight more like those of two internationally renowned reef breaks he'd read about in Ireland and Madeira, which had both been saved from plans to build marinas by a savvy group of terminal lobbyists?

The Lankans went on pretending not to understand a word he said, merely offering a facetious shrug of the shoulders before continuing to load their booty into the makeshift rubber raft. A bit more abuse followed, with idle threats coming from both sides, before the disgusted Frenchman finally turned shoreward, refusing to let these 'deek-eds' deflate his mood any further, although he'd still have loved to deflate that fecking tube of theirs.

Years before, Yannick might have called the police if he saw this going on, but he knew now that things were never that simple in Sri Lanka. It wouldn't be in police interests to lock these guys up – but rather better just to demand a fine (well, a *bribe* actually, although we all know that no truly crooked person will ever officially use that most taboo of words) of an affordable amount each time they got caught. This way the law would be assured a surplus income for the rest of their days on the 'job', while the illegal coral trade continued to prosper.

Another reason not to bother involving the police had been the wily reef bandits turning up at Jai's the season before, threatening violence if anyone called the cops again.

'Ze bastards will always be taking coral,' Yannick would tell you, before getting too wound up and ordering the subject to be closed for the rest of the day. 'We've tried everything. In the end they say "If you pay us, we will stop taking coral". They want three-hundred rupees a day – that's what they would earn selling the coral on to businessmen. What to do?

'Anyway, our countries have robbed them for tea and spices since hundreds of years ago, so don't you think it would be a little hypocritical now to tell them how to manage their resource?'

Yannick the Franco-Sinhala, not by blood descent, but by such dedicated study of the culture to have undergone some sort of metamorphosis: Midigama Kingpin, Western-Buddhist sage, local businessman and top-class spear fisherman. Since he first visited the place in search of enlightenment towards the end of the nineties he had almost single-handedly decided to embrace the village's future. He was the unelected mayor, the Godfather, and Jai was his right-hand man.

Besides a couple of monks in the hill country, Yannick's premier 'mentor' was Tony Hussein – the man responsible for pioneering the surf breaks of Midigama, and the first documented person to surf there in the early seventies. Tony shipwrecked into his fortune, literally running aground at the sight of a world-famous Maldivian left-hander now known as Pasta Point. Originally bound for Africa, he decided to stay at his new find for the next few decades instead, holidaying in southern Sri Lanka and 'working' in the Maldives. He now runs the lucrative Atoll Adventures surf camp, leaving the well-being of Midigama in the hands of Yannick, returning annually to spend Christmas surfing the Lazy Left and eating at Jai and Sumana's.

Since Tony first helped Jai transform his trade from ramshackle bits-'n'-bobs shopkeeper into as best an impression of an accommodation tycoon as can be done in an Asian village that still suffers from daily power cuts, the Subodanee building had grown to epitomise wealth and, I suppose, the 'Lankan Dream', whatever it may be.

'Jai rich,' said the coral thieves and equally amoebic tuk-tuk drivers, 'so Jai can afford to give us money.'

'Peace is a bummer,' some travelling surfers would joke, meanwhile. 'There were twenty people in the right-hander this morning. I'm over it. Next season I'm going to Indo instead, or Central America. Gonna get some real waves, with nobody in the water.

'This place is a fuckin' joke,' they'd go on. 'Fuck Wickramhrasinghe. Come on Prhbahkaran. Come on the

Tigers!' But peace was no joke to Jai, Yannick or the rest of Midigama's aspiring businessmen. You only needed to look at the sign over the doorway of a newly set-up Ayurvedic therapy centre to see how welcome the foreign coin now was on Sri Lanka's commercial front-line:

AYUBOWAN

```
We welcome you to resplendent Sri Lanka
- the paradise in the Indian Ocean.
We wish you to enjoy the Sun - Kissed
sandy beaches, the scenic beauty, the
salubrious climate and our koledoscopic
culture enriched with traditions of per-
colonial periods.

We pray (to God) for your health and
happiness through out your stay with us
without even a miner (Affection) distress
due to sore feet aches and pains of
joints or even a mosquite bite. We wish
you a happy tour.
```

Not all the local businessmen were able to stay as on top of their game as these literary masters, though: sulky Sugath would sit by the Midigama railway track, bemoaning how Jai's place could be full while nobody had yet checked into his 'traditional homestay'. Across the road sat Sandun the tuk-tuk driver, who had taken to lobbing pebbles at the clued-up foreigners who had begun refusing to pay the special 'tourist rates' that he and his equally greedy competitors had too obviously set about 150 per cent higher than what was reasonable.

And Yannick and co were praying (perhaps to Buddha) that the coral bandits would be the next to suffer.

'My friend from Matara,' said Yannick, 'has a friend who is working for the Coastal Preservation Authority – ze Government. He say that he is coming to Midigama to look at the reefs, then maybe ze Government will listen and the penalty for stealing the reef will become bigger – more steeper.'

What he really meant was that the authorities might finally do something now that the country had another, much mightier source of income to protect – tourism. Destroying the environment through coral poaching? Fine. Damaging surf tourism by reef stealing? Unthinkable!

Come to Sri Lanka, they were now saying. *It's safe, beautiful and has good waves.* The tourist board was reaching out to surfers, treating the southern surf zones like a commodity; equal in value to the ancient religious sites. Ask any Lankan in the know and they'll tell you: 'Garvanment policy! Bring in the dollars euros pounds!'

And once Yannick convinced the right people that dollars euros pounds needed surf-making reefs to attract them, the little coral scam would end.

But, as everyone knew, that was still likely to be a while in coming – for now, the 'deek-eds' with the inner tube could have their coral. This was Sri Lanka after all, where everything prided itself in moving at snail-pace (except maybe the traffic).

'What to do, what to do,' mused Yannick. 'It will 'appen. It will. Maybe not zis year, maybe not next year – or even the year after that. But it will. Midigama is changing. Let's just hope the waves are not!'

In the meantime Yannick had greater concerns anyway. His beloved left could be just moments away from being destroyed by something far worse, and much more immediate. Crowds – peacetime crowds. After all, the recent saga of Ram's Right, Robocop and Mr Narrabeen had affected us all, and was still very much on everyone's minds...

The morning Robocop arrived was, like many before it, just another fun-sized session in one of my favourite waves. A long-distance Indian Ocean swell was lining up behind the pot-holed reef, before breaking in precisely the right spot to turn the zippy inside section over. The bigger waves were perfect for slapping down a big carve, the mid-range ones were naughtily hollow and the smaller ones as whackable as any beach break. It can be a pretty lethal wave, but when the swell direction is good and the tide is right, it's quite simply a playground.

Over the years, though, the precious wave that broke into the beach behind Jai's cousin Ram's back garden had been growing increasingly crowded. It hadn't been a problem so far, because some of the seasonal regulars – a stern but fair group of Cornishmen and Aussies who, given that no Midigama natives surfed, were essentially the wave's local crew – always did a good job of regulating the line-up. They had laid down an effective system of turn-taking, flaring up whenever the occasional idiot decided to start snaking people (stealing right-of-way to the next wave by paddling rudely past people who are already in position). The good thing about Ram's Right was the way it had safely avoided any sort of descent into the bitter turf wars of the main peak at Hikkaduwa – another popular wave an hour up the road. As far as I was aware, the atmosphere at Ram's had so far been not much different to what I remembered of it from my last stay in Midigama. It was therefore with interest as much as concern that I responded to the reports that started coming in that day during a post-surf fruit salad:

'There are Israelis in the right-hander! Six of them, and they say they're moving in!'

There's nothing wrong with Israelis as people, but as surfers, most of the ones that visited Sri Lanka were a nightmare. It's a bit like the way Argentines are known for being dirty soccer players, or Eastern Europeans are known for having the disciplined mind-set required for gymnastics – both are generalisations, but both have their foundation in some sort of home truth. Similarly, it is safe to say that, in Sri Lanka for some reason, the Israeli *surfers* were some of the rudest, most aggressive people you'd ever come across. Whatever their ability, they would attack a line-up as if it were a contest area. They'd paddle you out of position, shirk any responsibility to take turns, and instantly turn a mellow session amongst friends into a savage free-for-all.

As if it were days ago, not years, I immediately remembered the crew of Israelis that descended upon Midigama during my first trip there with Richie, a grommethood friend from South Wales. With a total of only about ten surfers staying in Midigama at any one time (thanks to there being no sign of any Tamil cease-fire back then), more than four people in the water at Ram's Right was considered a crowd – so you can imagine our horror when three others rocked up on motorbikes, paddled out and decided to pick a fight with us straight away.

Sometimes, when someone is really taking the piss with their line-up etiquette, the only option is to take off in front of them on a good wave, letting them know your frustration, like that Spaniard had once done to me.

'Why you drop in, man?' one of them asked Richie, after my friend had administered just such treatment on the very next wave.

'I dropped in on you because you paddled inside me like a clown,' Richie replied.

'Was my wave, bro. That's the rule!' Technically speaking, the guy was right. Closest man to the peak should always have right of way. That's how they play it in a surf contest anyway.

'Yeah, but if you'd watched for even one minute before paddling out and sitting straight inside everyone like a fuckin' twat you'd have noticed that there's only two of us in here, and we're not bothering with your pissing 'rule'. There's

plenty of waves to go round, so calm down!' Richie was
definitely in the right here, no pun intended. This wasn't a
contest, and therefore it didn't matter who sat where. What
mattered to us was the fact that three scowling morons had
just turned up and destroyed a fun session by turning it into
an aggro-fuelled paddle battle. We caught another handful of
waves, before deciding it wasn't worth the bother of surfing
against these guys – which is what you invariably had to do.
We'd both done our share of contests, and could have easily
turned the tables on them if we'd wanted – but that wasn't
what people migrated to Midigama for the winter to do.

We'd also both been to Hikkaduwa some weeks before,
and Richie recognised one of the guys from a fight he'd seen
on the beach there. Some sort of dispute had erupted in
the water, and then continued on land. Fighting over waves;
what was the world coming to?

'Yep, it's definitely him,' Richie noted as we arrived back
on the small beach. 'Thank fuck they're on motorbikes is all
I can say. It means they've probably just come down for the
morning from Hikkaduwa, and won't be staying long.'

'Ah, we've had a good surf already anyway. Let's just leave
them to it.'

Richie agreed and we sat down for a fruit-shake, before
heading back to Jai and Sumana's to hide from the merciless
afternoon sun. Stalling for that fruit-shake proved not to
be a very good idea, however, as it gave our new 'friends'
time to leave the water, climb up the rocks to the south of
the right-hander, head onto the road and wait for us to walk
back. They'd obviously taken what Rich had said to heart.

'Whassup?' said the prick responsible for Rich's little loss
of temper earlier. They looked a lot bigger now on land
– as if they'd spent years in the army (which, considering
Israel's national service policy, they probably had), and were
unimpressed by the sight of two skinny Welshmen who
didn't want any trouble.

'What did you say to me in the water then, man?'

'I just told you to fuckin' chill out!' Rich was on the verge of shouting again.

'You fuckin' chill out yourself, man,' the guy said, his voice sinister and calm.

'Whatever you want. We're not interested.'

'Not interested in what?' Surely the first punch was about to be thrown.

'Not interested in any of it,' Rich replied, trying to give the impression he'd be willing to stand up to them. It was working so far, because neither of us had been hit yet.

We turned and carried on walking towards Jai's place, and they followed behind laughing, and whispering to each other. We had avoided a fight, but the visitors still had the rest of the day's waves to themselves – Rich and I not wishing to tempt fate twice.

Besides a plethora of other scare stories, which may or may not have been based on any truth, that had remained my one and only experience of Israeli surfers in Sri Lanka. Rumours of their return had cropped up from time to time over the weeks that followed, but none ever turned out to be true. There was always an unwritten law about surfing the breaks along Galle Road: if you wanted a fight, a heavy night's drinking or a crowd, then you went to Hikkaduwa. On the other hand, if you just wanted to surf, eat hot food and do little else, then you went to Midigama.

How much things can change in three years...

On the morning Robocop turned up for the first time, Ram and Jai had estimated that over sixty foreigners were staying in Midigama – and more than half of these were surfers. Three years is also long enough to start forgetting things, and since I've always tried to selectively recall surf trip details (leaving out the bad, such as mosquito bites, fevers, sunburn and fights; while dwelling on the good – i.e. waves), it was about another fifteen minutes before the full impact of what I was told got processed by my over-surfed, over-chillied and over-sunned brain.

'There are Israelis in the right-hander! Six of them, and they say they're moving in!'

Yes, Ram's Right had, once again, developed a crowd problem with a twist.

'Robocop' was the head of this ultra-aggressive new crew. A towering, stiff, broad-shouldered cyborg of a man whose attire was straight out of the deepest darkest eighties. His black, long-sleeve lycra rash vest and matching cycling shorts would have been enough to stop you from ever forgetting him – without the help of the custom-made saltwater shades that he wore over his chiselled face regardless of sun-levels (hence the nickname). He also carried a fluorescent blue surfboard with a full deck of snazzy traction pads (a strict no-no for anyone with even the vaguest knowledge of surf fashion) and a set of New Age fins that looked as if they should have been on a hydro-foil boat. His manner was every bit as wooden as his namesake's, and he chose to leave most of the heckling to his cronies; an equally cold-faced bunch of wave-poachers.

Their first morning in the water was as dog-eat-dog as that other session three years earlier – except that this time, nobody was going to dare tell them where to go. Robocop's size and stature had seen to that. For the next week, he would just sit there staring forward, or maybe even at us – the shades prevented you from knowing exactly where he was looking – while the rest of his crew dominated the line-up around him, taking full advantage of our obvious reluctance to piss any of them off for fear of invoking the formidable wrath of their boss.

We were at a loss. Urgent strategy meetings began taking place, with various factions of the Midigama surfing community debating the best plan of action.

'I reckon someone should try talking to them,' said one guy. 'Just politely explaining to them that we could all get along fine if they weren't quite so damn greedy.'

'Tried it. They just grunt back, then steal another wave off you,' came another voice.

My plan, though, was to leave them all to it and begin surfing the Lazy Left, where Breige was surfing, instead. It worked fine, until a couple of others followed suit, causing problems there as well.

'Why have you brought all your hassly mates over here?' Breige complained.

This was a disaster for me. As part of a surfing couple, the absolute worst thing you can do is be responsible for your other half having a bad session – it causes distress to both parties. Like I said, Breige took the sport up shortly after meeting me, and had since improved in leaps and bounds. However, at this stage, she liked to avoid crowds, looking for easier conditions.

This was supposed to be a major perk to life in Midigama – the Lazy Left was, according to the sales pitch I gave her before we decided to come, a brilliant stepping-stone into the world of reef breaks. It broke softly, it ran for a distance, it was easy to paddle out due to the deep channel of water alongside, and it was uncrowded. Breige could surf there all day without any trouble. Meanwhile, I had planned to head to Ram's Right just a hundred yards away, and we'd both be content.

Having a partner who surfed was great, as it meant they actually understood and sympathised with your obsession, but it also brought with it some paradoxes. Surfing is, whatever anyone tells you, supposed to be an individual pursuit – pure selfishness most of the time. Which makes it difficult when you care as much about how someone else's session goes as you do your own. Whenever I'd surfed with friends, it had always been preferable for them to share the same mood, but that was as far as it went. Whether or not they enjoyed themselves was their problem, not mine – if a mate had a bad surf when I had a good one, or vice versa, then it was tough shit. But surfing with Breige was different. Only by both of us having good waves could I now feel the same satisfaction as before – giving a new meaning to 'How was it for you?'.

She was getting much better at dealing with crowds in the water, having stolen waves off pros back in the beach breaks of France, and was growing more comfortable surfing over rock bottoms too. But throw a reef break and a competitive line-up into the equation together at once, and she wasn't so happy.

'The good thing about the left is that it's still got a mellow crowd,' she explained one afternoon. 'And then you and all that lot turn up and start paddling past everyone. It's rude – not just to me, but to all the others who surf there too.' She was right; we had become what we hated.

Filled with guilt, I headed back over to Ram's the next day, intent on finally forcing my way into the crowd. Things had only got worse. The atmosphere was filled with ill-will, as hordes of grumpy Israelis and Aussies circled around the take-off zone like vultures. Little skirmishes would crop up from time to time, and oddly enough most of the best waves were sneaking through unridden – the constant crowd movement meaning nobody could get in place to catch them.

Divisions in the line-up weren't even limited to Israeli vs non-Israeli any more either. About quarter of an hour into the session I saw one of the Americans that had been staying nearby with a local family get hideously burned by a middle-aged Aussie. Paddling back out, I heard one of the Aussie's mates, in full hearing distance of his victim, say, 'You just dropped in on that guy a corker.' The dropper-in, looking pleased with himself, just shrugged his shoulders and replied, 'Ahh, fuck 'im, eh!'

It was time to find somewhere new to surf.

There was another spot just up the road, called 'The Rock'. It was an A-frame peak that could get quite big from time to time. The sets would refract around a large rock stack about a hundred yards out to sea, after which the place had been named, and then overlap, causing the wave to throw out a big lip that plunged forward and down, like a guillotine of water. On a good day you could pull faces at your mates through the peak.

The first time I went there was three years previously on the back of a log-carrying pickup truck with another school friend, Rhyd. He'd been in Sri Lanka for two months before Rich and I got there and knew a bit of Sinhalese. The driver was paid off with a few loose cigarettes and that was it; we were alone on a beach, with no surfers in sight and the waking dream of four- to six-foot spitting waves – as idyllic a scenario as I have ever encountered.

After two hours of sky-blue tubes, we returned to find our flip-flops stolen – which took the edge off the morning as it meant we burnt our feet walking back to the road. But it was still a surf I'll never forget, simply because of the feeling we got from 'cheating' the rest of the surfing world. It was impossible not to feel smug. While across the world people were leaving the water frustrated and bitter after scrapping for waves against hundreds of others, we were taking the liberty of passing up the ones that weren't *absolutely* perfect.

Sadly, though, all good things come to an end, and The Rock was now one of Sri Lanka's most overcrowded waves. Coach loads of Japanese surfari holidaymakers were turning up every morning, while their Sinhalese hosts, tastelessly blinging from head to foot like anyone who's grown rich overnight, just sat and smirked. *'Fuck you,'* they seemed to be saying. Whatever job you do in countries like Britain, Australia, the US or Japan, you are a rich man in Sri Lankan terms, and therefore deserve to pay 'tourist price'.

The Rock, for all its early secrecy, could still be seen from the road if you were lucky enough to drive by during a good set and glance to your side. It had always been inevitable that the place would one day be discovered. If there had been other spots then, there would be other spots now. Surely, along the reef-littered Galle Road there would still be a wave that could remind us of that breakaway feeling.

The problem with doing anything out of the ordinary in Sri Lanka is laziness. It's too hot to move in the afternoon, and in the mornings the waves on your doorstep are too good to ignore. When you do go anywhere after midday then the routine onshore winds will mask potential surf spots anyway. If we wanted to find another spot, we'd probably need to give up a morning of good waves. Even with the territorial pissings taking place at our 'home breaks', it would still take a mammoth dose of conviction; a big sacrifice.

Thankfully, we didn't need to. I'd heard that an old friend, Imco the Searching Dutchman, had arrived in Sri Lanka and set up a business in Unawatuna, the Surf City Internet Café. Sure enough, Breige and I made our way up there during the afternoon onshores to find Imco engrossed in a game of 'carrom' – a cross between pool and tiddlywinks – against one of his local employees. He looked a little startled when I pitched up, but it's a small world when you're a travelling surfer, and bumping into people happens more often than you'd think.

'Have a drink,' he told us, gesturing towards the serene shack/bar that extended out of the café and virtually into the ocean. 'I'll just finish here. We've got some catching up to do – and I've got some *soopa* secret spots to show you. We've been having some *great* waves!'

Bingo.

In fact, Imco's place was only a few hundred yards from a little right-hander; a weird and wonderful wave that bounced off the foot of a Buddhist temple, mimicking a tidal surge. We tried it out one afternoon. The steep hill behind the temple kept the wind out, making the wave strangely glassy for the time of day. The take-off was interesting – exactly the same whitewater scramble as that of the Severn Bore back home – except that the wave would then wall up allowing you to skip along it. It wasn't a hollow wave, and looked nothing like the sort of thing you'd get on a plane for, but the atmosphere in the water was refreshing. The only other person there was a local kid on a battered, decaying hand-me-down board. He introduced himself as Charith, and, like any locals at a rarely visited surf spot, was delighted to see new faces.

Both Imco and Charith said that the wave only really got good during the off-season, but we had fun anyway.

After that little taster, it was time to get down to business. 'So, these spots?' I began.

'Ahhh,' he smiled, tapping the end of his nose. 'There are several, but one in particular is really, really gooood. It works in similar conditions to The Rock – but you can't see it from the road because there's something in the way...'

Even though we were good friends, he still didn't want to give too much away. It's a common dilemma: how much information to disclose about secret spots, and who to share that info with. New surf spots have to be nurtured like a child prodigy. Too much early exposure can lead to burnout, as crowds set in and the original soul of the nearby towns and villages is destroyed.

Over the years there have been several high-profile burnouts in the field of surf discovery, and while other surfers rocking up to your spot is inevitable, it is wise to put the event off for as long as possible. The trouble is, though, that you still want to share a place with your friends, like Rhyd did during The Rock's heyday. It's a tightrope all right.

I've only ever given away the location of a new surf spot twice. The first time was a real lesson, as I was forced to watch one of the best forest-hidden peaks of the French summer turn into an absolute shit-fight. The second time, however, was a different deal altogether. The Orkneys are so far from anywhere, and so cold, that any surfer dedicated enough to go there deserves a little nudge in the right direction. It'll take another ten generations of road-building and improvements in wetsuit design before that place ever gets a crowd problem – even though the waves are mind-blowing.

But Sri Lanka is on much shakier ground than Scotland. It's been a surf destination for years, and is only going to get more popular. While some might even grumble about my mentioning Midigama and Hikkaduwa (places that have definitely now reached saturation-point), I'd probably have to go into hiding if I gave away any information leading to the discovery and surfing of either of the two spots Imco told us about that afternoon. Let's just say they are both located somewhere between Hikkaduwa South and Dondra Head, Matara...

Spot 'A' was a simple affair; a big peak, not as good a wave as The Rock, but allegedly empty of any surfers.

'Next time you see that Midigama has waves breaking over head-high, give me a call and I'll take you there. It breaks all the time.'

Imco must have just jinxed us by saying that, because for the next two weeks Midigama didn't see another overhead day – a real absurdity for the time of year. During which time the surf politics of Ram's Right had been growing ever more unstable (as the real politics in Colombo steadied), and a state of 'troppo' had begun setting in.

'Troppo' is the nickname surfers give to the madness derived from too much downtime in a Third-World tropical country. It's usually caused by a combination of excessive itching and sweating, constant bad guts, too many flies parking on you, not enough surf and next to no Western mod-cons. The symptoms are basically the same as conventional madness, if such a concept exists, and I have even heard the term 'Midigama Madness' batted around from time to time.

Breige was studying in the afternoons (she went to uni a year later than me), and was soon set to fly back earlier for her university finals, so she for one didn't have the luxury of going troppo. The decision to change my ticket for the same departure as her and turn my back on Sri Lanka's west side forever would have been made but for one saving factor. In fact, it's probably safe to say that my case of troppo would have descended into a full-blown bout of Midigama Madness if it hadn't been for one thing: Spot 'B'.

With the date for the visa run now just four days away, a few of us decided we'd had enough of the small-wave delirium, and decided to go in search of this, the trickier of Imco's two spots. Both Math and Splinter were friends from home, and people that could be trusted with highly sensitive information. Math went to school with me, and was now a pretty regular travel companion. I have the utmost respect for him for one main reason; he made a late switch to surfboard-riding after having bodyboarded for years. Since Math had been well on his way to becoming one of Britain's top 'sponge-riders' at the time, it was a feat that took some courage. He went overnight from the peak of local pecking orders to the absolute bottom, rising slowly over the years to become an excellent stand-up rider too. Strangely enough Rhyd, the other school friend who first took me to The Rock, had done exactly the same. Maybe it was something to do with how much stick the rest of us gave them over the years for lying down when they could have been standing.

Splinter, on the contrary, was still a sponger, who saw no shame in the fact and had consistently resisted all calls to start standing. And as a reward for his commitment, he actually *was* one of the best bodyboarders in Britain. Although we joked about his career having been made considerably easier by the early retirements of Math and Rhyd, you still had to give it to him. He ripped, making a sport that many surfers virtually ignored into an impressive display of acrobatics, power and *cojones*.

Breige stayed behind for two reasons. Ever a fan of smaller waves, she'd surfed too much in the previous two weeks to have done any uni work, and was looking forward to getting me out from under her feet so that she could finally plug in the laptop and begin climbing Dissertation Mountain. Secondly, Spot B was meant to break extremely shallow, and over a reef that sported both live coral (a totally different ball game to dead coral), and worse still, urchins. Accomplished though she may have been, such factors would still place the wave beyond her idea of fun.

And so it was that on another sweltering and almost flat morning at Midigama, the three of us boarded the train to undertake the first leg of the journey to Spot B. Imco was not with us, but his map was. As the train pulled away from the platform at Midigama station, we began anticipating what sort of waves we might be about to find.

Train rides in Sri Lanka are every bit as eye-opening as road travel. People live all along the track, and must have to teach their kids to avoid thundering locomotives from a very young age. It's not uncommon to see youngsters running alongside you waving, or asking for school pens. Apparently Sinhalese children aren't allowed into school unless they bring their own pen – making the basic biro nothing short of a golden ticket to a better life.

The families that live by the railway often lay clothes out to dry on it – which is why the locomotive's driver constantly blew his horn. Among other reasons, he was letting people know that they needed to take their clothes in.

There was rubbish everywhere, and people stared at us out of huts made from mud and straw. Some had walls of corrugated iron, and others no walls at all. Towns drifted by, one virtually indistinguishable from another. Sri Lanka is a mélange of rundown post-colonial squalor and modern materialism. Tuk-tuk drivers, who can barely afford a fresh fish for their wives to curry, will often have fitted the most elaborate sound systems to the insides of their humble metal rickshaws. Open-doored sweat-shops run straight into airstrips and five-star hotel complexes. The Asian coming-together of cultures really has to be seen to be believed.

People often envision the East as mystic, bypassing Western technologies, and easily maintaining its diverse and powerfully expressed cultures. They think it is the epitome of unspoiled landscapes, beauty and cleanliness. The reality is different. You can expect to spot more Coca-Cola, Fanta, Nestlé, Sony and Fuji Film signs in Eastern countries than anywhere else. Greed and avarice are equally prevalent, as the merciless touts that ferry the Japanese to The Rock demonstrate only too well. Rubbish is dumped everywhere, laying bare the extent of confused and threatened cultures – the toxic by-product of an ongoing struggle with the contagious lure of Western influence. While elements of the myth are there to be found, reality hits hard – harder than the smell of sewage and burning rubbish. The montage of lifestyles we saw on that journey summed up the state of hellish modernity that the wannabe East had caught, like a bad case of dengue fever, from the West.

Amid images of poverty and filth lay grand mansions and palace-like complexes. There's wealth in Sri Lanka, but it's highly concentrated, and often earned abroad.

Away from those stately homes, Math, Splinter and I were unfortunately the closest most Lankans would ever see to wealth, though, and must have looked like walking pound signs as we moved through the turnstiles at the station of our destination, where we were promptly mobbed by people selling everything from oranges to sex. Rich as we may have been in their reality, we were still on a budget – as the aggrieved tuk-tuk drivers soon discovered when Math refused to pay their insultingly high price.

Nevertheless, we still ended up paying way over the odds for the short ride out into the jungle and into the lap of the elusive Spot B: a stomach-turning reef pass with what did indeed look like a potentially world-class right-hander about a kilometre from shore. You couldn't really judge the size of the waves from the beach, but this place definitely had a bit more surf than there had been back in Midigama. Imco had warned us that you needed to go there on a small swell, because the reef would easily 'max-out' – meaning that it couldn't hold a swell of much size.

We'd have gone out there right away but for the fact that the afternoon onshores had arrived early and blown the place to smithereens. No one, not even the fearless Splinter, fancied trying to surf a new reef break with the reputation for being shallow, in a less than favourable wind. It would have to wait until the evening, when the cooling of the land would swing the wind back offshore, cleaning the wave up for us.

Spot B wasn't that far off the beaten track – but still a good deal less accessible than Midigama, and at that point almost devoid of anywhere decent to stay. There were two places there that both looked as if they never scored any guests at all. Representatives from both of them ran into the street as soon as our boards could be seen on the side of the tuk-tuk, and a fight nearly broke out over who was going to get the honour of putting up these 'rich' men for the night. It was impossible to decide, until I spotted a sign outside the place on the right that read, *'Come and Try the Best Chinese Food in the Indian Ocean!'*

This statement alone deserved our custom.

'That way,' I said to the tuk-tuk driver, and in we went.

There wasn't much to do at Jai's apart from surf – but this place was even more ghostly. We were the only Westerners in the area and had, in the rush to catch the morning train, forgotten to bring anything to read. Splinter had a Game Boy, but Math and I were buggered.

'If the wind doesn't drop I'm going for a paddle anyway, just so that I can sleep tonight,' said Math.

There were still about two hours of daylight left when we set off from shore. It took about twenty minutes to reach the line-up, where we could see that the wave was barely clearing the reef. It was an odd set-up. Waves were coming through at about head high and running down the reef pass perfectly – but choosing them was a risky business. Half a foot too big and the wave would break behind the reef, doing nothing at all, while half a foot too small would make it break onto dry coral. Imco was obviously right about how you couldn't surf the place with too much swell. If you did the sets would just wash the line-up out, completely ruining the exact balance of water depth needed on the reef to make the right ones break.

The rideable waves were mind-blowing though. They were fiercely hollow, but with enough wall to let you squeeze in a few turns – which was a relief given the fact that tube-riding there was super sketchy. The barrel was staying open, but changing shape far too much to keep up with on your feet. Splinter was in heaven. 'Yet another wave where stand-ups can't ride the tube,' he gloated, before sliding down the face and into another soul-shaking water pit. The prone position does let bodyboarders fit into parts of the wave the rest of us can only dream of.

I asked Math if seeing a 'sponger' getting so tubed was making him regret getting a surfboard. 'Yep,' came the reply.

Considering our equipment handicap, the pair of us still managed to snag a couple of good waves. Math, being a goofy-foot and having to surf with his back to the wave, had every reason to give himself a pat on the back, but my situation was a little different. As a 'frontsider' who, according to friends, 'talks a good surf whenever it's barrelling', I felt as if there was something to prove. A good set appeared on the horizon just as we were on the verge of deciding that it was getting dark enough to head in.

The wave stood up in exactly the right position for me to catch, and I wasted no time smugly placing myself in the take-off zone. Nothing went overtly wrong, but as the wave jacked up I remember two things. One was Math screaming at me to go for it, and the other was a feeling that this wave was a little different to the others. Within a moment of getting to my feet, it became obvious that something was wrong.

The smaller wave in front had pushed a little too much water onto the reef, making the one I'd now paddled for slip further inshore than usual. The water from the first one had then run back off the reef, leaving a wave that had now sucked into an impossibly shallow position.

My surfboard barely made it down the face, tossing me forwards towards the coral. Math and Splinter were cheering like the bloodthirsty audience of a Roman amphitheatre as the washing-machine effect took hold. It is possible to be lucky in these kinds of situations, re-emerging without even touching the bottom – but that was not going to be the case this time.

Thud! The first part to hit was my knee. Once you feel yourself get cut, survival mode kicks in. It just becomes a damage-limitation exercise. The knee is one of the worst places to razz yourself, because you use it to push off the board when hopping to your feet. The only place worse than the knee is the bottom of the foot, which is what hit next. That one didn't feel too bad, but I could tell the reef was still near. The third and final blow was definitely the worst, despite only being on the side of my ankle.

The other two were delighted. From their point of view, someone else had paid the necessary skin-tax that most surf spots usually demand as a gate fee. They also knew that the cuts would need cleaning – an event that always draws an audience, although this time we were the only three surfers around.

Back on dry land, a closer inspection revealed that the skin on the bottom of my foot hadn't even broken. That was excellent news, because a cut there often means an automatic lay-period. The knee wasn't too bad either, but the scrape on my ankle was serious. It was quite deep, and even had a small piece of souvenir coral wedged inside.

'It's a scrubbing!' the other two declared gleefully. When a cut has coral microbes in it, you need to scrub the wound with a brush to ensure their removal. Coral is a deadly poison, and can lead to all sorts of horrendous infections like golden staph. Both Math and Splinter were dying to perform that task, but I was having none of it.

'Not a prayer,' I told them. 'I'm doing it myself.' The only brush on hand was my toothbrush, which I submerged in hydrogen peroxide for a moment, before moving in for the kill. Just for good measure, one of the other two poured some peroxide over the wound too, making it fizz like hell. After taking a deep breath, I began slashing the toothbrush across the base of the cut, racing to get as much done as possible before the pain grew too much.

The peroxide agony is a very specific one, with a delay of between five and fifteen seconds, so there was plenty of time to scrub away before it hit. After that there's little you can do besides gritting your teeth, looking away and waiting for it to stop. I'm sure putting a cigarette lighter or poker to your skin would be a more comfortable feeling than that of a flesh-eating dose of H_2O_2. It's like the pain of iodine, but only deeper. It doesn't last long, but is intense and carries a come-down not unlike the one you get after eating a ballistic chilli, or jumping into freezing water on a hot day.

It also leaves the area a little numb – which was kind of nice after having spent the last fifteen minutes paddling back from the waves, through a bacteria-filled tropical lagoon, with an open gash. At least it was clean now.

The come-down reached its calm phase, and I filled the wounds with antibiotic powder, bought from one of the many prescription-waiving pharmacies along the Galle Road.

If there was going to be any chance of me surfing tomorrow, I'd need a lot of that powder and plenty of waterproof tape. The last thing you need is to re-infect the cut and have to go through the whole peroxide ordeal again.

All the fun and games had made us hungry for some Chinese food from the Indian Ocean, over which we reflected on the session just had: the hero of the hour was definitely Splinter, who had, as usual, shown that it was possible to lie down and still charge hard.

As soon as dinner was over, the restlessness from lack of entertainment again kicked in. By night, this village was as feral as they come. Monitor lizards (a relative of the Komodo dragon) plodded past our door, while mosquitoes circled the room like vultures. The fan had obviously broken years ago, and the light bulb was on its way out too – although it was still bright enough to have a swarm of insects orbiting it like little moons.

Itching for our lives, we all agreed that this was going to be the only night we'd spend at the sweaty home of the best Chinese food in the Indian Ocean. If conditions weren't better over the road, or our surfing luck didn't change dramatically, then we'd be making our way back after the morning surf. To add to that, I could feel the humid, disease-ridden air searching hard for a way into my ankle. Open wounds can take days to dry in Sri Lanka, because of the amount of moisture in the air, and sometimes months to heal. Keeping a scab is an uphill struggle.

After little over an hour of sleeping, and about ten of not sleeping, morning did eventually arrive. Splinter went to check the surf, while Math and I looked at the other 'accommodation'. Far from being better, it was probably worse than the place we'd just stayed in. The room looked like a dungeon, and there was a smell of sewage in the courtyard.

'Let's have a surf and then decide what to do,' Math suggested, and so we embarked upon the marathon paddle for the second time, all feeling pretty ratty towards each other, too much discomfort and little sleep having taken their toll.

'It's gonna take something amazing to make me want to stay another night,' I told the others, looking down at my heavily strapped ankle. They showed their agreement by nodding – saving the rest of their energy for the paddle.

In the line-up we found something truly unexpected – another surfer, and a damn good one too. As we arrived in the channel, he stuck four critical backhand smashes into a very compliant wave. He kicked out right next to us and came over to say hello.

'Hey man.' His accent sounded like pidgin-American, and he had dreadlocked hair, gaunt features and a soft, stoner voice.

'Any waves?' I asked him.

'Ho! Yeah, man. It's going off,' he replied, nodding under the effort of talking.

'Are you staying here?'

'Nah, man. I'm just passing through.'

'Oh yeah – where are you from originally?' I asked, suspiciously. So often in places like Sri Lanka you can ask people where they're from, only to be told 'all over', or something else similarly pretentious.

'Is-rael…' The way he intoned the word like a question gave away that he had raised his guard.

Fuck! I thought, sucking up my dismay.

'Oh, cool,' was my reply though. 'Nice one.' Who'd have ever thought that telling someone where you came from could be such a conversation-killer?

Yet the next few hours turned out to be all about reversing generalisations. 'Ron', as he told us his name was, was actually one of the warmest people I'd ever met. He wasted no time in showing us that he wasn't like the guys back in Midigama. He had impeccable line-up behaviour and tons of surfing ability.

He and his girlfriend Mira, it emerged, lived in a kibbutz whenever they weren't travelling to various surf spots around the world. He was a slender goofy-footer who had, like all surfers who impress me, obviously spent a great deal of time thinking about his style. That can hold some riders back a little, as they become too obsessed with presentation and grow stale. Not Ron, though. He had a bank of flashy moves that he could almost pull at will – airs, slides, various rotations and a strong, fast carve. He reminded me a little of the world-famous Californian maestro Rob Machado, and almost wept when I told him so.

'Tenks, man,' he sniffed. 'If somebody wants to say that about my surfing, I'm gonna be really happy. He is my favourite surfer ever and I always wanna surf like dat. I don't know what else to say.'

The other generalisation that I'd been working under until then was that Imco was full of shit. Before paddling out, I'd decided that both his secret spots were never going to deliver. Again, this was not to be.

The wind, although dying down, had obviously still been affecting the waves when we'd paddled out the night before – but now, with over ten hours of calm having passed since then, things had changed dramatically. Although you still had to be really picky about which waves you chose, the right ones were now far, far better than before – good enough to make me forget about the cuts and bites accrued over the last twenty-four hours.

The visuals were a lot different now too, with the high midday sun making the water seem like little more than a thin sheet of vapour on top of a multicolour reef. Fluorescent parrot-fish drifted through the wave faces, their reflected colours skipping around the changing water surface as if thrown off some sort of disco ball.

When we weren't riding waves, the four of us would put our faces right up to the surface, staring in awe at the details of the reef below, which could be seen almost as clearly as if we'd been looking through glass. With only three others in the water, you could afford to dally about between catching waves – and dally we did. By the time the wind arrived it was as if we'd known Ron for years.

The session had been enough to make me totally forget about the uncomfortable night that had preceded it, and so we elected to stay another.

The wave broke again that evening, and the following morning, but we never topped that second session. Revitalised by our little break, Midigama felt once again like ours for the taking. Ron bade us farewell, promising to stop by and try talking to Robocop one day – but each of us knew it was highly unlikely that we'd ever see him again.

The return journey was a little more complicated. The 'hotel' tried to overcharge us, claiming they'd paid the tuk-tuk driver extra on our behalf and then added it to our bill.

'It's amazing the shit people will try and pull,' said Splinter.

Despite the frustration of knowing that the locals would always try it on, it was still memories of great waves that circled my head as I watched the real-life theatre show fly past my train window once again.

A few stations along the way, we stopped to change drivers – a lengthy delay since the next one hadn't finished sleeping on a nearby bench yet. A couple of shoeless kids were playing cricket, using a stretch of old railway for a crease. They'll make a game out of almost anything; sticks and stones, poles, discarded shoe-soles, but these ones had their own bat and ball, and were yelling for us to join them.

'What your name?' one of them asked Splinter.

'Michael Atherton,' he told them. They'd probably never seen a cricket match on television before, and therefore had no way of knowing what one of England's most famous cricketers, now retired and a couple of decades older than Splinter, looked like. However, being as the sport was almost like a religion in Sri Lanka, they still knew the name, and instead of laughing as he'd expected, these kids were actually ready to believe that this travelling bodyboarder was in fact a professional cricket player. Not for the first time that trip, the Sinhalese again began fighting over us – except that this time it wasn't over our money, but rather the privilege of being bowled at by 'Splinter Atherton'.

Knowing full well that he'd be exposed as a fraud the moment the ball left his hands, Splinter offered to bat instead. It wasn't going to be hard to impress these pint-sized fielders, and so he swung for the ball with all the energy he could muster. Not a wise idea, because it went flying over the nearby wall, and off into the streets behind.

We started berating him for his unnecessary display of force, but the kids didn't seem to mind at all. As far as they were concerned, *the* Michael Atherton had just wellied *their* cricket ball into the back of beyond. They cheered his six-point smash, turning and running after it as fast as their legs could carry them. One thing that definitely runs in Sinhalese blood is the gene for resourcefulness – these kids wouldn't give up on finding the ball.

The train wasn't going anywhere fast, so we were still there when they got back, giving the mighty Splinter a second chance to practise his new favourite sport. This time he went easy on them, slogging high into the air, but not very far. It was a day of dreams for the lucky kid who caught the ball. 'Howzaaaaaat!' they all shouted together. Splinter, deflated, climbed back onto the train carriage.

'That kid is going to be telling his grandchildren about today,' I told him.

After that we were mobbed. More and more kids started milling around the carriage to get a glimpse of the world-famous cricketer that their little mate had just caught 'out'. By the time the train finally pulled away again it was actually a relief to be leaving. A handful of them ran after us down the track, waving and shouting.

'Hello sir! Wherarugoing? Ten rupees? School pen?'

'I'm gonna be telling my grandchildren about this train trip too,' said Splinter.

Back in Midigama, we could tell that something was afoot. According to Jai, we'd just ridden one of the last trains before tomorrow's national strike, but the look around the common room told of more line-up trouble.

'Do you want the good news first, or the bad news?' Andy, another of the Welsh guys staying at Ram's, asked me.

'The good.'

'The Israelis have left!'

'No way! So we're back in business.'

'Er, not quite. Ask me for the bad news.'

'Let me guess. Four more have turned up to replace them...'

'Not quite,' Andy began, 'but there was this one guy, an Aussie. As we started paddling out he was just screaming at us, shouting all sorts of shit. "Get out, you fucking kooks", "Fuck off" and all this. Well, we tried talking to him, but he was just a total wanker. "This is a high-performance wave, mate," he said at one point. "You's all shouldn't be in here!"'

'So what happened then? Did anyone tell him to fuck off, or what?'

'I did, but he just started saying more shit. He called one guy a fat cunt, and then started having a pop at this young Cornish guy. He was saying, "I'm from Narrabeen, mate. Where I'm from you's all'd just get run out of the water."'

I had to laugh at that. Narrabeen was one of Sydney's highly localised beach suburbs. All sorts of stories about gangs of surf nazis emanated from those areas – and I'd even met a guy from Maroubra once who'd claimed to have a gang tattoo on his sternum – all in the name of a couple of waves!

I wandered over to Ram's to find out more. The boys over there were laughing about it – as if this idiot had brightened up their day. Apparently, when someone called him a wanker, he'd replied by saying, 'I'm the biggest wanker you'll ever meet in your *life*, mate! My dad's a wanker, me brothers are wankers. We're all a bunch of total bastards, mate, and you'd better believe it.' It sounded as if this guy had *arrived* with the Midigama Madness.

He had promised to return tomorrow, with a few of his 'mates'. Perhaps it was just as well Breige and I had to go to Colombo on the visa run then anyway – maybe I'd still manage to miss this fool altogether. But had the legacy of Robocop actually been replaced by something far, far worse? Was this the death of a surf spot?

★ ★ ★

It's amazing how quickly some things can fade into memory, I thought to myself as Akalanka saved our lives from yet another murderous oncoming driver. The train strike had been for real, leading everyone out onto the roads. Speeding buses buckled under the weight of all those extra Lankans. They say you never know what is around the corner in Old Ceylon – and on this day the phrase was proving to be literal.

It was hard to imagine having been at Spot B only fifty or so hours before. We hadn't taken any photos of the place beyond those in our minds, and the Colombo journey's main surf-talk was so far centred on Mr Narrabeen. Was he mentally ill, or just ignorant and a bit troppo?

The visas were sorted, after about another two hours of waiting during which Johan decided to go and buy an English-language newspaper. According to reports in the paper, the strike was over a tiny amount of money, making me suspect that the goals were more likely to be political than financial. It was just an attempt by rebel factions within

143

the ruling party to undermine the president before the upcoming annual elections. Even in peacetime, Sri Lankan politics were still a disaster waiting to happen.

The trains had stopped, and buses were set to go within the next few days too. Elephants had been ordered down from the mountain provinces to replace the striking airport barges, and were expected on the runways the next day (they don't walk quickly).

Ahh, that's what this area needs again, I thought selfishly. A bit of good old-fashioned political instability. Joking aside, though, it was a grave affair. Akalanka had been listening to the radio on the way back and was worried.

'Hmmn,' he frowned. '*Beeeg* problems. Always saying peace lasting never.' You could tell that this stuff really mattered to him (and not least by the fact that Boney M had been temporarily shelved). His business, his lifestyle and his dreams were tied up in this peace. I'd heard the other day that he was planning to go on a once-in-a-lifetime trip to Australia one off-season soon. He'd apparently sat all the various visa exams and now just needed a few stable years in which to save up the cash.

I began to feel guilty. After all, the Tamil troubles that had made the place so serene from a surfing point of view were widely believed to have been caused by British foreign policy. When the island fell under British rule in the early nineteenth century, the colonialists found the laid-back Sinhalese to be awful workers (actually, laid-back is probably an understatement – the Sinhalese have more national holidays than any other race on earth). So the solution to this problem was to bring in a Tamil workforce from Southern India. The Tamils and Sinhalese started bickering, and the British solution to this second complication was typical – they buggered off. Using the guise of generosity that was an offer of Sri Lankan independence, the stiff-lipped masters turned tail and ran, washing their hands of the problems they had created, and leaving the country in turmoil. And ever since then, the Tamils who occupy the north of the country have wanted independence, while the Sinhala have kept claming that they, as first settlers, should have the right to continue governing. (The Tamils were probably there long before the Sinhalese, but only as passing 'transients', so neither can really claim absolute rights over the other.)

It's hard for us Westerners to imagine what it must feel like to be in Akalanka's shoes – spending your whole life longing to do what so many of us take for granted. Not knowing if you will even once be able to leave the land of your birth and visit a different culture. You come across so many people in poor countries who say they want one day to go to France, Italy, Great Britain or somewhere else. Some of them get really hung up about it – reading about London for years at a time, sticking posters of Welsh Guards and Buckingham Palace on their walls. Akalanka's main wedding photo showed him and his new bride superimposed in front of the Taj Mahal.

The girl in the stall over the road from Jai's was just as keen to travel, although she was less particular about the destination. Breige was chatting to her and got talking about Bristol University. The next day the girl showed her some pictures of Bristol that she'd printed out in a Galle Internet café, and claimed she was now going to apply for one of the courses there!

The more I thought of it, the harder it became for me to see how, in any way, we had a right to hope the number of visitors here wouldn't grow. Who cared how many people were in the water anyway – to the people who lived here, surfing was a way of life now. It was from surfers that Akalanka and co made their living, and if all went to plan and peace did last, then it would be partly through surfers that he might one day achieve his own dream journey.

Akalanka rarely furrowed his brow for long, and was soon giggling about something unrelated. Some used to say that Sri Lanka had been placed under a *Brahmana* Curse – thus leading to an impossibility of peace ever thriving there, but our chirpy van-driver didn't believe that. Even if there were a few weeks of chaos to follow, things were ultimately going to be OK, because this time the *people* really wanted peace. That was a first – particularly amongst the Tamils in the North. Jaffna and Trincomale had been open to foreigners for the first time in decades, allowing people to see just what life could be like when you weren't living from one conflict to the next.

The country was growing up, and so was Midigama. What we'd been seeing over the past weeks, along with the bigger picture of political changes, had been a surf destination coming of age, and the inevitable loss of innocence that came with it. For me, it signified a need to move on too. In more ways than one, my work was done here. I'd experienced the adventure of looking for new waves, I'd seen a town and a surf culture grow almost from scratch, and I'd ridden most of the waves the area had to show. But as much as the Lazy Left was a stepping-stone into the more advanced Ram's Right, so was Sri Lanka itself meant to serve as a stepping-stone into heavier reef breaks and, ultimately, J-Bay. By the time I'd seen out the remainder of the season in the 'new' Midigama, it was certainly going to be time to find a new surfing challenge.

Yet for the next month and a bit, Midigama was home, and the only thing to do was embrace the town, and its brightening future. One of the old guards, an enigmatic Queenslander who called himself 'Emerson X', was stoked to see things finally working out for the Lankans. He'd been there at the very beginning, surfing the east coast's Arugam Bay back when it was uncharted territory. 'They can't go on fighting over waves forever,' he said of the surfers at Ram's.

'But while they do, I'm not gonna surf there.' The turf wars didn't worry him. He still savoured his tales of old, moonlit night surfs with his buddies out at the left – watching those big shadowy waves on the inky horizon. Emo knew that things had changed, but Sri Lanka still charmed him as much as ever, and he chuckled warmly at the Sinhala and their quirky ways.

A couple of seasons after this trip there was another event that showed the benefits surfing could bring to villages like the ones I visited. We all saw the devastating tsunami that hit that fateful Boxing Day while most of us ate rich food and drank sherry, and the many hopeless scenes of destruction left in its wake. Unfortunately, Midigama took a hit from the freak wave too. There were casualties, some of whom would have been familiar faces to many travelling surfers, although every character named in this chapter was still alive and well last time I asked. The tsunami was a big blow, but Sri Lanka and its burgeoning businesses remained determined not to get knocked off course – and one of the great allies of the southern coastal towns proved to be surfing. For it was through the surf communities in Europe and beyond that a lot of re-building funds were raised, with Midigama being virtually adopted by some of the French, Welsh and Cornish surf communities – so much so that Ram and Jai were open for business by the following season.

Akalanka was accelerating into another bend, and the other three were chatting – about something other than Mr Narrabeen now. Breige and Johan were talking about going in the Lazy Left for a quick surf when we got home to Jai's. She was going back in just a few days, and was therefore at that part of the trip where you cram in as much water-time as possible. At the end of the day, you were still guaranteed a daily surf here, whatever happened.

'Ah,' said Chips, as Galle dropped into the background. 'You can feel it in the mood. We've arrived at that stage of the journey where everyone is feeling like they're nearly home…'

Sri Lanka had fallen into my plans as a warm-up to Indonesia, and like everything else in my surf journey so far, it had become so much more.

But I would soon be ready to leave it behind. The next trip was appearing on the horizon.

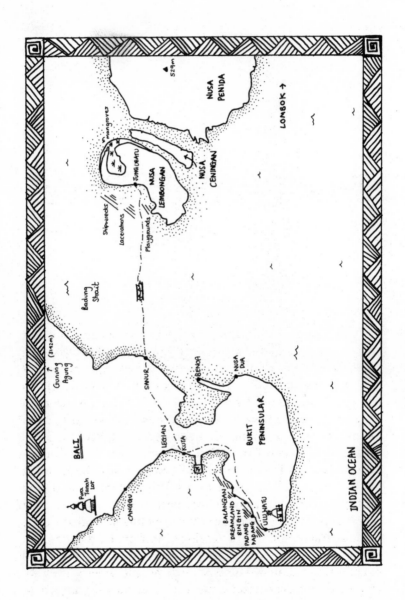

5.
The Perfect Wave:

Indo

S o is there such a thing as the perfect wave? This has to be surfing's ultimate question. Something you can discuss for hours and hours, without ever arriving at a definite answer. Some may say 'six foot, warm water, no wind and only me and a few buddies', but that just seems a little too straightforward. The whole reason we go to such extremes can't be so simple – or can it? If Plato and his illustrious 'company' struggled so hard to find the definition of a perfect form then surely a bunch of surf-bums can't just go and do it in thirteen words. What people who define perfection often overlook is that perfect surf is a quest; the actual act of wave riding only the conclusion of that quest. The surfing itself is only a fleeting sensation, hard to commit to memory – which is why the adventure of the voyage is equally important. If you ask most people where, if at all, they've found the perfect wave, they'll usually list anywhere they've been *except home*! There seems to be no such thing as the perfect wave at home.

Everyone thinks their local waves are at best average – no matter where that is. Brits aren't the only ones who moan about the drawbacks of home – I've heard guys from California, Australia, France, South Africa and any other place with great waves saying that 'home sucks', that they will never experience the perfect wave there. But why? Simple: when you go searching you must find. Only the nature of a search, or a voyage, can lead to that adrenalising thrill of discovery that is associated with the perfect wave.

It's like a pilgrimage. The hardship of the journey and the insecurity of the search is the only way to experience true reward. The Buddhist temples I visited in Sri Lanka were often located at the tops of hills (which is why they were all spared by the tsunami and then used as refuges for the homeless). Besides believing that the altitude brings pilgrims closer to the heavens, it is hoped that the feeling of accomplishment in completing a climb will cause a sense of euphoria – which is then compounded by a breathtaking view. Pilgrimage.

Perfect surf may have as much to do with the circumstances of your session as it does the waves you're riding.

Returning from Sri Lanka, I was well aware that one pilgrimage stood out in surfing. Malibu, Mundaka and J-Bay are all important milestones in any surf-traveller's career. Some will keep total faith in one of those waves and put it in a permanent mental shrine. But be that as it may, as far as journey and exploration goes, there is one place all surfers must visit. A place where, even today, with enough determination you can still explore virgin, wave-rich coastlines for yourself – and that's Indonesia. Before finally searching out my own perfection in South Africa, it seemed like a place I needed to have been. Surfers with Indo trips under their belts are better equipped to take hold of future perfection. It's a place to gain both travel savvy and experience of thumping reef breaks and open ocean swells. If I could surf some proper Indonesian waves, then I would be ready for J-Bay.

Amongst the 17,000 islands that make up the archipelago, probably at least half of them are surrounded by surfable waves of all variety, from playful little points to life-or-death reef breaks. Indo is the surf of fantasy, what most grommets will draw inside their schoolbooks when the maths teacher stops making sense. It's where almost all of those seductive *Search* posters have been shot. Indo has become the very ideal of surf discovery and rightly so. It has *everything*. You can go there on a shoestring, or on a playboy yacht. You can sit in a Westernised bar, or go to a cockfight. You can get a massage on Kuta beach, or 'feral out' at Bingin. The choices are entirely yours. There's as much exotic culture as you want, right on tap. A hotel room with MTV, BBC News 24, CNN and ESPN Sports is never too far away if you choose, but it's also possible to go far enough off the beaten track to put most Victorian missionaries to shame.

A film crew from Huntington Beach, near LA, once went so deep into the Javanese jungle in search of the perfect wave that they were killing their own food, boiling their water over and over to get rid of the risk of diseases (which still left them helpless against the malaria-carrying anopheles mosquito), and slowly going mad. Ahead of their footage, they sent *Surfer Magazine* a few taster photographs of the resultant discovery, making a cover shot that no other publication on the planet could rival: a hopelessly skinny Robinson Crusoe lookalike slouching in the throat of a wave so perfect that I shiver to recall it. They called one of their spots 'Orgasms'.

Rumours abounded that on their return to California all three of them suffered from depression and reverse culture shock; their hopeless addiction to waves that Huntington Pier will never produce had sent them into cold turkey. Returning from their wave-rider's Eden, the commercialism and hysteria of the Western Vanity Fair got to them badly. They'd seen sights of such supernatural bliss that their psychological make-ups had been severely altered, forever. What kind of perfection entitles a wave to be called Orgasms?

That's what was on my mind boarding the final leg of the marathon journey that is London to Indo. As the sights of Bangkok dropped away from me, and sky vapour filled the plane window, I was running through the various names that travelling surfers have given to their Indonesian discoveries. Naming rights always fall with the first guy to paddle out, and the results tend to be either silly references to in-jokes shared along the way, or profound metaphors alluding to the very nature of the wave itself. I don't know why, but there's never any middle ground. The names of the most significant spots in Indo tell the story of decades of ecstatic moments of discovery. The perfect wave, hundreds of times over.

Orgasms was just the latest in a long line; Racetracks, Dreamland, Padang Padang, Shipwrecks, Lacerations, Scar Reef, Thunders, Playgrounds, Pit Stops, Periscopes, Super Suck, Steroid Nias, G-Land, Greenball, Depth Charges, Macaronis, No Can Duis, Lances, Indicators, Impossibles – and on it goes.

As the plane touched down at Denpasar, another glance out the window revealed, as I had been told it would, that the waves at the less cleverly named Airport Reef were firing. That apparently means that every other spot throughout the whole Archipelago is also doing what it does best. In the peak season of May to September, the waves in Indo are never worse than very, very good, and usually ranging from excellent to out of this world.

A small airport, with a relatively mellow customs section, and in the queue with me awaiting my first Indo stamp was a large selection of obviously like minds, everyone itching to get out of the air con and into the thick of it. Some, like me, just eager to get their first Indo trip underway, and others awaiting the latest fix in a lifelong addiction to the place. Indonesia is one of the most frequently returned-to surf destinations around – leaving most people with a feeling of unfinished business that can last a lifetime, no matter how many follow-up journeys are taken.

Baggage arrived quickly too, and I made my way to the door with a brisk pace, hiding my excitement so as to avoid looking like a fast buck to the taxi drivers. Running the gauntlet of hawkers and overpriced bemos (Balinese-driven people carriers) that swarmed around the airport exit, I eventually found someone who looked reasonable.

'You need trans-porta sir?'

'Can you take me to Kuta?'

'Yes, yes. Kuta, Lovina, Nusa Dua, Belangan, Jimbaran...'

'Kuta. Poppies Lane Two, please.'

'Poppies Two! One hundred thousand rupees.'

'We'll see about that mate. I'd rather go by the meter, please.'

By the time the yellow cab had scraped its way down the narrow Poppies Lane Two, that meter hadn't exceeded sixty thousand. Kuta's taxi drivers were yet to realise the best way of pocketing their earnings themselves would be to offer un-metered rides for *lower* than the standard rate, not higher. Bali is the London Town of Indonesia – everyone goes there, from all over, with dreams of getting rich. Thousands upon thousands of Indo Dick Whittingtons pour in every year from Java, Sumatra, Lombok, even Timor, in search of those gold-paved streets. Usually the only gold they find is the writing on the bottles of fake aftershave they end up selling for a living.

Kuta is a cacophony of cultures. It's kind of a West-meets-East tourist town, but then there's that age-old surf travel vs beaten-track tourism thing going on. Quite a few of the 'Balos' surf (some very well – there are several Indonesian pros) and are very culturally aware indeed, as are some of the foreign surfers, but then there's still a million people from both sides of the fence that don't understand each other at all. Expect to find hoards of inconsiderate louts, aloof rich people who complain at restaurants for a hobby and idiotic rugby teams searching for trouble. Touts and hawkers are always on the lookout for a quick scam and the main industry is fake designer merchandise. As in Sri Lanka, traffic is ridiculous, and brief sewer-flavour wafts are likely at any time and any place.

To mix things up, there is one single, very upmarket 'high street' right in the heart, as well as a Hard Rock Café and more multinational Western fast-food eateries than you can shake a big-wave board at; all overpriced as hell. Oh, and surf – lots of it.

Right in the middle of 'Halfway Kuta', the stretch that encompasses the ultra-high-performance set of beach breaks, are two roads that run onto the beaches like veins from the jugular street of Jalan Legian. It is in this part of the town that most Indonesian experiences inevitably begin...

★ ★ ★

After taking every second of the compulsory lie-in that is needed the morning after a long journey east, I surfaced from a very deep, fan-assisted slumber to the sounds of the Kuta horror show already in full flow. A brief stopover in Bangkok had had the opposite effect to that intended. Rather than breaking up the journey and resting, I had neurotically attempted to 'do' Thailand in four days, subsequently arriving in Bali absolutely fucked. The waves had been good when I arrived, but not quite good enough to compete with the option of sleep. Eastbound jetlag has no cure other than stoic suffering.

After forcing myself to eat breakfast, it was time to step out into the madness of Poppies Lane Two to see if I might be ready to try settling in. The Poppies Lanes are the centre of Kuta's surf culture, and the only place to stay if you really want to get into the spirit of things. Each one leads from the beach to town, and has hundreds of cheap restaurants, shops and accommodation. The prevailing noise is that of the scooter, the main form of transport in one of the most densely populated places on earth.

Bemo drivers slouch against each stretch of flat wall or tree-trunk begging you to give them something to do. 'Belangan...? Surf good today, you need go to Bukit!' The Bukit Peninsula is where it all goes down. A brief drive from Kuta, it's where a succession of world-class – and deadly – surf spots line a four-mile stretch of sharp coral. At the tip of the peninsula is the majestic Uluwatu Temple, one of the island's many sacred places. At the foot of the cliffs lies another of them, for surfers at least – Racetracks and Padang Padang – two of the best waves in Bali.

Padang Padang is supposedly the hideout of the Queen of the Southern Seas, who occasionally abducts surfers to be her lover. The tale says that she likes green, and to this day surfing in anything green is a dead no-no – sometimes even literally. Statistically more people drown in green than any other colour in Bali; eerie considering the fact that only a few brave individuals ever wear it. From Padang Padang the Bukit Peninsula then runs into the mind-warping waves of Bingin, Dreamland and Belangan, before the coast turns to face west at Jimbaran Bay with some of the best (and most basic) fish restaurants you're ever likely to come across.

Once I knew my breakfast was definitely going to stay down, thoughts began turning towards surfing. Some friends were due to join me, but their flight wasn't coming until the next day. Here was my chance to get rid of those cobwebs, and provide them with the reassuring sight of a settled-in person, who they knew well, to show them the sights and sounds of the place. After that we would embark upon a new journey, together. I unwrapped my boards – always a hair-raising moment as you wait to see what damage the ruthless airlines inflicted in transit – and got ready for a surf.

It's a lovely feeling, walking towards a beach in nothing but a pair of boardshorts. Although it was only late August and home was relatively warm, little could compare to the balmy, bath-like water of Bali. As in Sri Lanka, the freedom of ocean that requires no wearing of a wetsuit is such a pure source of euphoria.

Kuta Beach was filled with surfers who, like me, had recently flown in and were anxious to get some practice in a sand-bottom spot, where the consequences of a mistake were nil, before heading off in search of heavier waves. Most of the waves in Indo break over super-sharp coral, and are big and heavy. The beach break warm-up is vital if you don't want to spend your entire trip watching from shore, nursing brutal reef cuts, as your mates get great waves and have the time of their lives.

There is another type of surfer in the water also: the tanned and smiling cat that's got the cream – guys who've just completed their time in Indo and are having one last surf before cruising over to the airport where their next goal is getting home as quickly as possible to develop any films, and make all their friends jealous with stories of perfect waves. These guys are there to show you what you'll be like in a few weeks' time.

After a day of fun surf and another long night's sleep, it was time to welcome the crew, three friends from home who had all just quit their jobs and flown to Indo with their savings (en route to Australia, where they planned to rent an apartment and then 'see what happens). The person I knew best of the trio was Richie, the same grommethood friend who had been on my first trip to Sri Lanka. Sri Lanka had done the same to him as it had me, and Rich had since been travelling at every opportunity he could find. The other two were friends of his; Andrew, the loud one, and Pete, who during the first few days of the trip only ever spoke up in order to make fun of, disagree with or insult Andrew.

Already to me they looked pasty-faced. The smog and some inedible food in Bangkok, coupled with a day of surfing at Kuta had given me the look – gaunt and tough-skinned. As for the newly arrived; they had over-relaxed Western waistlines and soft faces. But that would soon change. A boat-ride was calling us...

* * *

Nusa, Nusa, Nusa. Nusa Cenningan, Nusa Lembongan, Nusa Penida. The greedy travel agents who lay in wait along the Poppies gangways, touting sketchy exchange rates for your rupees, had started to call them Cenningan *Island*, Lembongan *Island* and so on; but *why*? Balinese and Bahasa are such beautiful languages. All those 'y's, 'ak's and 'ng's. Listen to the names of the dishes and tobaccos: Nasi Kampur, Gudang Garum, Nasi Goreng, Sate Lilit, Tum Ayam. Such rich language. Why should they give in to the dictionary of the tourists? At least the surfers still say *Nusa* Lembongan.

But now there was the 'Bounty Cruise'; a chance to see the beauty of Lembongan without having to risk touching, or smelling. Just like seeing the place on Sky Travel, or an airliner's in-flight advert programmes. Surfers can sometimes harbour a bitter hostility towards mass-market tourists, and this is the sort of reason why. Indo is threatened, goes the voice of surfing reason. A look at parts of Bali could certainly make the alarm bells ring. Buildings were sprouting out of the ground like weeds, and the vibe of Kuta's nightlife had started losing its utopian edge as irresponsible Aussie rugby boys pounded each other, fuelled by Bintangs and Arraks. Lembongan was still relatively virgin (considering its proximity to Bali) – and a perfect example of how, despite having been visited by surfers for decades, Indonesia can still give you that sense of adventure and discovery almost as soon as you leave Kuta. The expensive, banana-yellow Bounty Cruise had started to hover ominously off the northern shore once every two days, but its cautious human cargo was yet to spill onto the beaches. Unlike the surfers, who hadn't wasted any time.

We caught the boat to Lembongan a few mornings later, after a brief but stuffy bus ride from Kuta to the eastern side of the Bukit Peninsula. A youthful human chain transported our boards from the shoreline to the minuscule vessel that relied on two stabilisers to deal with the mighty Indonesian swell problems. Because of this, we dubbed these boats 'pond-skaters'. The fact that this thing was going to attempt to take us across the Lombok Strait would have been funny, if this wasn't real-life.

But we were in Indo, and a certain suspension of belief seemed to hang about the place. So off we set, the boards laying at one end of the gondola and we at the other. Our captain, having already launched us into the mercy of the ocean with a push of his staff, began the delicate process of starting the outboard motor. Eventually it coughed into motion and we were off.

As soon as we left the bay and hit open ocean, it became obvious that the waves were really *pumping* their way across the sea. Our boat was climbing and dropping some forty feet at a time as massive cyclone-created swell lines, sent with love from somewhere off the Cape of Good Hope in the Roaring Forties (the same storm pattern that sent waves to J-Bay), marched sternly up one of the deepest stretches of water on the planet. The Lombok Strait is the point at which the Australasian and Asian tectonic plates meet, so beneath us was basically a crack in the Earth's shell. The flora and fauna of Lombok is that of an entirely different continent, since water of such depth has, for millions of years, served as a great divider – before some Indonesian genius invented the pond-skater.

Bali disappeared from behind us and a new land came into view. It had actually been disappearing and reappearing for about an hour before finally dropping from sight, as the ruthless ground swell blocked out the horizon (and at one point even the sun) repeatedly. For a while there followed the stomach-churning feeling of being in a tiny boat in the middle of huge seas with no visible land in any direction, before another island began to bob in and out of our range of sight. We began timing the intervals between the waves so that Pete could clear the spray out of his binoculars and pass them on to the next person in time to catch a few seconds of view. The intervals between rises were steady, and dramatic. This was some swell.

Richie had struck up a conversation with the captain, who invited us to the cremation of one of his uncles in three days' time. We accepted, naturally. It would be something to look forward to between surfs.

Nobody ever talks on boat rides, I've noticed. Everyone just sits and absorbs their surroundings, feeling the rhythms of a sea they will later be riding, running through their own personal anticipations of what adventures the land mass creeping towards us may hold. Dialogue doesn't normally resume until the boat has landed and everyone is off. Eventually the boat arrived inside a lagoon.

'Boys, did you see the size of the swell?'

'Yeah, it's gonna be sick!'

'Where are we gonna stay?'

'Dunno. In front of the best wave, I suppose.'

'Boys, I dunno about you but I'm in there straight away.' This was the eager voice of Andrew.

'Are you sure?' – the reply from a tentative Pete.

'Are you mad? It's the best surf you're gonna see in a long time. What are you waiting for?'

'I might watch it a bit first, you know. Just to see where the waves are breaking and all that, you know. It's fucking big out there, and I'm gonna just warm up slowly on the beach, drink some water and get out there in an hour or so.'

I favoured Pete's stance, as did Richie.

'You're all a bunch of poofs, boys!' Andrew was bitterly disappointed in all of us. 'You come all the way to Indo and then don't wanna surf!'

We were in the right on this one, though, and everyone knew it.

'He's stupid, man,' noted Pete as another pond-skater pushed off towards the reef pass, carrying Andrew on towards the waves of his dreams. Most waves in Indo break on coral reef passes around the islands. This means that the actual beaches are usually tranquil lagoons (ideal for winding down after a long session in scary surf).

'That reef is a long way out, man. Further than you think. And it's bigger than it looks too.'

Welcome to Shipwrecks, so named because a rusting WW2 ship lies grounded on the reef, yards in front of where the waves break. Shipwrecks is a treacherous wave, shallow and tricky, and it was about to enjoy making light work of Andrew.

After warming up and stretching a bit, we arrived alongside the waves in another one of the ferrying pond-skaters to join him. These boats pull up alongside the reefs, anchoring in safe, deep water to drop off a fresh group of surfers and take another in. As we all prepared ourselves to jump off the boat, the biggest set of waves so far decided to charge towards the shipwreck. Andrew had just tried to catch a smaller one and failed. He was about twenty yards too far inside of where the bigger waves were breaking. As he turned to face the monsters, we all began hooting and cheering. A massacre was going to unfold before us. He was old enough and ugly enough to look after himself, so all we were going to do was sit there and enjoy an 'I-told-you-so' moment of *schadenfreude*. 'Your friend not surfing again thees treep,' mumbled a similarly humoured boat driver, as Andrew got washed over the reef and into the shipwreck.

'I told him,' Pete grinned.

Bloodied and out of breath, Andrew accepted his fate. There would be plenty of relaxing in the lagoons as his cuts healed, but no more surfing – not until we got back to Bali, anyway. First, however, was the agonising (or highly entertaining, depending on your point of view) job of cleaning the coral cuts. Hydrogen peroxide bubbled and fizzed, and then the pond-skater turned round and bore the martyr back towards the beach – while we all had a great surf, for hours. Another crucial part of a trip to Indo: one of your crew must get injured very early on in the trip and then have to watch from the beach, an example to all to look before you leap.

Halfway through the session a vicious tropical storm set in. The surface of the ocean came alive, dancing under the impact of millions upon millions of dive-bombing raindrops. The rain stung my bare back and smashed my eyes half-closed. Nobody rode any waves. We just hid underneath our surfboards, hoping the wave that got Andrew didn't have any relatives. Thunder got louder and louder, until fork lightning pierced the ocean surface only a few hundred yards away from us. Thanks to the height of swell lines, it didn't find our flesh and gave up, moving on up the Lombok Strait to terrorise the poor old Bounty Cruise.

After the storm, the waves were even better. Liberated from the humidity that usually encircled them, the lips of the waves were able to freely jump forward onto the reef, making huge almond-shaped cylinders of moving water roll towards the deep-water channel. Cylinders big enough for us to stand in, untouched, surrounded by water, enveloped in energy. The waves looked like they were breathing, firing spray out of the tube into the crisp air, like the blow-out from a moody whale. It felt as if the ocean had turned itself up a level.

The cleared air also brought Bali back into sight – or rather the volcano Ganung Agung, about 80 kilometres north of Kuta. Usually the tropical sea air is too thick to see over the Lombok Strait, but now we lay in the lap of a monstrous decapitated mountain, who watched over us menacingly. Sea-level Bali was below the horizon, but Agung rose high above cloud level, causing you to tilt your head in order to see its crater. I welcomed the feeling it gave you of being completely at the mercy of capricious nature.

As the sun dropped, we opted to paddle in across the lagoon, passing up offers of a boat ride. The water was so warm you could have stayed in there forever. 'Don't care if I die,' claimed Pete.

The next day was nearly a carbon copy wave-wise, except that instead of a storm arriving in the afternoon, it was just the trade wind. With surfing off the agenda for the rest of the day, Scott – a talkative Aussie staying nearby who had been offering to help the other three find apartments when they got to Australia – suggested that we go to watch some cockfighting. I was intrigued. The others weren't interested but Scott argued that cockerels had been keeping us awake every night, so he wasn't going to mind seeing one suffer. They were noisy buggers, you had to admit. Last time Andrew came to Indo he had been woken up in the middle of the night by a cockerel and taken a pot-shot at it with a sling. Accidentally, he killed it – the village's prize-cockerel! He left that day, and still won't go back to Sumba, the island where it happened.

Three days of holiday had been declared in honour of the ferry captain's uncle, so what better way to celebrate, thought the Indonesians, than cockfighting? Scott had arranged for guides to take us, so we jumped onto the backs of some mopeds, put on blindfolds (cockfighting – and any gambling – is illegal, but we were rich in their terms, and so more than welcome) and waited until they were removed. I began to regret the decision the moment we arrived at the small glade in the jungle. Hundreds of men were screaming aggressively at a fight you could tell was in progress from the flying feathers, but couldn't yet see. Our guides parted the crowd for us to stand at the front, and there it was: violence, real-life violence. Death, blood and pain. There you go, I told myself, you've got what you wanted, now you're stuck here until they take you back. Unfortunately, my guide had no intention of leaving for quite some time, and we still had to live up to his expectations – by spending money. About three great British pounds left my pocket that afternoon, and nothing came back. That was largely because my guide placed all my bets for me, any winnings from which he presumably pocketed. Even if my cockerels had won I didn't care, and would never have discerned so from the mélange of 'ng's and 'ak's being shouted anyway.

Cockfighting is one of Indonesia's favourite pastimes, besides following British Premier League football. Champion cockerels are held in reverence, and often fed better than their owners. Two cockerels are placed into the ring together with daggers two or so inches long strapped to their heels – 'spurs' apparently. The owners (the real competitors here) then proceed to wind each other's bird up. This is done by holding one blindfolded while the other is allowed a free peck, and vice versa. Once the roosters are obviously angry enough to start fighting, they are unleashed. And that's when the gore begins.

Cocks tend to start fighting by fly-kicking with both feet. However, since they now have blades on their ankles, the results can be messy. In the second fight the two birds both fell to ground with these spurs embedded firmly in each other's chest. A scramble began, with the birds desperately trying to regain control of their feet but unable to work out why they could not. Both died. Looking over at Scott, I could see he was grimacing too, but had found videoing the whole thing a good way of detaching himself from it.

Actually, most of the fights don't turn out to be fatal, as birds can often concede defeat, in much the same way as dogs playfighting down the beach may do. However, in one instance towards the end of the bill, two equally stubborn cocks, too battered to fight on, were causing embarrassment to both owners. One had lost an eye and could only walk in circles but still wouldn't submit, and the other couldn't muster the energy to finish him off.

The situation was resolved by a small, primeval Lembonganese man, with cruel features, a grin that was certainly *not* the mark of happiness, and a home-made cigar stuck firmly between rotting teeth. He took a basket and placed it upside-down over the two birds. The effect was that both were able to draw on a second wind of energy, probably stimulated by fear and changed surroundings. After about half a minute of flying feathers, everything went quiet and the man lifted the basket up again. One-Eye had delivered a single fatal blow, against all odds, and was lauded like a big-time sports star as a result. The loser lay in the dust, a dark trickle of freshly spent blood growing into a pool around his neck. This would be One-Eye's owner's victory meal for the evening. But the real winner was the bird. By losing an eye and winning a fight at once, he was now guaranteed a healthy old age, free from having to fight again, or from ever getting eaten. One-Eye would recover to keep tired surfers awake in the afternoons for the rest of his days. Some sort of justice, I supposed.

Still, you'll never begin to know what a relief it was to finally get away from the place and back to the familiar setting of the beach.

Despite a naughty afternoon wind having blown the waves to shreds, I had to venture down to the south of the island and a spot called Playgrounds – just to get the blood off my mind. Playgrounds wasn't really living up to its name, though, and all I did was bob around for half an hour, catching nothing much, before heading in again feeling no better, or maybe even a little worse. It was probably no help that Scott was showing his new camcorder footage of the cockfighting when I got back.

'If you think this is rough on the eyes, you wanna watch some of the dog-fights I filmed in Taiwan,' he was saying. 'That shit fetches a few dollars back in Oz.'

It took the rest of the day to get over the fights, and some of the evening too. In the end I could only be saved from my new demons by the purifying power of surf-fatigued sleep – which had been in abundance ever since my arrival in Indonesia. Thank God for surfing, I began to think, but fell asleep before thought formed any definite shape.

Mornings in Lembongan are made for the quintessential yawn-and-stretch, as you stumble up the sand to take in another day of paradise. In front of me an island went to work; Nusa Lembongan is a seaweed-farm-cum-surf-camp, and life there is ruled by the tide. At low tide the surfers relax while the waves drop off in size and start to close out, but the locals use that shallow water to wade out across the patchwork quilt of seaweed allotments beneath the lagoon. The seaweed grows well in Lembongan because of the Lombok Strait's high salinity – a product of the low rainfall. Its main use is as a gelling agent in foods and cosmetics. At high tide the farmers then rest while the surfers come out to play. We played at Shipwrecks for another two days until the swell finally subsided and it was time for the cremation.

As we waited for the boat captain to come and get us, Pete paced nervously up and down convinced that we wouldn't be welcome, while I concentrated on hammering Andrew, still wounded, at chess. When the captain showed up, he was carrying some garments – headscarves and sarongs. We were asked to remove our shoes and to dress accordingly. The captain's uncle, it seemed, was a very respected gentleman.

He then led us through a small alley, onto a street that ran parallel to the beach some fifty yards back into the jungle. Things hadn't started yet, but already a lot of people were congregating at the roadsides, all dressed in the same robes we had on. More and more people kept emerging until, by the time proceedings got underway about half an hour later, the numbers lining the streets must have been in the thousands. This was how a funeral should be – a celebration. At no point did we see the captain anything other than joyful. First came a procession of elaborately dressed women bearing all manners of gifts, from glorious tropical fruits to spare pairs of Reebok trainers. This procession went on and on, and on and on…

… and on

… and on

… and on. As I said, Indonesia is one of the most densely populated places on earth, and quite how so many people lived on this tiny island was hard to fathom. Thousands of women, both young and old, were laying down gifts in a carefully crafted pile that formed the base of the pyre. Meanwhile, some nearby monkeys were occasionally daring to try and steal some of the departed's death-rights.

Then came the sound; drums and bells, distant at first but growing with the same sort of rhythm as the cyclone swells that frequented the reef pass behind. Coming from the jungle was this din that brought your blood to life. Hundreds of percussion instruments from kettledrums to xylophones were being thrashed by an erratic marching band. The men were sweating and shaking in the midday heat, but their faces burned with dedication. This band also went on, and on (you get the message), until I began to think that other islands – like the whole of Java, maybe – had come over for the funeral. Andrew, Pete, Richie and I had seen thousands of people by now, and the body hadn't yet arrived.

When it did arrive my guess was the accompanying noise could have been heard as far away as Singapore. A tower, covered in decorations and memorabilia, came towards me, borne by forty or so men, heaving and chanting. At the top of it stood a priest of some kind, bellowing in that beautiful language. He was holding a microphone, connected to a sound system that was rigged to the tower. Under his balcony lay the body, royally clothed but with a face made up like some kind of clown – part of the ceremony, apparently, although the captain didn't know what it meant. On either side of the corpse sat a pair of trembling old men, one playing a xylophone and the other a lyre or something similar. The frailty of these guys was shocking, yet they clung ably to their swaying places as if a precipice to the centre of the Earth lay below them.

What really lay below may have been worse. The bearers looked like a primitive army, grimacing and gurning under the buckling weight of the tower, but they weren't just carrying the thing. No, they were *shaking* it violently. We had to look twice to be sure, but the sight didn't change: holding onto a criss-cross mat of bamboo sticks that formed the base of the structure, they were raising it high, and *shaking* it.

The heat generated by all that activity was enough to make the temperature of the day rise momentarily as it passed by. Any women who were not involved in the march ran up with buckets of water, which they threw dutifully against the tortured men. Steam rose off them, and then there was the sound of their feet; a terrifying stampede. If either of the elders sitting on the tower aside the body fell, death by trampling would be a certainty.

But despite their desperation to balance, these gentlemen still managed to play their instruments. There they stood; brittle, almost old enough to join the pyre themselves and wobbling as if they were riding a bucking bronco, but still gaily tapping away at their instruments, which couldn't be heard at all through the wall of noise made by the percussion, the cheering of the crowd, the stamping of feet, the splashing of water, the barrage of 'ak's and 'ng's emanating from the microphone on high, the groans and moans of the bearers' determination to throw them to doom and the density of the afternoon air.

Two smaller coffins trailed behind, one a cheap wooden car and the other a model boat with puppets at the helm. The smaller groups of pallbearers were shaking these coffins frantically too, stopping, running back the opposite way – anything they could do to disorientate the soul of the man inside – the same reason for shaking the main pyre. Hindus believe that a departed soul must never find its way back to the village again, so they shake, shake and shake the body until they are sure it won't.

The reason there were three coffins at the same cremation was because these ceremonies were, I was reliably informed, too expensive, and too *tiring* to perform regularly. Instead, most dead people wait (the only thing dead people do well) until a major figure dies, and then get cremated alongside them. This saves their families money, and adds to the importance of the main man's funeral. The other two cadavers were the support group at the captain's uncle's gig. I was later horrified to learn that they had been *exhumed* for cremation after several months! That explained the tremendous smell of disinfectant that swirled around them, fumes filling the air so thickly that the wooden boat wasn't far off being able to take to its own and sail unaided to the pyre.

After hours of marching back and forth, disorientating more than merely the deceased, the tower was fitted onto another wooden base at a clearing on the south end of the island, just behind the beach at Playgrounds, the other two coffins attached to either end, and then together torched. The flames danced high into the purple, sun-setting sky, while the bearers one by one dropped to the ground with fatigue, where they would still be lying the next morning as we deftly stepped over them on our way to the surf. Shipwrecks had decided to turn on again.

As if the powers that be knew about the funeral, the waves had laid off for a day. Now they returned with a vengeance. A new and freshly lined-up swell was thumping its way down the reef at Shipwrecks. The surf was big, and I mean big. As we set off on the long paddle out (we decided the exercise could warm us up better than the lazier boat option – nobody wanted to join Andrew on the sick list), somebody dropped into a wave that was easily three times his own height, if not more. And these waves weren't just a good size. Oh no. They had *pulse* too. The entire ocean was throbbing with this swell that had been travelling for thousands of miles, originating somewhere off Antarctica, and accelerating the whole way across the Indian Ocean with one goal in mind: to scare surfers in Indo out of their wits.

Fortunately nobody was shy to admit their fear.

'It's good for us all that we're freely admitting to being scared,' Pete explained as we finally approached the line-up. 'It means we're not going to dive in gung-ho and do something silly, not mentioning any names of course. Fear is OK. As long as we've got it under control.'

'Shall we get on with it?' Richie interrupted.

The term that has always seemed most fitting to me when talking about the waves in Indo is 'full-on'. Everything about it is full-on. The reefs are sharper, and more alive than anywhere else. The waves are often bigger and more powerful. Yes, it can be safely said that with a few exceptions (namely Hawaii, Western Australia and the reef passes of Tahiti), Indo is home to the most full-on waves on earth that a human can still paddle into, and however hard you try, you will never quite force that to the back of your mind when arriving at your first big swell there. Regardless of how many times you've seen it before, there is always a learning curve to be got over, as you adjust to the waves, the boards you're using to catch those waves (bigger waves need bigger boards, otherwise you won't manage the paddling speed needed to get down them or the stability required to hold a powerful turn), and the competitiveness of the line-up. Once the surf in Indo is more than two times head-height, you can guarantee that everyone in the water will be an advanced, experienced surfer.

'Apart from us,' Richie joked. 'We haven't got a clue what we're doing really, have we?'

Shipwrecks turned out to be surprisingly user-friendly, though. The take-off stage of a ride was a big deal, but after that you were left with a dreamy wall of water to carve or smack at your leisure. Richie, surfing on his frontside, was playing around with grabbing his rails (the edge of the board) as he turned, while Pete, surfing backhand, was going straight down the wave faces and then straight back up – a pretty valiant attempt considering the place was meant to be a frontsider's domain. Pete said it best, having also been to Sri Lanka in previous years: 'It's Ram's Right, Midigama, but on steroids!'

When the tide dropped further, the wave went mental, running extremely shallow on the inside section, starting to suggest that we should maybe quit while we were ahead, and go in for some food before our rapidly-weakening shoulders gave that reef the chance it needed to double-cross one of us. The boats had stopped running, so another long paddle lay ahead.

'Our motivation for this paddle,' I began, thinking we might need it, 'is to get to the beach to wind Andrew up about what he's just missed.' As we arrived, his face told us that we didn't need to. Despite the distance, you can still get a fair view of Shipwrecks from the shore, and he had seen every wave.

'Don't,' he said once we were within hearing distance. 'Just don't. OK?'

★ ★ ★

A great wave is a great wave, but a couple of Indonesian discoveries have stood out among the others. There is the fabled left-hander in the Javanese jungle near Grajagan, which, if J-Bay is the natural-footer's one compulsory pilgrimage, is often labelled its goofy-footed alternative. 'G-Land', as it's better known, is one of the fastest, hollowest spots yet. There are also famous waves on the islands of Nias, Lombok, Sumatra, Sumbawa, Sumba and parts of Timor. And, more recently, the era of the boat trip has led to more finds in the Mentawai and Simulue Islands. The most timeless of these discoveries, though, is the set of waves off Uluwatu Temple that run down the Bukit Peninsula, conveniently located back on Bali.

Uluwatu's iconic backdrop of rugged cliffs strewn with oriental plants and other tropical shrubs, and the crumbling monkey-filled temple at the top, have had more of an effect on the waves than just shaping them. Uluwatu, or 'Ulus', was one of surfing's landmarks; an idyll. It represented another aspect of the perfect wave – and duly became part of the history of the search itself.

Once the early twentieth-century surf spots like Malibu, Waikiki Beach and Makaha started to get busy, surfers began realising that they no longer needed to stick to these few beaches. People started migrating in search of places where they could surf without the crowds of Hawaii and California. A place where they could experience a rebirth of the innocence once found at the old homes of surfing. They went to Australia, France, and then further.

Surfing was already a lifestyle that demanded as much commitment as any marriage. Part of its lure, besides the pleasure of actually riding a wave, was the wait – the excitement of reading weather conditions and tidal charts, the devotion of always keeping an eye on the ocean so as to be ready to drop everything and paddle out as soon as the right swell turned up; a series of life sacrifices that made the reward even sweeter. But the introduction of travel added a whole new dimension. Why wait for the waves out front to get good, when you could go looking elsewhere?

Many had still been doubtful that a wave could be found to rival Malibu. At this stage, the journey was merely a search for something rideable of any kind the other end, the actual quality of the waves still relatively unimportant in the face of the enrichment that journeying had given to the surfing experience.

Until 1963, that is, when Bruce Brown set off to make his canonical surf film *The Endless Summer*, in which the idea of a perfect wave first began to take form. Bruce took a group of young men on a worldwide odyssey to find new spots, but this time the idea was not only to find surfable waves, but *good* surfable waves. And once Brown's trip was completed and the stories of his discoveries made public, surfing's ultimate goal began to take form. The mile-long lefts of New Zealand's Raglan Point rivalled Malibu all right. And the journey there, via Senegal, Ghana, Nigeria, South Africa, Australia, Tahiti and Hawaii, gave it that vital element of quest – the obligatory climb to the top of the mountain; the pot of gold at the end of the rainbow.

Most of my generation grew up completely unaware of *The Endless Summer* until Brown released a sequel in the mid nineties, three decades after the original. *The Endless Summer II* was an instant hit, and I saw it for the first time in a cinema near Hossegor, during one of my teenage French trips. The sequel includes a trip to J-Bay, and between the two films, the story develops of how the wave itself was discovered. As Pat O'Connell and Robert 'Wingnut' Weaver, the two surfers chosen to star in *The Endless Summer II*, step up to the sight of the point at Jeffrey's breaking as good as it gets, Brown explains how close his original expedition had come to being the first to find and ride the place.

Ironically, one of the dreamy discoveries made by the crew of the original film was a right-hander at Cape St Francis. At the time, another example of a perfect wave. Content with what they'd already found, Brown and friends had no idea that they were surfing only a few miles up the coast from the yet-to-be-ridden Jeffrey's Bay – arguably today's pumped-up version of that same perfect wave. For that concept has indeed changed through time, which is what enabled Uluwatu to have such an impact. As boards grew smaller and lighter, allowing surfers to discover new and more complex lines in increasingly critical parts of a wave, so the very definition of perfection began its own metamorphosis.

In the beginning boards had been ten feet in length, making a long, gently spilling wave like Malibu ideal for 'hanging five'. The actual term 'hang five' comes from the act of draping your toes over the nose of one of those big old Malibu boards – hanging five is getting one foot over and hanging ten both feet. To this day people still ride these longboards, also known as 'Mals' – short for 'Malibu'.

But then along came pioneers like Nat Young and David Nuhiwa, whose visionary attitudes to board shapes involved shaving them shorter and shorter by the week. Tube-riding – placing yourself inside the pitching wave – became easier, and as a sensation more revered than noseriding, the act of hanging your toes off the end of the board. Out on the wave faces, the new in-thing was 'hot-dogging', the term first given to developing performance manoeuvres like fast slash turns off the top of a wave (which has now given way to the aerial and fins-free manoeuvres of today). Surfers like Shaun Thompson, Rabbit Bartholomew and Mark Richards (who won four consecutive world titles – a feat only bettered by Kelly Slater with five in a row) began to really push the boundaries, and the search for the perfect wave had to pretty much start over.

This is where Uluwatu came in. Ulus was the first of the new family of perfect waves. A section as long as Malibu or Cape St Francis, but *hollow* throughout. And just down from it, the cavernous single peak of Padang Padang – a wave that broke so shallow, and was based so singularly upon being able to tube ride to avoid the cliffs, that it wouldn't have been considered rideable until only a few decades ago.

Surfers had been toying around with Kuta beach for a while already, and a few had even taken pond-skaters to nearby reefs, but it was only when another film-maker – the Australian Alby Falzon – turned up to make *Morning of the Earth* that anyone ventured out to the Bukit Peninsula. Falzon took two of his surfer-subjects, Rusty Miller and Steve Cooney, to visit the temple at the headland by Uluwatu, and inadvertently made one of the best moments of discovery in the history of surfing. Below the cliff were unmistakable swell lines, leading around to a totally virgin line-up of thumping, empty tubes. They frantically scrambled around looking for a way down to the surf, to the eternal amusement of the villagers, until they landed upon a cave which lead directly into the line-up. If that Queen of the Southern Seas legend is to be believed then maybe she left this cave as a lure to draw her surfer prey into the water – without it Ulus would have been nigh-on inaccessible.

And not only did Uluwatu have great waves, but a great backdrop too. A set of lefts that rolled across sacred ground.

A temple above and a cave below. It became a symbol of the era, setting off a new generation of boardbag wanderers, each inspired to find their own Uluwatu.

The bit I really loved about the Ulus story was the way people had carried on blissfully surfing Kuta for years prior to Falzon's discovery, completely oblivious to what had been breaking unridden for thousands of years just a few miles away. That had been exactly the case with J-Bay too. I thought of the innocents frolicking in the waves of Kuta and Cape St Francis, content in their ignorance, like the people of Pompeii before the eruption, unaware that they were living life on the fringe of history.

But, for me, the drama around the way Jeffrey's revealed itself had been even better, because a major perfection quest had failed to find it first time round. The *Morning of the Earth* crew had been more clinical than the team from *The Endless Summer* – they were venturing further out into an already surfed area, and were going to find Ulus whatever happened. Jeffrey's was, rumour has it, actually first ridden when a couple of Durban travellers took a wrong turn on the way to Cape St Francis while trying to mimic the *Endless Summer* trip. And then there was the apartheid travel boycott that had made everyone forget about the place, until the chain of events that led to its renaissance.

But that was just me. Jeffrey's was *my* quest. And Ulus another vital part of the seemingly never-ending dress rehearsal. Like Mundaka in Spain, it was another prototype of the modern perfect wave for me to try, but this time further from home, heavier, shallower and holding a higher place in the lore of surf travel.

I had to make a visit there.

There was another few days to go before the next boat back to Bali, during which the swell dropped a little. Shipwrecks was still offering a staple diet of playful peaks, but it was definitely time to move on. Back to Kuta and then off on our own individual paths. The other three were going to head to Sumbawa, before continuing to Australia, while I made my way to the Bukit Peninsula.

The boat journey back was a mellower affair, and the clearer skies made it possible to see both Bali and Lembongan at once for a while, with the unmistakable might of Ganung Agung again peering down at us – reminding me that a lot of surf destinations are the product of volcanic activity, perhaps demanding not so much a 'thank you' as meek respect. It seemed like a fitting end to the week.

Kuta hadn't changed at all, but we had. We were darker-skinned, more aware and charged up by the waves we'd just been riding. Back on Poppies Lane three groups of fresh arrivals were wandering around in the mayhem, their bags and boards the heaviest they'd ever feel, and their sweaty porcelain-white skin attracting touts like flies. Although we also had our bags, nobody bothered us.

I indicated to one of the Bemo drivers to come over.

'Tomorrow morning,' I explained, 'I'll be needing a ride to Uluwatu.'

★ ★ ★

'Steve McQueen', he called himself, real name Nyoman Wayata. But he certainly didn't drive like the Hollywood icon. The plan had been to arrive at Ulus just after dawn, but, then again, I should have guessed that Mr McQueen's idea of 'just after' could easily stretch to an hour or two.

Nevertheless, the wind was still half a day away, if it came up at all, so I had time. We arrived behind the ever-growing collection of warungs (restaurant buildings) that had sprung up around the cliffs in front of the most famous section of the wave, 'Racetracks', where you'll also find the cave. Although the waves weren't visible until the last moment, I knew this was the right place. All the locals were dressed in various surf labels, probably donated by visiting pros.

The deal with the warungs was that you could leave your stuff in them while you surfed, as long as you bought food and drink there. Some even let people sleep on the tables. Ulus doesn't need much swell at all to be good, because it's so exposed to the full range of Indian Ocean storms. While Kuta had been only a foot or so the night before, there was a solid swell running down the cliffs. I watched it for a few minutes, but that was enough. Time to get in there.

When I emerged from the cave to check my reef boots and start paddling out, it began to look even bigger – the view from above had been deceiving as usual. The waves at the top of the reef were way overhead, but then they'd run into the Racetrack and just reel around the corner at about head height, barrelling two or three times before running out of juice, leaving some people with a paddle back that was probably almost as long as paddling on to Padang Padang.

The cave now had a couple of wooden steps in it, but must have one day seemed terrifying to the two Aussies who first surfed here, all alone and with no guidance. I remembered how well they had ridden it in *Morning of the Earth*, drawing smooth lines across a screaming wave face, unfazed by the reef, the cliffs, the rips. Then coming ashore to camp in the dangerous tropics, away from medical centres, phone lines and other perks of civilisation. I tried again to imagine what it must have felt like to look off the end-of-the-world cliffs to see perfect lefts peeling away, day after day without another surfer in sight, before sliding down to where I was now and looking the line-up in the eye. I knew the feeling of finding virgin waves from the Orkney Islands, and some of the spots in Sri Lanka, but stumbling on Uluwatu – one of the greatest discoveries in the history of surf travel – must have been something else.

It was still an intimidating enough spot to paddle out in even now, despite the security of knowing people had been surfing the place in their droves for decades and that no movement would go unseen, no wipe-out unchecked, and no wound untreated. If I'd thought the backdrop to Mundaka could put the willies up you with its wide-open valley, deep-water estuary and the menacing shadow of the grand old church looming over you, then Ulus was off the scale. The Guernika estuary was now the edge of the Indian Ocean – a mass of water that could do as it pleased, when it pleased – the Basque valley now a cliff-face, the medieval church now one of the most revered temples in the Archipelago, and the sandy river-bed now razor-sharp coral.

And yet again, the locals were running the show. Every wave you caught at Racetracks was with the permission of the Balinese. In a line-up like Ulus you needed to be seen as willing to take off on waves from the outset, otherwise the locals would look down the line at you and just drop in, like Richie had done to the Israeli back in Sri Lanka, or that Spaniard to me before throwing a punch. So when the first wave came through that I was in position for, there was only one option – get busy. If I'd gone there straight from Kuta then the place would have likely claimed skin at my first attempt, but the week on Lembongan had given me the chance to sharpen my reflexes, and remember well the old rule: add a few extra paddles to get over the ledge of a heavier wave – since they move faster than usual, you have to work harder getting up to speed before jumping to your feet.

Despite the aura of the place, Racetracks was a phenomenally good wave, and again relatively easy to surf. As long as you didn't do anything stupid, then it would be great fun. You start getting into a rhythm in these kind of conditions, and even the paddle back up the point is part of the ritual. A solid slog against a bit of a rip is often a good time to reflect, your head flooded with endorphins. And now my mind was again going over the history of Ulus and its legacy.

When I got to J-Bay it would be the same, I realised. The wave wouldn't have changed. When there was a swell, it would do exactly what it had been doing since first it was ever ridden. As simple as this place – paddle out, pick a wave, turn around and go for it. And, like that, you could be up and riding the very waves you've grown up dreaming of, experiencing exactly the same sensation as anyone else who'd ever caught one there.

Another set stalled as it reached the end of the cliff-face corridor, churning over itself as it got ready to begin its run down the Racetrack. Someone had been shut down way back, leaving me next in line. I moved to face Padang Padang, and began paddling. Drop safely made, I started tentatively to work my backhand turns closer and closer to the hook of the lip each time, gaining momentum as the wave reeled on. Here was a wave that, like Jeffrey's, lined up walls of thick water for section upon section, with no need at all to pump the board with your feet in an effort to go faster. A wave where the issue was not finding speed but coping with it. The repertoire of lines you could take here had no limit, and nothing seemed to matter at all. I kicked out and began to paddle back up the reef again. Right then, surfing Racetracks, I realised I was ready. I could surf this place, therefore I could surf Jeffrey's Bay. It was now time to get on with the one trip that would complete my own ride.

For the first time ever, I got the feeling of being in one place but genuinely dreaming of another. Indo was now a temporary fix at best. Its waves could have such an effect on you that you may never see the world the same way again – many had come here and promptly lost interest in anything or anywhere else that this life had to offer, and it was easy to see why. But for me, the experience was doing something else.

Seeing spots like Uluwatu, that had previously been fantasy to me, now materialising in front of my eyes, touching and feeling them, as real as anywhere else I'd ever been, was making me realise it could just as easily be J-Bay.

More lefts lined up in front of me. Again I picked one off, getting right through to the end of the wave, and paddling back towards the take-off zone while constantly reminding myself that this was one of the best waves on earth. I could tell I was close to the perfect wave now. It could have been the end of the road, but not for me – it wasn't Jeffrey's.

Under no illusion, though, as to how enviable a situation this was, I continued surfing for hours more, until hunger and sunburn became unbearable. I caught one across the reef and aimed for the cave. There was no doubt that on this trip so far I'd scored several of the best surf sessions of my life to date; waves that would stay with me forever. But there was still a hunger for something else, and I knew exactly what it was.

I climbed back out of the cave, stashing my board in the corner of the warung my sandals and T-shirt had been left in. Lunch was on the agenda, followed by sleep and then another surf. There would be several more good sessions ahead on this trip to Indo, and that suited me fine, as I'm sure it would anyone else in their right mind.

But try as I might to ignore it, from that first go-out at Ulus onwards, my list of priorities had become crystal clear; see time out here, go home, save money, and get to South Africa.

Which I almost pulled off.

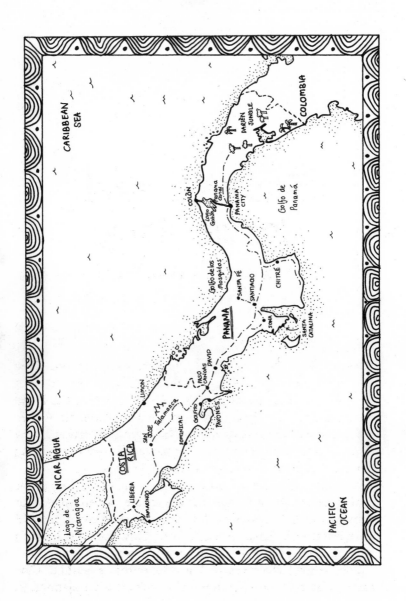

6.

Panama and Costa Rica:

A Spell in Dry Dock

I knew right away my leg was broken – but not quite how broken, which was perhaps for the better, otherwise it'd never have been possible to keep so calm. But everyone had heard the cracking sound ripping through the dark winter air. Within what seemed like seconds the laughing gas had arrived, and a drip was connected to my arm. The paramedics were reassuring in manner, but wouldn't commit to saying I was OK.

Nitrous oxide does funny things – enabling you to be philosophical about things that are severe. When the doctor showed me an X-ray of my left shin smashed clean in half I am rumoured to have just said, 'Well, I always knew I wasn't cut out to play football. I probably deserve it.'

The irony hadn't escaped my 'teammates' either. One game, a bit of a mess around – that was all we'd planned. A local novelty match where we surfers had decided to play a reserve team from a nearby football club. The problem with surfers practising other sports is that we can easily forget water is an exceptionally forgiving opponent, and end up being a little too gung-ho at times. After nominating myself for a role in central defence, I decided to wrap my left leg around someone who was running flat-out, the plan being to scoop the ball from under him, before initiating a counter attack (when I do follow football, it's always Arsenal, and I'd seen the likes of Tony Adams and Patrick Vieira do it on television a thousand times). As you can probably guess, it didn't work. As my foot connected with the ball, another player from Team Surf came flying in innocently and my leg got sandwiched between the two, soaking up tons of pressure. I've done the maths; two fully grown men running into each other at full speed and it's no wonder it snapped like a matchstick. Even the goalkeeper the other end heard the noise.

What a bummer. I'd always known to stay away from competitive field sports, and was now paying the price, hobbling out of the Princess of Wales Hospital in the early hours of the morning with a heavy plaster cast up to my hip and a long, long stint out of the water to look forward to. No use to anyone.

When I did learn a few days later that the sentence was nearly a *year* out of the water, it didn't really sink in.

'If you can sit totally still for three weeks,' said the orthopaedic surgeon, 'then hopefully you won't need any metalwork.' One in four victims of the 'tibial nail', a horrible rod that gets inserted from knee to ankle in the case of bad breaks, suffer chronic knee problems afterwards.

I did as he ordered.

'Good,' was the reply three weeks later. 'Now just three more, and we'll let you move your knee again.'

Again, I followed doctor's orders.

'Excellent! I'd like to see you do another fortnight with that knee still locked, though.' Predictably, the next few months were a nightmare.

My father had returned from his stretch in California, and was living in South Wales once more. Although I was injured and unable to do much work, he had a place for me to stay at least. Perhaps my parents' individual obsessions with North America was simply a coincidence, but my mother in the meantime had moved away to Toronto, where she had married an old university friend.

Friends – especially the one who'd been involved in the tackle – came around with surfing videos, books and fruit. Occasionally I went down the beach to watch them ride a few, but in general it was a long, boring recovery. Eventually I was cleared to bear weight, but still confined to 'several weeks' in plaster (sixteen!). By then it was the darkest part of winter, early March, and I had itchy feet – although I could only scratch one of them.

And so it was that instead of the usual process of inventing my own procrastinatory detours en route to J-Bay, I ended up having a trip thrown into the mix by circumstances beyond my control. The flight money I'd already saved before the injury had to be used somehow, and just because I couldn't surf for a while it didn't have to mean staying home for the year.

Like most of my friends, I was by now trying to take at least one major overseas surf trip per year, if not several. It was the absolute bare minimum needed to guard sanity. In order to keep this up, I'd done hundreds of jobs, boring, hard, fun and silly: golf-caddying, caravan cleaning, confiscating maxed-out credit cards for banks, selling posh evening wear, assistant painter and decorator, mobile ice cream seller, television extra, along with the usual stints in a local surf shop, a couple of restaurants and bars, and, as happens to any serious non-professional surfer at some point, production operative in an electronics factory.

We worked hard for our trips and, now unable to do much of use to anyone, there was no way I intended to waste the latest funds on staying home feeling sorry for myself. I had to go somewhere, as had been the case every other year from leaving school until now, even if there would be no chance of going in the water.

Breige had continued her swift progress towards expert surfer in the last eighteen months, and had just landed a job in Costa Rica teaching the sport she now loved – an amazing opportunity anyone would jump at. I was almost as stoked about it as her, even though she was going on her own – or so we thought at the time anyway.

J-Bay was off for another season, that much was clear. So once my plaster was brought below the knee, and I was cleared to fly (it's forbidden to go on an airline with an above-knee cast, like the one I had at first, due to the risk of DVT), I decided to go visit Breige after all. It was my first ever trip abroad without surfboards – but then all good runs have to come to an end eventually.

'Panama's only a bus ride from where I am in Tamarindo,' she said over a delayed phone line the day before I set off. 'D'you fancy going there once you arrive?'

'OK.'

'Good. How about doing a bit of filming, then? This is gonna be a real role-reversal – you relegated to bimbo behind camera.'

I couldn't think of many occasions when Breige had stayed out of the water to film me – it just wasn't her style – she was someone who had to participate rather than watch. But we had always commented on other couples in which the girls didn't surf, but waited loyally on the beach, video camera in hand.

I thought too of plucky old Ed back in the south of France, and his dilemmas with filming and surfing – how we all took for granted that he'd spent half of the best days in Scotland on land with a camera, instead of out there with the rest of us. This was going to be a real test of strength, but it was sure to give me the resolve needed to make that final push to J-Bay the following season. In fact, maybe one more diversion was going to do me good anyway. At least I'd have a chance to put my plans into perspective in a much more reflective way than getting mindlessly tubed in Indonesia.

And anyway, a trip away to *film* surfing would be better than no trip anywhere, I reminded myself. And so the reply: 'Sounds good. Bet you I don't grumble even once.'

And with that, a friend was ordered to drive me to the bus stop, where the Gatwick Airport shuttle was due at midnight.

★ ★ ★

The growth of women's surfing had been spectacular since the late nineties. Girls were starting to show up and hold their own in all sorts of line-ups – big and small, cold and warm.

When Breige started, I'll admit, it had seemed kind of novel. She'd have a go for a laugh and that would be that, I thought. But the determination she showed to get competent as soon as possible was inspiring. Ever the modern man, I welcomed the development, but most of my mates in a traditionally male-orientated sport could think of nothing worse.

'I'd hate it,' they would say. 'Surfing's where you go to get away from the missus, and turning around to see her in the water would suck the big one.'

'Yeah, but she understands the obsession,' I'd reply. 'If the waves are pumping, I don't get in trouble for cancelling things – because she normally beats me to it!'

There had been several big changes towards the end of the nineties, both in the way women saw surfing and the way surfing saw women. One major architect in this was Florida's Lisa Andersen, who surfed well enough to win several world titles, but with a uniquely feminine grace. I remember that an accusation levelled against women surfers was that they tried too hard to surf with the styles of men – which, given the difference in muscularity between sexes, was challenging to say the least. Since body-torque has so much to do with good surfing, women who struggled to match the physical strength and aggression of men were not getting as much power into their turns, producing an awkward, flat-footed style of surfing.

Lisa Andersen changed all this, pulling the extreme manoeuvres the men were doing, but with a stance and style that was beautifully female – a fresh dance altogether. And she changed women's surf fashion too, in a quite unexpected manner...

Along with equipment and the definition of a perfect wave, the shape of boardshorts had also changed with time: boards shortened and shorts lengthened – getting dubbed 'baggies', and coming down almost to the knee. Women hated wearing them, leaving few options for those who weren't keen on going everywhere in a bikini. At a get-together of various surf clothing industry big-wigs one day, former two-time world champ Tom Carroll was laughing at an old pair of shorts he had once worn in the neon-hell days of the mid-eighties – tight, hip-hugging bathers that resembled rugby or cycling shorts more than the modern icon of freedom that was the 'baggy'. Turning away briefly, Carroll didn't notice Lisa Andersen try them on until the last minute. 'Look,' she said. 'A perfect fit. These would be great for us chicks.'

After that, Roxy, the feminine version of Quiksilver, reinvented beachwear – all from a pro surfer who tried on an old pair of shorts for a laugh. It was a simple concept really; the more leg on show, the more the media wanted a slice of female surf culture, ushering in a new era. Suddenly girls looked good on a wave, and women's surfing started hitting the big time. On my way to Central America I even saw a photo of Lisa Andersen doing one of her trademark frontside re-entries in a pair of Roxy boardies on the side of a London bus.

And following Lisa's lead were a generation of talented *femmes*, sticking it to some of the gnarliest waves on earth. Girls like Rochelle Ballard, Keala Kennelly, Chelsea Georgeson and Sofia Mulanovich – all of whom most guys would dread competing against in heavy conditions.

Simultaneous to all this had come another movement in surfing; the 'Rebirth of Cool'. Centring around longboarding, this involved a resurgence of old beach fashion; label-less neoprene tops, beaver-tail wetsuits and classic toes-on-the-nose wave-riding. Walking down the trail to Malibu with my dad a few years previously, I remember feeling kind of left out of it all. People were sharing waves, hooting rides, paddling back up the point on their knees; all the sort of stuff I thought had died along with 'free love' decades ago. Longboards were for old people, or so my generation had been brought up to believe.

You couldn't share waves on a shortboard very easily (they need to be ridden in the most critical parts of a wave, where there's usually only room for one track to be made) so I had a frustrating time – until the old man, who'd been living 'upstate' for a while and had surfed the place plenty already, got out and lent me his own 9'6" noserider. A two-hour session of revelation followed, as Malibu decided to let me in.

Beyond learning that longboarding could be great fun even for younger surfers, I also saw for the first time the way women were getting into the sport of surfing. For the best waves all afternoon had been consistently scooped up by two girls, also on longboards. They would cruise down the line like ballerinas, fluttering eyelids at any guys who looked like getting in their way, stealing all the sets, and getting none of the grief you'd normally expect a *guy* to incur for being so greedy. Girls leading proceedings at one of surfing's most ancient sites of worship: Malibu. Our Mecca, our own

Palace of the Emerald Buddha; surfing's Mt Horeb; a place where shoes were removed as a mark of respect the moment you arrived – being dominated by a couple of girls in their early twenties. I should have known – Southern California has always been stuck in both the past and future at once.

Leaving the beach and heading towards LA, I pulled into a gas station just outside Long Beach. A porky man stood by the magazine rack, his skin-tight, stonewashed jeans overlapping a pair of pointy leather boots (I didn't want to look behind him for spurs). A tiny denim waistcoat stretched around his white T-shirt, shaded by a dreadful crop of shoulder-length black hair.

'Hey, man!' he called after overhearing me speak to the cashier. 'What's that accent? You sure aren't from LA, huh?'

'Er, I'm from Wales?'

'Oh yeah! England! I know. I got a coupla' friends from *Wales*. Catherine and Michael... You know, Zeta Jones and Douglas? That's right, man! I was with them downtown last week. Oooh yeah! Cool guys. I'll say "hi" for you.'

With that he about-turned and left the shop. In the forecourt an old, bottom-of-the-range BMW convertible sat pitifully at the foot of the gas pump. Of course it was his. Out he pulled, onto Highway 101, spluttering dirty petrol emissions and carelessly cutting up another, much newer-looking car carrying four wet-haired girls and a roof-rack piled high with longboards.

Prick, I thought, until to my great amusement the offended vehicle pulled up alongside him at the next traffic lights, still in perfect view of where I was standing. They were close enough for me to make out a suntanned arm coming out of the back window of the newer car. The arm was holding something – a soda, which was promptly thrown at the BMW convertible, soaking the prat's denim costume and probably damaging the upholstery too. He'd have trouble impressing Catherine and Michael now!

From then on I began to take women's surfing very seriously.

That said, this was still a position I'd never previously imagined: sitting on a bus going south from San Jose to Panama City with my girlfriend, her friend Anne and two sets of boards, neither of which belonged to me. I'd spent a day or two in the place that had become Breige's home for the past season – the town of Tamarindo in the north of Costa Rica – but there had been hardly any waves, and so my patience hadn't really been tested yet.

It was on this bus ride that the real story of our Central American trip began to bloom – when a vital part of the engine decided to drop out, leaving us stranded in the mountains just south of San Jose.

I'd seen a bus-sized turbocharger sitting on the floor of the depot just before leaving. It was lying there drenched in fresh oil, like a recently extracted vital organ – and I pointed out this ominous sign to the other two.

'The one they just replaced it with is probably dodgy too, it looked pretty worn.'

And sure enough, just as we were starting to feel that San Jose was really behind us there was a popping sound and a sudden loss of all power, not far off the summit of a hefty climb. A vital part of the engine had dropped out, leaving us stranded in the mountains. The only other non-Latino person on the journey, a well-dressed blond man in his early forties, was quickly off the bus and speaking to the driver in Spanish.

'Any idea what it is?' I asked.

'Yeah, he says the turbocharger went.'

'So now what?'

'He's gonna go phone the bus company.' Before he even finished speaking, the driver had begun running up the hill, disappearing around the corner, from which he didn't return.

During this time the 'Ticos' on the bus (an American nickname for Costa Ricans), remained in high spirits, singing choruses together in both English and Spanish. One even serenaded us four 'gringos' (Tico nickname for Americans, although they tend to use it for any foreigner) with a solo rendition of 'Disarray, it's OK'. Breige and Anne applauded him, but the other guy – Canadian, I guessed, from his soft North American accent – was starting to look a little tense.

'Where's that damn driver got to? I bet he's drunk by now,' he cursed.

When the driver did eventually return (sober, I should add), it was only to roll us all back down the hill a mile to a bar and restaurant in which we would wait for another bus to come from San Jose – three hours behind.

'Has it left yet?' I asked the Canadian. A quick exchange with the driver did not return the answer we may have hoped for.

'He says it's leaving "soon". We've got no chance of reaching the border before it closes for the night.' He introduced himself as Jim, and sat down with us to eat a buffet of nondescript canteen food, as the now freezing night air began creeping through the open doors and into our temporary safe haven. The only threat to our well-being was the sharp drop in temperature that happens at such altitudes – something our clothing choices hadn't accounted for. On a daytime bus the mountains south of San Jose would be easily bearable in shorts and T-shirts, but by night it was colder than most of Europe – we're talking about an area that is over 3,000 feet above sea level. Wrapped in towels and shivering uncontrollably, all we could do was keep moving and drinking hot tea until the new bus arrived.

During the wait, we learned that Jim was the owner of a golf course near Toronto. He even knew the street in which my mother now lived – a pretty good ice-breaker really. He kept us well entertained with tales of rounds with Tiger Woods and various actors, singers and former US presidents.

'They all love to hit one, man!'

Jim had that slightly pampered look on his skin that denotes a wealthy person – the complete lack of stress lines; smooth cheeks and a cushioned neck, probably a product of a healthy diet; neatly cropped greying blond hair; along with immaculate white teeth and a briefcase which we noticed he wouldn't let go of at any cost – not even to take something from his pocket or look at his watch.

Despite the up-front persona, though, something didn't add up. A rich golf course owner riding the red-eye bus to Panama City? He said it was cheaper to fly to San Jose and drive down to the border – but surely there was no need for someone like him to bother with this extra hassle.

'Drugs,' whispered Anne when he went back to the bar for another cup of tea. 'Panama City airport is getting harder to smuggle into as a passenger.'

Breige didn't agree: 'Nah, he's travelling the wrong way to smuggle. We're going against the flow of most drug-trafficking routes now. Customs are only interested if you're coming *from* Panama.'

I was forgetting that Panama had been part of Colombia for centuries, and that there was still no road between the two – just the inhospitable Darien Jungle, which had resisted all roads and commercial development and was home to the Embera tribe. The Embera still lived as they would have done in the times of Christopher Columbus and Sir Francis Drake (who are both pirates according to most Latin American histories). They even continued to hunt animals with blow-darts dipped in the gland of a poisonous frog. The only effective way to cross the Darien was to float down streams in dugout canoes – proper boats would draw too much attention.

'Perhaps he's just got money in the briefcase,' Anne continued. 'Maybe he's on his way to pick up…'

It did make you think. Still, there was bound to be a logical explanation, and probably one that we would never learn of.

At around midnight, the new bus finally choked its way into the yard outside, not a minute too soon. Any longer and hypothermia would surely have come knocking.

By the time we finally reached the frontier town of Paso Canoas and crossed into Panama, the journey had already lasted twenty-two hours. We'd been told back in Tamarindo that, as with all Centro American border customs, it would be a stressful experience, but it wasn't, as it was early morning and we were the first bus to be admitted across. Our bags were only briefly searched by some half-interested teenager in plain clothes, who took a quick peek inside before snorting and nodding us on our way. The boardbags made it through with even more ease – a quick nudge with the foot to make sure they had something solid inside and that was all.

Jim, on the other hand, was given the Spanish Inquisition. His briefcase was handed into several different rooms for inspection, all without him being allowed to watch, before someone else older, and this time in uniform, frog-marched him into a small office at the end of the corridor.

'He's a drug dealer, I told you,' said Anne.

If he was, then his ability to keep calm was admirable to say the least. Loading our own luggage back into the hold of the bus, we could see him standing inside the office gently touching the sweat off his forehead with a handkerchief. We were at sea level again now, the sun was out and the heat was back.

After almost an hour, he was allowed to get onto the bus, with an apologetic look to the Ticos, who at some point in the night had finally started to show signs of impatience.

'OK,' Jim said, sitting down and wedging his briefcase back under the seat. 'I could have done without that. Highly embarrassing. I'm so sorry you guys had to wait.'

'What did they want?' I asked him, causing Breige to nudge me hard on the good leg. She hated my tendency to ask these sorts of prying questions. Jim didn't seem to mind at all, though.

'You're right. I'd better tell you. Well, you know I said I ran a golf club in Canada...'

'Yes,' came the three-strong chorus, its tone as leading as we could possibly be without making him backtrack on the decision to spill.

'Well, it's kinda more than one golf club, and I don't have to do much to run them – people do it for me...'

'OK,' again, three voices strong.

'Well, I don't really do that much these days, to tell the truth, and 'cause I'm sorta all right for money, well, I got some toys.' He paused for a moment. 'Like my yacht in Panama City. That's where I'm going now. Those guards were funny back there 'cause I got some cash in the briefcase – gotta pay for some work I've had done on it...'

Telling other people you've only known for a day that you have a suitcase full of cold, hard US dollars on the Panamanian highway may seem stupid, but he obviously trusted us, and the decision to share his burden was evidently an attempt to feel more secure – almost like the way you tell the coastguard what time you plan to come home when going boating. Perhaps he thought that informing us about what he was carrying gave him three more pairs of vigilant eyes.

Still, it was all the more baffling as to why someone like this was riding the Panaline express from San Jose with the riff-raff.

The curving land mass of Panama doesn't support the usual swathes of uncontrolled palm jungle that you'd expect to see close to the equator. Because of its particularly wet climate, the vegetation consists of smaller plants and interspersed bushes that cling to the mountainous isthmus. The Pan-American Highway (a branch of which drives straight past

Malibu and over the Golden Gate Bridge if you stay on it long enough) winds cleanly in and out of the various slopes, passing only the occasional village and town all the way to Santiago. From there on it's increasingly urban, with touches of North American life everywhere; big SUVs, cinemas, potable tap water. We were now approaching what used to be the 'Zone'; ex-US territory inside Panama, the purpose of which had been to enable the safe running, and military defence, of the Canal by the United States. The Zone had, a few decades ago, spiralled into an embarrassing foreign policy dilemma.

General Omar Torrijos, one of the many colourful characters that line the halls of Panama's history, championed the cause in the seventies to bring the Canal back under Panamanian control, heaping on the pressure of public opinion until Washington could no longer stand by and do nothing. Torrijos was a controversial figure, whose support of both Cuba's Fidel Castro and the Socialist Sandinista movement in Nicaragua caused a few eyebrows to raise among Latin America's many CIA operatives. Torrijos was eventually killed in a plane crash, which may or may not have been an accident. It depends who you speak to – just like almost anything else in Panama; truly the kind of country the magical realists such as Gabriel García Márquez and Salman Rushdie would say had 'multiple versions of history'.

Torrijos's legacy was easy to identify, though. He had done his bit for the Republic. In 1977, amidst growing unrest among Panamanians who saw the Zone as a purely imperialist venture, the General had managed to get the then US President Jimmy Carter to sign a treaty promising the return of the Canal to Panamanian hands at the start of the year 2000. This was duly honoured despite the protests of many 'Zonians', who thought the most important shipping lane on the planet would fail to run properly if left to the locals.

So far, they had been proved wrong; the canal was running efficiently and Panama's economy was slowly recovering from the handover (the US withdrew significant trade and investment at the same time, plunging large parts of the population into poverty).

As the bus swung into the outskirts of Panama City there were slums and old military bases on either side of us. Jim was telling us about General Manuel Noriega, another renegade ex-ruler, eventually imprisoned in the US for drug complicity. Noriega had been an understudy of Torrijos, and was rumoured by some to have been behind the fatal plane crash that finished off his mentor. It would have been a worthwhile death to engineer, as he promptly graduated to *de facto* leader of Panama. He was known for running a cruel regime of bully squads, nicknamed 'dignity battalions', or 'dingbats'. Despite having allegedly been on the CIA's payroll for decades, Noriega was eventually ousted by Washington during 'Operation Just Cause' at the end of 1989. The USA bombarded Panama City with firepower, killing some civilians and rendering others homeless. The operation eventually ended with the dictator being flushed out of Panama's Vatican embassy, by the use of blaring rock music.

'They used either Iron Maiden or Metallica,' Jim explained. 'I can't remember which it was. Just blasted out of loud speakers until he couldn't take it any more. It was one of the more interesting sieges you'll hear of.' Breige, who had already read about most of this, was smiling in agreement. Jim then assured us that the outskirts of the city were no true reflection of its character, and that the centre reminded him of Miami. I wondered if the inhabitants of the slums would agree, or whether they might think the up-market city centre was actually the façade, and these shanty towns the reality of day-to-day life here.

'Crack is big here,' Jim added, looking out the window at some of the faces staring hopelessly back from the dark, rundown buildings.

Then over the famous Bridge of the Americas, where I looked down to see a series of freight ships emerging from the Canal locks, a brief break in routine for the sailors, before they accelerated and pressed on towards the western horizon, and the vastness of the Pacific Ocean.

And moored just inside the estuary way below us, Jim's yacht.

'It's the one with red floats around it.'

Anne, who worked on boats and had just been sailing the Caribbean in something half the size, was getting excited. She'd heard about the type of boat before; Norwegian, only ninety of them made, fast and spacious with two 'heads' (bathrooms – apparently having two is the mark of a great yacht).

Amid the excitement and relief of finally finishing the bus ride, we agreed to come and stay with Jim the next day. He needed the evening to tidy the boat first – 'or to hide all the cocaine', suggested Anne.

★ ★ ★

Of all the ridiculous things that humankind has tried to build – pyramids, towers into the heavens, tunnels joining countries, palaces of pure gold and stadiums that only get used ten times a year – the Panama Canal has to take the biscuit. Twenty-six thousand people died, mostly of diseases, ensuring that we could sail clean through a continent – probably far more than would have otherwise drowned negotiating Cape Horn. But it's taken weeks off the time taken to sail from Europe to East Asia!

'Ladies and gentlemen,' began the chirpy Caribbean accent of the announcer at the Miraflores Locks, the nearest to Panama City. 'If you're feeling down about the weather, please think again! You're getting the chance to meet Panama Canal's girlfriend, the *rain*!'

Yes, and lots of it. It pours daily in Panama, which is a big reason the Canal was sited here. The 360,000 hectare drainage basin is the basic tool of this inter-oceanic waterway, the largest stretch of the Canal being an artificial lake, Lago Gatun, created by harnessing some of this watershed. The French made the first attempt, digging several kilometres from Colon on the Atlantic side to the foot of a valley that spanned the isthmus almost all the way to the Pacific coast. They then went bankrupt, leaving the USA with the opportunity to finish the job, by digging the opposite end of the valley through to Panama City, and flooding the entire basin. Lago Gatun is way above sea level, and has an eerie feel for the boatsmen negotiating it, as the corpses of submerged trees and bushes can often be seen directly below when the sun is highest in the sky. It's as though each underwater branch were another worker lost to tropical illness or accident.

Panama was originally the second candidate for the building of a canal. It was first planned to blast through Nicaragua, a country that already had an almost country-wide lake in its middle. But seismic studies recommended against it – Lago Nicaragua was home to two volcanoes, and the land seemed to be permanently vibrating in one way or another. By popular report, the French noticed a hundred-year-old unsupported archway in Panama City had never fallen down – proof that this area didn't succumb to earthquakes in the same way as most of Central America. The final decision to site the waterway here was made by Ferdinand de Lesseps, a national hero at the time for his success in overseeing the completion of the Suez Canal – a project he would soon learn had been a far simpler one. The French lost an absolute fortune trying to see the Panama mission through, and eventually had to concede defeat. Which, as I said, was when the Americans came in and took over.

Jim had brought us out to watch the locks in action, after we'd spent a day on his boat, watching gargantuan cargo ships sail past us, their wakes romping through the moored boats of the Balboa Yacht Club. (It was hard not to fear for the dryness of my plaster cast, which wasn't waterproof.) I had heard of people surfing the wakes of oil tankers somewhere in the Texan part of the Gulf of Mexico, where a sand-bank ran parallel to the shipping lane, giving a ride over a mile long. No such geographical phenomena in the bay here, though.

The vessels would also make you giddy as they went by, the human senses not well adapted to something of that size in full motion. But this was nothing compared to the effect they had on you at the locks, where it looked as if the boats were actually moving through dry land. There remained less than a foot to spare on either side of the biggest ones. Most modern ships are fitted to the Canal's specifications, known in the industry as 'Panamax dimensions', but not all can pass. US Navy Supercarriers are probably the most high-profile name on the Panama Canal's no-can-do list.

Before us were two ocean-liners called *Coral Princess* and *Norwegian Spirit*, both pushing the lock to full capacity. All the clientele were out on their balconies cheering and waving at us and the twenty or so others who had been admitted into the upmarket Miraflores Restaurant (Jim's shout).

'Where are you coming from?' yelled an onlooker.

'New York!' someone on the cruise liner called back.

'And where are you going?'

'San Francisco!'

I'd always thought cruises were the domain of pensioners, but right now it was impossible not to envy the people in front of us. Doing the Panama Canal by boat. Anne had often talked about the wonders of shipping, saying it was amazing to think how the hulls of the ships in the Caribbean had probably seen all the waters of the world in their time – the frigid waters of Scandinavia and the North Scotland oil-fields, the South China Sea, the Suez Canal, the Grenadines and now the freshwater lake of Panama. It'd be nice to think that one day about the hulls of my surfboards, I thought. As a surfer, you have an affinity with sea, and part of the thrill is the awe-inspiring size and variety of the planet's oceans.

'It will cost me like thirty grand to sail my boat down the Canal,' Jim explained.

'No way. How much would that make it to take one of these things through then?' I asked him, pointing to the passing liners.

'Oh, about three hundred grand a boat. It's measured by weight – and you need to pay a pilot from the Panama Canal Authority to navigate it for you too.'

'No way!'

Breige had been doing her reading-up again: 'D'you know what the cheapest fee ever paid was...? Seventy cents, by a guy who swam through for fun.'

The Miraflores Locks could just as easily have been located in the heart of Middle America. All around us on the way to and from the locks were the cosy buildings, manicured lawns and neatly aligned palm trees of the old Canal Zone. A place where for decades North American family life had run smoothly, without interference from the outside world. Zonians had done everything they ever needed to do with other Zonians. Their kids had gone to ordinary US-style high schools, the road signs and markings had been the same, the suburban architecture identical to that of somewhere like Atlanta. The Zone had, in effect, been like an extra state. Until the hand-over took place, whereupon the tropics had slowly began to encroach.

'If you guys fancy it, I'll show you around the Old City tonight,' Jim suggested after we'd spent another hour or so in silent awe watching a freighter named the *Iver Excel* drift by. 'And my buddy from the boat club wants to come too.' Why wouldn't he, I thought; two young surf girls, boyfriend in plaster. I evicted these cynical thoughts as quickly as they surfaced.

And anyway, if my plaster was a sign of weakness, then I wasn't alone. Jim's companion from the boat club, Henry, had a limp too – a permanent one from a sailing injury incurred in the US Navy. It had forced his retirement and he now hung about the boat club, tinkering with yachts and 'whatnot', drinking cold afternoon *cerveza*s and enjoying a life of leisure.

'Tell all your friends Panama's still not safe,' he laughed. 'We love it that way – all to ourselves, man!' Such talk sounded familiar – wanting to protect the exclusivity of his little find.

'Yup. This country's the place for me,' he went on. 'It's one of the only places where a fifty-five-year-old guy like me dating nineteen-year-old girls is perfectly normal!' No threat to Breige and Anne, though, because he was apparently meeting one such honey immediately after joining us for a drink.

Henry was proud of his penchant for young girls, but knew where to draw the line. 'One of the waiters back at the boat club has this saying: "They old enough when they leave school, and they leave school at three o'clock." That's not my scene, though, man. I limit it to eighteen. That's the youngest I'll date.'

Casco Viejo (Old City) was, according to Jim, 'purest Havana'. Thick air, multicoloured, antiquated Euro architecture – and a sinister edge that made you feel alive. Jim and Henry knew what they were doing here, and sat us down outside a seedy café where they ordered drinks from the Haitian waiter.

It was an extraordinarily multicultural city, mostly from the legacy of the Canal. Chinese, Filipino, Indian, European and African workers had set up their families here, where there was little overt racism. A real mix of human migratory patterns. Henry was telling us about the tolerant attitudes of Panamanian society, although I couldn't forget John Le Carré's quip about how faces grew paler here the higher up through society that you got – 'altitude sickness' according to the spy writer. Indeed, the scourge of corruption was still rife throughout the country, with politicians well practised in the art of self-preservation – rarely did rich men need to answer questions. Paul Theroux believes working classes in Panama, more than almost anywhere else, truly are 'the silent men in history books'.

The latest additions to the Panama melting pot were the Haitians. Most had come over in considerable numbers after the US deposed their ruling Junta. Haiti's economy had fallen through the floor since, and these guys were desperate for any spare change you had. Most of those we met were endearing in manner, often speaking beautiful English, French and Spanish, but still Henry had deep reservations about their arrival.

'Dangerous, man,' he claimed. 'One by one the bars in the Old City are getting scared out of opening 'cause these guys are running around causing all kinds of shit.'

Panama City's structure represented the two great colonial ages of modern times. The first phase was where we were now sitting, a remnant of the age of European greatness: Casco Viejo. Here was the city that the Welsh pirate Henry Morgan had once ransacked before becoming Governor of Jamaica, where the Spanish had stationed themselves in the early gold rush, transporting loot over to Colon before taking it back across the Atlantic in pre-Canal times. This style of architecture remained only in the outskirts – the commercial centre was the new face of Panama, visible on the other side of the bay from us. The Metropolitan topography of that modern city was the next colonial age in bloom: America.

The Presidential Palace, a low-key building that was guarded pretty lightly for a Head of State's home (the pet storks at the front looked sterner than the security services), was located in the old half of the city – with no plans to move operations to the new sector any time soon. Not sure if this was supposed to signify the Republic's desire to resist the US culture that had already had a massive influence on daily life here.

'Well, man,' Henry began. 'They say China's gonna be the next world superpower, you know. And there's tons of Chinamen in this city, man, so it'll happen here first. Things always do, man.'

I didn't have a clue what he was on about, but gestured through a mouthful of *cerviche* for him to elaborate. And he duly obliged: 'In maybe another two hundred years we could be looking at a three-part city. Europe in the *Old-Old* City where we are now, America in the Old City, over there, and then the new part would be all Chinese architecture and whatnot...'

He then started asking us about surfing, and sounded like he knew a bit about it, unlike Jim. Anne asked him if he might know where to go looking for waves around here. But his first response was to chuckle and say, 'Jim knows all the surfing areas in Central America, man!'

The Canadian shrugged, and gave Henry a stare.

'You should do anyway, man. After all, you've fucked around with every inch of this coast no?'

'No.' Jim looked annoyed. Surely this was Henry ratting on a little contraband game of his. His number had to be up now.

'No?' Henry wasn't going to let him off.

'No.'

'Oh yeah, it was Mexico, El Salvador and Costa Rica, huh?' Jim had to be a drug runner. Nothing else could explain his immediate caginess.

The atmosphere was tense again. This time, under his wing in a dingy part of Panama City, it was a little more alarming to think he may have something to hide.

Jim clearly saw the need to clear his name. 'Henry's cornered me into telling you the story of how I got my boat,' he moaned.

'Yeah, man. It's a fuckin' good one. You haven't told them? Oh, it's fuckin' awesome.'

'OK, I'll tell them.'

Truly a master of revealing himself in tantalising stages, Jim decided to go and get another drink before continuing, leaving us to wait in awkward silence with Henry.

There were actually a few surf spots inside the bay here. At dusk we'd seen two surfers riding clean two-foot peaks directly in front of Plaza Franzia. Every part of the panoramic view could have been a postcard.

As there was only a half-hour of light left and their gear back on the boat, the girls didn't try to go in. The waves looked great, though. 'Ideal for longboarding,' said Breige.

One of the two surfers, both local according to Henry, was pretty adept at riding the small waves. Probably only about five feet tall himself, the kid was smacking the lip with agility and flow. He had a great style for small surf, coiling himself low over the tail of his board as he moved down the wave face, before unleashing all the stored energy into an explosive series of moves. He rode the right part of the wave to be a great surfer too – coming from behind the foam on each turn to neatly take the corner off the spilling lip.

'The water looks as warm as piss,' I said.

'That's 'cause it probably is piss,' said Henry. 'You think all those ships and locks don't cause any pollution? Those guys are mad to go in there.' I didn't care, though. The water back home was dirtier than this, and there was nothing anyone could say to stop the ocean looking very inviting. I wondered how long it would be before I could feel sea water on my left leg again.

'How's that, watching a surfer when you can't do it?' Anne asked.

It felt fine. At least I was still having some sort of involvement in the act, breaking down the technical details of this Panamanian youngster's approach and style in a way that I hadn't done since the 'grom training' sessions at Cardiff's Sofia Gardens sports academy years ago.

Having been out of the water for a while, I could think about surfing more intensely whenever I chose to, but push it to the back of my mind with greater ease when it wasn't needed. It was as if the addiction was receding, or rather lying dormant until I chose to entertain it once more. At the Canal and on Jim's boat I had been totally absorbed by what was going on around me – while it was Breige and Anne who felt the urgency and pressure of needing the next wave.

If the little session they saw outside Plaza Franzia almost tipped them over the edge and into total wave desperation, the rest of what Jim and Henry had to say that evening certainly did.

'Well, where to begin the damn story really,' Jim mumbled on his return from the bar.

'The fuckin' beginning, man!' Henry snorted before almost falling off his chair in self-merriment.

'Well, I had this friend in Mexico, who was always getting himself into all sorts of shit. A kinda entrepreneur, you know. Often selling a bit of coke to get himself by and whatnot. Well, he got himself into being a run-around for some biggish drug dealer guy – who was really starting to shift some serious stuff. This guy I knew ended up becoming like his personal assistant.

'So my buddy's getting into it all, but he's also got a bit of a habit. He was always one of those guys in the thick of it, if you know what I mean. Anyway, the guy he's working for gets arrested…'

'Arrested? Who? The drug dealer?'

'Yeah, the big Mexican drug dealer he's working for, right. Yeah, he gets arrested. So my buddy's having to lie low and all that. But he's got a bit of a habit, and expensive tastes. So he's not too happy 'cause he can't trade or do much work. And it's not his style to just go back to Florida, where he's from, so he just kinda hangs out in Mexico getting himself further into the shit.

'Anyway, this dealer guy is gonna go to jail for a while, and the fuckin' drug squad are gonna take all his property off him, like all his cars, vans, boats and all that. So he starts trying to asset strip – giving it all to other people so that things can't get taken off him, so he gives the boat away too...'

'To your mate with the habit?'

'Right. So my buddy's wandering around with all this stuff. But like I said, he's got a habit and he's starting to owe all kinds of people money and whatnot. And the boat's costing a whole bunch of money to maintain too – you gotta pay harbour fees and all kinds of shit. So he starts thinkin' of ways out. Ways to get home to Florida without people coming after him or his family.

'Anyway, in order to leave and pay off all his debts he needed to raise some money, so he sold the boat!'

'To you...'

'Right. To me. Last time I was there. And that's the boat we're talking about back there in the yacht club. And I got it for like a quarter of the market price.'

'A fuckin' steal and a half, man,' nodded Henry. 'Jimmy got himself a fuckin' deal all right!'

'It came with some baggage though, man,' Jim continued. 'The drug dealer guy's family turn up next, with papers saying they own the boat.'

'And did they?'

'No way! As soon as I bought it I flew back to Canada with all the papers and got it registered as a Canadian vessel in my name. You gotta register boats, like you do cars. So all my papers are legit, but in Mexico money can buy you fuckin' anything, and this guy's family have got loads of it. After all, they got most of the other assets when he went to jail. And they sold their stuff too, of course.'

'Why didn't they get the boat, though?' I asked.

'Well, because this drug-dealer guy trusted my buddy,' Jim went on. 'Although he shouldn't have 'cause after selling loads of his property, he turned around and testified against him – to keep the guy in jail so that he couldn't come after him. I mean, that drug dealer has gone down for fucking ever now, like twenty years before he's even up for parole, man!

'So anyway, the family turn up with fake papers, and my solicitors are like, "You're gonna get that boat back, but it's gonna take like four years." And the drug dealer's family are saying the same thing, going, "You're loaded man, forget it and buy a new one."'

'Which you didn't want to do, I take it?'

The filthy rich almost always get that way by being shrewd – pennies taking care of pounds etc. – and Jim certainly had been here.

'No way. I bought the fuckin' boat, and I got it for a good price. I like getting a good deal and that boat was mine!' He looked exasperated at the thought, and paused briefly for breath before going on. 'So this family turn up with the Mexican police and all that – who they may or may not have bribed. And they get the boat taken off me with these fake papers of theirs and put it in some harbour where they think it's safe. So me and another buddy decide to take it back one night...'

'You stole it back?'

'Well, I wouldn't say "steal" 'cause it was my boat, but we took it back. Just sailed it outta the harbour in the middle of the night. As long as we got it into international waters by the time it was reported missing then we'd be fine!

'So we sailed it out to sea in whatever direction felt like due west. I don't know shit about sailing – but it's one of those things where you just learn as you go along, so we had a go anyway. The oceanic current alongside Central America is meant to go south, so we figured we'd sail it down towards Panama and then maybe into the Canal and through to Canada – I could park it along the East Coast there and just go sailing from time to time. And anyway, I could break the whole Caribbean into a big long project – just flying over and moving the boat on bit by bit.'

Henry was laughing again. He knew the story inside out.

'So we figured we'd sail outwards until we were in neutral water, and then if we just sailed back east again the oceanic current would mean we were out of Mexico by the time we saw land again. And that worked – I think we got back to the coastline somewhere around the border between Guatemala and El Salvador. And then just began hugging it all the way down towards Panama.'

'How did you know where you were?'

'Well, we didn't. Which is funny, 'cause me and my buddy were awful sailors then – we didn't even know about satellite navigation or anything. We just figured the Bridge of the Americas and Panama City would be so easy to recognise that the plan was to keep going south until we saw it. Only we didn't quite have the patience, so after like fuckin' ages we started worrying that we'd gone too far and were lost along South America.'

Henry was still laughing.

'So we tacked back to shore and ran aground on some random beach.'

'And where was that?'

'Er, well...' Jim looked slightly ashamed, and Henry's amusement was almost uncontrollable now. 'It turns out we were only in Golfito.'

Golfito was a horrid little place in the southern part of Costa Rica – a semi-lawless, ex-gold rush town in which people would stumble out of bars with broken bottles stuck to their temples without anyone batting an eyelid.

'So you just ran up the beach in Golfito?'

'Yeah, we just ran up the beach. And then I paid some South African guys I know to sail it to Panama City for me. That's why I rode the bus from San Jose – I booked a return flight from there to Canada and figured I might as well use the other half of the ticket on my way back. I mean, I'd already paid for it, right...?' That shrewd rich-man thing again.

'And now the boat's here in Panama City, and some other guys I know have changed the name, repainted it and put a new deck on.'

'And they done a great job,' added Henry.

'Damn straight. Teak – cost a damn fortune. So now if that asshole family come lookin' for it they won't find *shit*. And soon it'll be in the Caribbean, and then Canada. Hell, I might even make it to Europe one day. Can I sail into the town where you guys live?'

Henry was beginning to get a bit restless now that Jim had come to the end of his story, and was looking as if he wanted to find something he could tell us himself. And that was when the tip came:

'So you guys are surfers, right?'

'Yes...'

'Well, there was a bunch of guys from some Cali surfing magazine here last month. They chartered a boat from the yacht club at Balboa. I spent a fair bit of time with them – took them around the city a bit.'

The effect of this on Breige and Anne was instant. They went from mildly interested to forcefully inquisitive.

'Really? Did they say if they got any good waves here?'

'Yeah, man. They said this place was fricken awesome and that they found loads of good surfing along the coast. I got all their coordinates from that trip if you guys wanna go try and find the waves yourselves. You'll need a boat for most of those places, but the best one they said they surfed you can get to in a four-by-four...'

Was this for real? Had we just heard him properly?

'And I know a guy that works for one of the best car hire places, man. He might be able to get you a special rate.'

Sometimes you go on surf trips and everything is an uphill struggle – which usually happens in places like Panama, known for good waves but not really as tried and tested as others. That was the appeal of Indo – you just know it'll be pumping day in, day out, and that you won't have to do much to surf a lot. And then sometimes you get those strokes of luck that lead you right into a great find. This was one of them. Only I wouldn't be able to enjoy it myself.

A few more beers went down before we retired to Jim's yacht for the night – getting asked forcefully for a dollar on our way to the taxi by another smiling hobo with perfect English grammar. A particularly disruptive ship wake woke us the next morning, whereupon we hailed a water taxi back to land and set about getting a four-by-four. This lead from Henry had to be followed up.

The otherwise brief drive to Chitré was slowed by the daily rains coming a little earlier than normal, soaking us to the skin even inside the car – the fault of a gap made in the door seals by board-straps. My plaster cast was getting soggier, but it would dry again.

Driving in Panama was better in the rain anyway – it would slow the other cars. When dry, the roads were lethal, as illustrated by a campaign one of the national newspapers was running. Every day they were placing totally uncensored coroner photos of the previous day's fatal accidents on the front pages, along with the headline 'La matanza continúa' ('The killing continues').

The spot Henry had tipped us about was a wedging beach break at which we were assured to find no other surfers at all. This was fine by me as it would spare me from having to explain time and time again how I'd decided to travel despite my injury, batting away the usual questions about whether it was killing me to watch other people surf etc., etc.

The truth was, I was looking forward to it. I could still share the thrill of the find, still engage in the session even if it was from land. And anyway, I had always got a real satisfaction from watching Breige surf, as I had seen her learn from scratch. Since the injury, there had been an abundance of time to think, and one idea I'd formed was that surfing is a gift you can give people. It's such a difficult sport to really get into properly, especially in South Wales – you need to know about tides, wind directions and swells, which equipment to use and most of all what to do once in the water. So ensuring someone does make the right moves to become totally hooked, and a good surfer, can be a life-changing act. The sea had been in my family for generations, so I'd always known where and when to go, getting beyond the basics quickly and catching the bug in a very short period of time, and had now been privileged to have a hand in passing that know-how on to someone else.

We didn't arrive near the area early enough to try making it out to the spot that day, and almost ended up all sleeping in the car but for an elderly woman of Mediterranean complexion, who offered for us to stay in a small condo for five dollars each. Air conditioning – excellent. The plaster dried, although I tossed and turned all night without the gentle rhythm of the sea underneath that had sent me to sleep the past few nights. I'd always fancied living on a boat – on a clear night you could sometimes hear the sea from the street I lived in back home, but that was nothing compared to the feeling of waking up on a floating vessel.

It would take about an hour of off-road driving to reach the cove in which Henry claimed we'd find waves. In order to be sure of beating the wind, and quite probably the rain, we moved early again, loading up before sunrise and leaving some money on the desk for the old woman, along with a thank-you note in basic Spanish. Even then, the sun had heated the day to almost 30 °C by the time we arrived on a completely virgin beach, which, as Henry had promised, looked to be a lovely set-up. Seeing my first sight of Panamanian surf, I didn't know what I wanted really. Did I want it to be good, for the girls to score? Or would I be content for the surf to be shit – the old 'if I can't then no one should' mentality?

It's a common sentiment in surfing. If you get stuck in a workplace, visiting relatives inland, are injured or unable to get in the water for any other reason, then it's perfectly normal to hope the waves are awful – so at least nobody else is surfing while you can't. When the waves get good, not being able to surf is a terrible feeling. I tried as best I could to wish for a good swell, light winds and well-shaped waves, and to be thrilled for Breige and Anne when it all came together. But regardless of any efforts to be noble, life would certainly have been easier if the waves had not been as good as this – the length of the beach was filled with clean, chest-high peaks.

Oh well, better put a brave face on anyway, I figured, setting up a video camera to give me something to do.

The waves were breaking shallow over a sandbar, in water so clear that they sent off all sorts of crazy reflections as they peeled along. Sand would run up the face of the inside section making the little barrels look dark and frothy – but cosy in the morning heat. It was the sort of conditions that could give you a whole month's dose of surf satisfaction in just a few hours.

Videoing gave me at least some sort of chance to interact with the session. From behind the lens, I found myself rooting for Breige to catch certain waves, and then going over the rides with her later in the day – a good way of improving your surfing. This could also let me 'mind-surf' waves, envisioning how each one could be best ridden, and then comparing the lines drawn in my head to those she would actually end up taking.

'A beach break wave like this is a little conundrum,' I found myself saying. 'You have to solve the puzzle of how best to ride it, whether to take off and then race across the face immediately, or whether to drop straight down and into a bottom turn. And then there's picking which ones to catch...'

But Breige was someone who always needed challenges, or things to learn, and in the last few months since swapping Porthcawl for Tamarindo, she had already worked most of this out for herself. One of the left-handers she caught just before the end of the morning session was a perfect solution to this beach's particular puzzle. The set lined up all the way through to the inside section, but she was careful to pick one that wasn't going to close out, and got around the fast beginning of the wave with expert dexterity and conservation of momentum, before putting in a couple of strong turns off the lip. I was thrilled.

We developed this routine of surfing and filming for a few days, taking advantage of the windless mornings and then spending the afternoons in shade, before returning to 'Henry's Cove' for an evening session. We would have stayed longer, but the swell direction must have changed – one morning the wave was no more. Coming here in the first place had been a bit of a gamble anyway, so we were content with what we'd found, and not too unhappy moving on.

Anne had to leave us, reluctantly catching a bus back to Panama City to fly home, while we moved further along the coast to a tiny fishing village called Santa Catalina, from which you could get access to Panama's best known wave – a spot that would not be so fussy about swell direction.

We got a little lost just outside the place, before Breige asked a local carrying a machete for directions.

'*Dónde está Santa Catalina, por favor?*'

Breige couldn't understand his thick accent, and repeated the question with more and more gesture, until the mad farmer opened the back door of the jeep and got in.

He was good natured enough, couldn't understand a word of English, or our attempts at Spanish, and didn't seem to have any desire to slow his own dialect down either. The machete remained a source of alarm for the duration of the journey, and the smell of freshly cut grass mixed with sweat made him hard to ignore.

To make things worse he tried to ask the owners of the Punta Roca guest house for commission when we arrived. Their Spanish he did understand, and the frustrated farmer turned to start the long trudge back to wherever he really lived, without a donation of any kind.

'He always do this,' said a smiling Panamanian man in chef's overalls, just as we were wondering if this outcome wasn't just a little harsh. 'You give him nothing, right? Good. Important he learn. Everybody find Santa Catalina, without help from him.'

The waves were onshore, fattening horribly (running into deep water and losing power) after about ten yards, and filled almost to bursting point with surfers. No surprise really, given the name of this village is just about all most surfers will know of Panama. It was rumoured that Tom Curren, the man who rode that wave at J-Bay in the *Search* film that sent me on this walk of life, had a house somewhere in the vicinity. Since that rumour first surfaced, surfers from all over had duly journeyed to see the spot supposedly good enough to make the legendary Curren buy, or build, a house.

'Tomorrow gonna be OK,' the chef told us, noticing the looks of concern.

Tomorrow began with a big increase in the swell size, but it still wasn't really much better. The wave didn't hold its shape well at all. Most of the travelling surfers seemed awkward too. Despite the attempts of some of the 'Big Wave Daves' at breakfast to put her off, Breige still paddled out to see if she could steal one of the waves, breaking at about three times her height, from an unfriendly looking crowd. Meanwhile, I sat back to listen to a barrage of bullshit from the various others that had been on the dawn patrol. The peak was breaking too far out to sea for me to film.

A couple of guys from Kauai, the Hawaiian island responsible for some of the world's top pros, were bickering about some Aussies and Argentines they hoped to be on for a fight with. I couldn't stomach it and went for a walk into the village.

Santa Catalina was beautifully primitive in appearance, a town of ants, clay, simple fishing boats and hypnotic regional dialects, but surfing was bringing changes. Apparently plans were afoot to pave the road into the village, and various guest houses and surf lodges were springing up. There had even been a rumour that one company wanted to buy the entire village. I stopped for a drink at a wooden café, where an Australian was boasting how great the foreign coin was going to be for the area.

As a visitor, nobody had a right to grumble, though. If Santa Catalina wanted to modernise, then who were we to complain? On the various trips taken so far, I'd seen many once primitive locales growing into sprawling surf towns, and wondered why some had seemed comfortable with it, and others not. Perhaps it was to do with wave quality – most places in Indo seemed totally content to embrace global surf culture, but then they really did have waves worth shouting about, something to be proud of. J-Bay would have been through all these stages, I was aware, but then I suppose when a wave's lure is that timeless it can override any on-land experiences.

'Mate, they've got a baseball team here now,' the Australian continued. I found it hard to imagine how the place could ever find the population to make a go of such a personnel-heavy sport. 'They're on the radio playing right now.'

Sure enough, on the table opposite us there was some sort of sporting event playing on an ancient wireless. A crew of locals were crowded around it, listening intently, many of them obviously drunk – it was the weekend after all. Within minutes the voice screamed something about a 'carrera Santa Catalina', and they all exploded out of their seats.

'I'm gonna open a restaurant here,' the Aussie went on. 'This place is too Yank-heavy. It needs the Aussie touch to make others feel more welcome here. My restaurant is gonna be a real laugh. I'm gonna make the menu funny – crude names for the dishes. Wanna know what "Mutton Shutters" are?'

I didn't muster a reply.

'Well, you'll see. "Docker's Tea Break" is gonna be a good one too. And "Vinegar Strokes".'

I drunk up politely, and left. When I got back the baseball team had lost by 'tres carreras a uno', and the Kauaians were still bickering, although now joined by another oik from Oahu, who we nicknamed 'Da Hui' after the well-known group of Hawaiian water vigilantes. Well, actually, he was from Santa Cruz, but had moved to Hawaii ten years ago, forcing us all to hear about how important being able to fight was if you wanted waves on the North Shore. I tried to cross examine him on that over a few beers, before Breige warned me that she thought there was a risk of him coming on to me if I wasn't careful – coming on for a fight, that is. The fact that I had a leg in plaster and remained civil in tone throughout obviously counted for nothing. The real Hui would have probably been ashamed

– word is you don't get into trouble with them unless you *really* deserve it.

His friends, who all still lived in Santa Cruz and didn't try to shamelessly pass themselves off for Hawaiian rippers, were easier going, and took Breige surfing to a nearby island with them the next day by boat. There was too much swell for most of the spots, though, and 'Da Hui' almost stayed home in protest at the thought of a girl coming on the trip.

We went for a drink with them again that evening, but ended up talking more to the bar owners, a down-to-earth Argentine couple, the male half of which, Breige informed me, had been the best surfer in the water. The woman told us the best tale I've ever heard relating to the origin of the term 'gringo': Apparently it came from Mexico, where people used to shout at US troops to 'Go home'. As the unwanted guests were usually dressed in combat uniform, they got nicknamed 'greens'. The phrase 'Green, go home' soon shortened to 'Green go', before the Spanish accent rounded off the metamorphosis to 'Gringo'. I didn't care if it was true or not. The story was great, and brilliantly told in a sexy Argentine voice.

Panama had been a real country of highs and lows. Panama City had an air of constant adventure simmering just below its surface. Waves being ridden in front of the Casco Viejo, and a great man-made waterway that felt like the gateway to a world of oceanic exploration. The secret cove we'd found courtesy of Henry seemed like a mirage compared to the horrible modernist vision of what Santa Catalina could some day become. The perfect wave for Tom Curren maybe, but it hadn't done its thing for us, and Breige believed a better offer was now on the cards.

We left the next morning, after looking at swell forecasts faxed to the chef by his friend working for the Panama Canal Authority, which were suggesting there would soon be a chance to score the fabled left-hand point break of Pavones, back in Costa Rica.

The four-by-four had to be dropped off in David, one of the hottest cities on earth. It was so humid there that when I got out of the car my sunglasses misted up instantly, before clearing again within ten seconds.

'That's water vapour in the air condensing on the lenses,' Breige explained. 'The AC in the car has made them colder than outside. And then it's evaporating again as they heat back up.' Before moving on we called into an Internet café, where she found out that one of the Americans back at Santa Catalina had emailed her a proposition to 'ditch the geek and come live in California'. She wasn't tempted, or so she told me.

'Let's have a look at the swell charts,' she suggested.

It turned out that when hiring it back in Panama City, we had paid up-front for an extra day with the car. The word 'refund' suddenly and mysteriously lost its Spanish meaning, and it would be a waste not to use what we'd paid for, so after visiting various Navy and oceanographical websites and discovering the swell situation wasn't too urgent (the waves were still three days away, we guessed), we elected to take a drive up to the hill town of Santa Fe, the home of the chef back at Santa Catalina. He said he often missed the place, and it wasn't surprising. Virgin Latino culture, hidden away at altitude. Traditionally woven *mola* outfits and Panama hats, families going to school on horseback, a village square, Catholic church, quaint community feeling – as close to García Márquez's fantastical 'Macondo' as real life may ever offer. This place would never in a million years look like the remnants of the old Canal Zone, or Santa Catalina. Shame it wasn't anywhere near the beach.

But there were still miles of unexplored coastline in Panama, we realised, looking over a map before driving back to David the next afternoon. Henry's spot had only been one of several that the surf magazines had tried out, and they hadn't even begun to look into the possibilities along the edges of the Darien jungle yet, although good old Ed in Bayonne had, and was refusing to tell *anyone* what lay there.

'If you want to find out the surfing potential of that place, you have to come on a trip with me there next year,' he had explained in the days leading up to my flight out here. 'Sod this J-Bay nonsense. Once you get fit again I'm doing Colombia, Cuba and then we might just have a look along the Darien Gap.' They called it the 'Gap' because of the way virtually all roads and remnants of civilisation stopped until after the Colombian border, meaning the area was allegedly a haven for drug lords and other outlaws.

'There's no risk of getting shot these days anyway,' Ed had added. 'It's far more worth the militias' while to kidnap you instead – then you *will* wish you were sitting on a crowded beach full of Americans, crying about a broken leg and watching your missus do all the surfing...'

I grabbed him a postcard in David, and filled it with satisfying insults and obviously fictitious tales of perfect waves breaking under the Bridge of the Americas, as we rode a bus to the border, going back into Costa Rica to pick up the well-tested surfer trail to Pavones, a place that was already comfortable about making the transition to full-blown surf zone.

* * *

The best way to Pavones from the Panamanian border, as the chef in Santa Catalina told us, was to sneak out the side of the customs complex. We got to avoid any searches or interrogations, the journey was quicker and it was cheaper.

The border village of Paso Canoas was a hell-hole by daytime. We'd gone through at dawn before, but now the place was thronging with all sorts of con men on the lookout for a scam. This was the point at which I felt least safe, although Breige was still totally comfortable with it all. She had become a firm Centro America-phile almost the moment she arrived, and had crossed Costa Rica's other border already, on a weekend visa-break with American girlfriends living in Tamarindo.

'Coming back in from the Nicaraguan border is much worse than this, I promise you,' she informed me.

A newly built but empty office complex was sitting deserted in front of us. Its intended purpose was, according to a bearded American who had appeared from nowhere and taken it upon himself to arrange our taxi, to let passport control and customs operate out of the same building. This was so that you couldn't just get your stamp from the one hut, and then dive out the side road to Pavones without passing a baggage check.

The offices weren't operational yet, though, so the short cut was still available. A stamp from one hut, five dollars for a sticker to accompany said stamp, and then out of there. The officials gestured you towards the customs hut the other side of the street, but took no notice when you went nowhere near it.

'John', as the bearded American identified himself, claimed he was now living at the border full time, and freely admitted that drug addiction was slowly killing him. We didn't need it spelt out– the desperation in his eyes was enough to see that something was seriously wrong. He made his money from arranging dodgy Tico taxis out of the Paso Canoas side-road – most of them for surfers.

'It's not that they've ever got any shit to hide, man,' he explained. 'It's just no fucker bothers running checkpoints along the road to Pavones, and surfers always tend to get searched, so it's a win-win situation. Anyway, it's cheaper to get to Pavones this way rather than riding the bus up to Golfito and heading back on yourselves.'

The Golfito route was hardly meant to be much fun; filled with crime and seedy characters, part of the old gold trail and, until recently, home to nut-cases like the infamous French adventurer Cizia Zykë, who blew the anarchic reality of Central American gold hunting open with his 1980s best-seller, *Oro* (Spanish for 'gold'). The gold miners focused a lot of their attention on the nearby Osa Peninsular, but the subsequent gringo culture had stretched down to Pavones, albeit in a slightly more relaxed form.

Pavones was supposedly first surfed by American smugglers in the seventies, who subsequently bulk-bought most of the land there. This led to aggrieved locals trying to take property back forcefully, burning several US-owned homes to the ground. It had all smoothed itself out eventually, and now a new wave of real estate dealers were moving in, trying to buy and sell little pieces of paradise. The popular line was that things would never regress again to the burnings and riots, but how could you be sure? Central America is a part of the world with a rich tradition of adventure, uncertainty and often violence.

For now, Pavones's new reputation was that of a mellow surf town, with welcoming rest lodges and one hell of a long left-hander. The taxi driver that was going to take us had to ward off a couple of crazed kids, who weren't even trying to hide the fact they wanted to steal my passport. They kept screaming at me in Spanish as I waited for Breige to finish getting her stamp. In the end I couldn't resist telling one of them to fuck off, in clear, forceful English. The kids skulked away instantly, and our driver began pissing himself laughing. This seemed to be the right tone with which to conduct yourself around here. Soon we were on the bumpy dirt tracks to Pavones, and it was all behind us. Thoughts were turning again to surfing – at least for Breige anyway.

The journey took no more than an hour, and we arrived in time to find a place to stay, and check the surf. It was about waist-high, and sectioning a little, but still looking pretty damn good. Breige ran back to get her surfing stuff, and I sat down on the point to watch the conditions for her. Crowded, but easy to get waves if you had a plan. We decided to work on one before she went in.

'There are about two or three real good guys in there who are getting any wave they want,' I explained to her. 'That's because they know where the end of each section is. They're waiting for the wave to shut someone down, and then taking off unchallenged. And if you're gonna paddle for a wave, make sure you catch it. Once someone sees that you are willing to take off, then you'll be given space to catch waves for the rest of the time we're here…'

She paddled straight out, and caught the first wave that came near her. I was filled instantly with a sense of pride at how well she could pick things up. We had a point break at home, but nothing like this. Breige was now catching good waves in her first ever session at Pavones – a competitive, internationally renowned Central American point break.

Within half an hour a torrent of rain came down, forcing me to make for the nearby bar, dubbed 'La Cantina', as quickly as could be done with a leg in plaster. The corrugated tin roof structure was filled with drunk Ticos, along with the odd gringo, and had a great view of the last section of the wave, which was being ridden by a couple of tiny kids and a woman in her forties. I could make out from eavesdropping a nearby conversation that this was the mother of one of them. They were soon joined by another kid, whose board looked familiar. A 6'3" Al Merrick, Quiksilver logo on the nose and two blue 'K-Fins' – the rear one missing at the plug. I turned to ask a middle-aged man who had come to sit next to me: 'Isn't that…'

'Yup. One of Kelly Slater's boards, dude. He was here like a month ago and broke the fucken tail-fin out, man. He gave it to that local kid there. It's his first ever board of his own, man, and he's fucken lovin' it! What a way to catch the bug, man – Slater's fucken board.'

The kid was surfing pretty well on it too, especially without a rear fin.

'This is the place for kids to grow up, man,' the guy went on. 'It's like a fucken dream, dude. I first came here in the early seventies, man. And now I just holiday here once a year. I live on Maui, man. What about you?'

Like everyone, he was amazed to see surfers from Wales, and immediately began quizzing me about it.

'I heard some of the waves in the UK are sick, dude. I saw a right-hander in Scotland, man – "Coldwater Nias" I think they call it. You know where that is?'

'Yeah.' He meant Thurso East. Inevitable magazine coverage of the place was making it a popular name – although I was still willing to bet hardly any of the Americans or Aussies who asked me about it were ever likely to brave the cold enough to go there. Instead most of them just commented how perfect it looked, likening it to another famous right-hander on the Indonesian island of Nias, before going on to say:

'It looks fucken cold, though, man! I dunno if I could do it, even though the waves do look pretty sick...' This guy was no exception.

Breige had spotted the sweet little waves that were now running into the bay at the end of the point, and had paddled down to take advantage of them. This meant I could begin filming her again, while still staying dry, and continuing my conversation with the guy from Maui – which pretty soon got around to J-Bay.

'Dude, that place goes off. I'm tellin' ya. You gotta go there, soon as you get that leg of yours fixed. Get on it. It's like this place, only a thousand times faster, and way hollower.'

'And it breaks the other way,' I reminded him.

'Yeah, tell me about it, dude. Although I fucken wish it didn't – I'm goofy. That place was a fucken nightmare on my backside. That's why I prefer coming here, to surf

on my frontside. This is a pretty good backside wave too,
mind you...'

'Yes, I had noticed.' This was a lot harder to deal with
than the beach break I'd filmed in Panama. These were real,
world-class waves. Despite all the internal resistance and
psychological preparation, I was feeling my loss. Breige was
clearly having a cracking session.

'But this is nothing, man. Wait 'til the swell arrives
tomorrow! Then you'll see some fucken *surf*!'

And sure enough, that was what happened. The following
morning it jumped to way overhead, with some sets looking
alarmingly big. Walking down to the beach you could see the
wave running along the point, partially masked behind the
grove of trees that hugged the start of the beach. Now it was
sectioning a lot less, holding its shape as it ran almost the
entire length of the point. Breige was animated, jogging on
the spot to prevent herself running off ahead of me, about to
try a world-class surf spot in full flow for the first time.

She chose to paddle out at the top of the point, near a small
rivermouth, figuring the rip would carry her down the point
a few sections before she started paddling for anything. She
got it dead right, arriving in the line-up at the end of the
board-snapping first stretch of wave, and just in time to
catch the dreamy, wind-groomed wall into the bay.

Waves ran through a second tube section as the tide
dropped, but the easy run-up meant it required far less
bravado than the tubes at the top of the point. Again, within
minutes she was on a good set wave, which ran for ages.
Most of the footage I got of the ride ended up being from
the rear angle, because the wave continued so far around
into the bay that I was standing almost behind it. Because of
this, I decided to walk down towards La Cantina again – and
anyway, at least I'd be safe from the rain clouds that were
building overhead too.

In Pavones, it rained even more than Panama City. The whole appearance of the place was rain-made. The centre of the village was a luscious green soccer field, that looked nothing like the dry, pot-holed pitches Breige had seen in Tamarindo. The beach was covered in driftwood from various floods, and decaying branches from the trees overhead – which frequently got so weighed down with water that they would just fall off. And they weren't the only things falling from the trees either; all day long ants were landing on me, as they lost their footing on wet foliage. All sorts of flying, crawling, squirming creatures were appearing from time to time, while on the beach everything seemed to be in motion. Lizards, ranging from the size of a finger to the size of an arm, wandered in and out of the waterlogged tree debris, while hermit crabs moved in all directions. Meanwhile, tap and shower water smelt strongly of sulphur – evidence of volcanic activity, and sometimes a deadly sign that you're about to be buried by lava.

The dark green backdrop of the mountainous Osa Peninsular would come in and out of view all day depending on the cloud situation, while the rain also moderated the wind, weighing the air too much to blow easily– meaning that the surf rarely stayed onshore (messy) for long. The buses in Pavones reserved the right not to run if the ground was too wet, which happened often.

Ticos have a reputation for being lazy, carefree and endearingly vain. You could even see it in the local surfing style – lackadaisical cruising down the wave, unwilling to compromise coolness by putting any real commitment into their manoeuvres. When they do decide to really go for it, it's usually in the form of a massive aerial or tail-slide that they've no hope of landing, but which looks extreme for a split second. They come up punching water, as if to say *FUCK! I can land that shit all the time normally. What's wrong with me?* It's believable until attempt number twenty. Within a day or two Breige had noticed that the hot local surfers were actually the best ones to try and poach waves from: they caught a lot and didn't care about blowing the ones they were on, which meant that nine times out of ten a Tico flying down the line at you meant the wave would be empty by the time you paddled for it.

'Fuck, man. That's one difference between here and J-Bay,' exclaimed yesterday's acquaintance from Maui, who had just returned to stand beside me. 'The locals here, they hardly ever try to ride the wave like the long point break it is. Instead they get a short burst of speed, then boost and blow it. You can't ride these waves like that. It's fucken wrong, dude. They got no sense of what they're doing. A surfboard treated properly is like riding a magic carpet, man, and don't you forget it! In J-Bay you'll see how they put together a real ride. Light carving turns, then building up the momentum as you go down the point...'

I'd seen this guy surfing by now. He practised what he preached, racing smoothly at the lip-line of the best waves he could catch, crouching ready to move from rail to rail with a traditional style, almost like a martial art, which fitted his long black hair and samurai-moustache. He told me that he and his Argentine wife visited Pavones every year, but before that he had surfed all over the world, and had been to J-Bay several times.

But by far the best surfer in Pavones that particular swell was another girl from Argentina, Laura. She spent the whole time flying along the first section of the wave, often getting tubes that would have blown minds in Indonesia, let alone Costa Rica, before throwing herself at the lip with graceful aggression, carving, smacking and gouging the wave all the way into the bay before getting out and walking back up the point. She was staying for the season, and trying to turn pro, working two jobs in both the surf shop and a nearby restaurant to save money with which to get to contests in the States. An inspirational surfer, dominating the line-up at one of the best waves in the Americas – and a girl in her early twenties.

On the second day of the swell, Laura took off on one of the biggest waves I'd seen break at Pavones so far. Coming around a menacing bowl of whitewater, she bottom-turned hard, before redirecting herself back towards the pit, jamming water up the face and causing the tube to throb open as her board's wake arrived at the lip. She then disappeared from view behind a curtain of water, and the wave reeled, seemingly empty, down the line for another few seconds. As a gentle plume of spit puffed out of the barrel, the girl flew back into daylight and safety, as spectators on the sand roared their approval.

Through my lens I watched Pavones's infuriatingly fun-looking wave rolling down the point at almost a right angle to the beach, pulling a few cobble-stones along the shore as it went. Even in a big swell, you could get into the line-up dry-haired with a bit of clever timing. Between sessions, I could prep Breige on who to avoid paddling near, who to snake at will, who to take off on, who not to take off on, and what waves would be the best ones to catch. Again, it was probably only for my own amusement, as she was already wise to everything I said.

My thoughts drifted to the collection of dedicated older guys that had done the same for me in the past; my dad, guys from the Welsh Surfing Federation, and the surf club I used to train with sometimes in Lacanau, France. These patient characters had sat there for hours on end, without needing an injury to keep them from wanting to surf themselves, filming kids surfing for no other reason than handing the gift of wave knowledge on through the generations. I had a sense if they'd seen me watching Breige surf here, they'd realise that at least one person had come to appreciate and understand the sacrifices they'd made, and the enjoyment they'd got from watching the bug catch on. But then I'd get frustrated, thinking this was enough thinking of other people, and just wanting to be able to get back in the water myself.

When it came time to leave Pavones, a strong sense of unfinished business had grown in me, and some of it bitter. I'd had enough of watching other people play around, taking it for granted that they had healthy bodies. It was hard not to start criticising people's rides, cogitating as to how each wave could have been better ridden.

'Don't worry about it,' Breige kept saying. 'Just let this make you keener when you get back into it. You'll have to come back here, won't you? That's all.'

She was right. I would need to come back. Pavones had given me a second mission – to return here next season and catch all the waves I'd missed during this swell. I was starting to see goals beyond J-Bay – 'life after Jeffrey's,' I took to calling it. I needed to get it over and done with now, to set myself free from the pact as much as anything.

Had I been scared that reaching the wave of my dreams was going to somehow take the reason out of my surfing? *Nah*, I said to myself. *You've done it all right. You're gonna surf J-Bay better 'cause you've been to Indo. You'll travel with the experience of all these other places.* Even though not part of the original plan, this from-the-beach perspective of Pavones crowd dynamics would help too. And anyway, it's only a broken leg. It could have been worse – knee ligaments, torn achilles, slipped discs or other injuries of a more permanent nature. I knew there was going to be something to gain from this trip, and that something was the fire within, the burning need to finally ride a wave at J-Bay.

No more messing around.

On with it.

★ ★ ★

On the bus to San Jose a few mornings later was a couple in their thirties with a big five-board travel bag. The guy was from California, judging by his accent.

'What did you do to your leg, man?'

I told him a cock 'n' bull story about fracturing my ankle in small Tamarindo beach break surf. It would be far easier than having to explain why I had still travelled to Pavones with no hope of even getting wet. My brief explanation concluded with, 'and anyway, I'm sure it could be worse'.

'Yeah, it could,' came the reply. 'I tell ya, I got malaria so bad once that I was literally minutes from dying.'

'Where?'

'Indonesia. And the Indonesian doctors had just written me off saying, "this guy is finished". They thought no one would get me out of there, and locals wouldn't survive this shit, so why should a Yank be any different. I suppose they were kinda right too. But then my buddy in Denpasar got me a Medevac transfer out of there, and it saved my life. I lost all my savings, and couldn't surf for nine months. Hell, I was in a coma for three. But I'm here now, and I tell ya there's not a day goes by I don't thank God it wasn't worse.'

The Californian couple introduced themselves as Greg and Helen from Ventura.

For the second time in recent conversations, I ended up talking about Scotland. Only this time it felt like there was a danger of making the sale. I'd previously gassed on about the place, unworried about the risk of crowding it out. But Greg had a look of conviction about him.

'Man, I've been planning to get there for a ages now. I keep promising I'm gonna go, but Pavones is just such an easy trip from LA. And I'm still so hooked on Indo too. I just gotta get myself motivated to make it out there, though. Perhaps next autumn. Is Scotland good in autumn?'

'That's the best time,' I told him. 'And warmest water temperatures, if you can actually use that word to describe a place colder than San Francisco.' That usually put people from California off.

'Oh, screw the cold, man. I wanna go there for the waves and the adventure. It looks like such an amazing place. Wild and cosy at the same time. That's the thing, man; people who don't surf will never realise how much more than just a sport it is.'

'It's not a sport,' Helen added. 'It's an art.'

'A *sporting art*,' Greg continued. 'But it's about so much more. It's about travel. It's about how you live your life. And I for one have no regrets about the path I've taken.'

He went on about how they loved their simple existence in Ventura, making money from painting and decorating, and travelling whenever they could. He also decided, on that stuffy bus-ride to San Jose, that he was definitely going to go to Scotland next year, in the autumn. He gave me an e-mail address and told me to send him some info on the place, inviting us to stay in Ventura whenever we wanted. He also suggested I joined him on his trip.

'I should be back from J-Bay by then,' I said. 'I'll be keen for sure.'

At the bus stop in San Jose we got into separate taxis, after having agreed to stay at the same backpacker hostel for the night. Breige knew a good place to go for a drink and some food too.

The evening lights of San Jose rolled by the taxi window, the mountain air outside inviting us to enjoy the luxury of a night in a pair of jeans for once. The first people we bumped into at the hostel were a couple of Swedes who had been at Pavones.

'Small world!' they noted in that friendly Scandinavian drawl.

But Greg and Helen never arrived at the hostel, and their e-mail address didn't seem to work either. Surely only a frustrating spelling error, and no doubt they had innocent reasons for not arriving. But I was worried about not being able to give him some contacts in Scotland.

'Ah, he'll be all right,' said Breige. 'If he's gonna make it there, he'll do it with or without any help from you.'

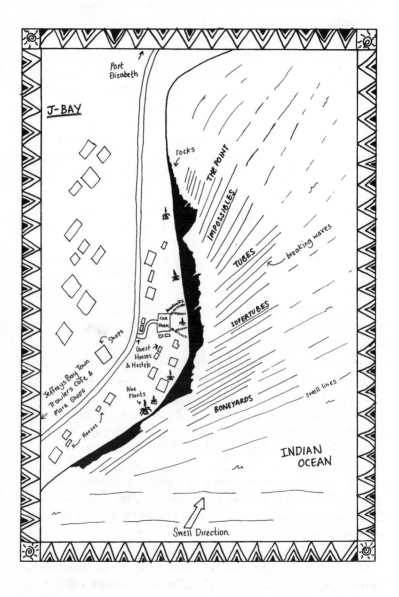

7.

The Perfect
Wave II:

Just Beyond Humansdorp

I t's a start…'
Adam didn't seem too impressed by the look of the
waist-high beach break waves, but was still easily
persuaded to come and give it a go with me. It was surely
preferable to just going back and hanging around 'Alcatraz'
until dark, and neither of us could be bothered to find our
bearings much more that day. Everything else could wait.

So a surf it was. No better way to wash a flight out of you
anyway. We stopped off to buy wax and a leash from one of
Durban's several beachfront surf shops, before going back
to get our stuff.

'That leash'll be eighty rand please, bru.'

'Bru… Rand…' The words echoed in my head. This was it:
South Africa, and although KwaZulu/Natal was a different

climate, province, culture and even consciousness to the cold and mystery of that fabled point beyond Humansdorp, this was the home strait. J-Bay was only a relatively short hop across the same land mass now.

Nine thousand down; one thousand to go.

'*Fark*, bru. That place is like nothing you've ever seen before,' the guy behind the counter of the surf shop carried on. It's surprising how little time it takes you to get onto the subject of a country's best wave. 'Yeah, it's farken sick. That place cooks. You'll have a ball, yah.'

'Yeah. Come on, Adam; let's get in the water. I'm gasping for a surf.'

'OK, man. We're out there.'

★ ★ ★

Since making a full recovery from injury, I had become the keenest surfer on the planet. Of that there was no doubt. Surfing, I realised, was something none of us would be able to do forever, so from now on life was lived more wave-to-wave than ever. Whereas before I might have only gone in the water once a day while at home, and possibly twice if the waves were good, I was once again all over it, regardless of the conditions – like a grommet. In the past small ailments like a minor earache, a bit of wetsuit rash, a hangover or a badly planned meal-time might have made me can a session that wasn't that good, but this was behind me. Nothing got in the way of surfing any more. Absolutely nothing.

When the cast came off it was like being reborn. Within half an hour I had hobbled down to the shoreline at my local break, Rest Bay, to experience for the first time in six months the baptism of seawater washing between my toes. The wave retreated, the pull of water allowing my foot to sink an inch or so further down into the soft sand, before the next one came up and splashed my knee. It was over at last.

The next ten weeks were spent working the stiffness out of my ankle, and coming to enjoy all over again the beauty of surfing and its culture. I spent most of my time hanging around the local Surf Academy where Breige, back from Costa Rica, was now working for the summer. I'd wind up the newest crop of grommets with tales of how much time I was going to spend in the water come September when the injury was well and truly behind me and they were all safely back in school.

Things had changed over the years. These kids now had a lot going for them. They had the support of Porthcawl Comprehensive (under a new and much more progressively-minded Headmaster) and in the Surf Academy they had a beachside base where they could leave bags and wetsuits, keeping parents happy. Interestingly enough, most of them seemed more tuned in to school, were brighter and less cheeky than I remembered my group of friends to have been, but they still had that enlightened grommet state about them. Watching them come and go as I sat stretching my ankle, it was heartening to know the groms were making the right choices:

'Once I leave school I'm gonna go to Indo.'

'I'm off to France this summer...'

'What's Sri Lanka like?'

I felt like one of them too, with my new devotion to surfing and anything related.

Besides the grommets, I also found myself reflecting contentedly on the other communities that can spring up around wave-riding – so awash with characters. South Wales was no exception. I remembered how my dad and his friends used to get embroiled in all sorts of professions alongside their relentless pursuit of the next swell. There was the Pilot (who became best known for flying a by-plane under the Severn Bridge one bored, swell-deprived afternoon), the Undertaker (called 'Duncan the Box' or 'Duncan Death', in whose mortuary the boys used to leave their boards, as it was closest to the surf and none of them had cars to lug their stuff around in) and the Surgeon (a good guy to have on hand for coral cuts), to name but a few.

As my healing leg slowly became more and more stable, I began looking for the right day to get back on a board. Halfway through August it came. A softly lined-up swell resulting from a middle-of-the range US East Coast hurricane, and I paddled out on one of the Surf Academy's soft-top beginner boards. The feeling was incredible. On my first wave I was too tentative to move my feet, but within a few sets, it all started coming back. Like riding a bike, but even more instinctive.

I'd never remembered my first successful ride as a kid, but this time it was different – unforgettable. The return to water and the energy of the sea washing away the months of injury and boredom, bringing me right back to where I'd left off. Indo's Uluwatu felt like it had only been a week ago. Within a month I was surfing normally again and planning a trip.

Irrespective of my resurgent love of surfing, my home town and friends, one thing was clear: South Wales was not going to be the place to hit proper form before going to J-Bay. And, as I was done messing around with extra destinations, the obvious choice was to move to Durban for a few months to train, with a view to travelling down to J-Bay once the season kicked in.

'Do it,' said Breige.

In the same way I had really wanted her to take the opportunity to go to Central America, she too wanted me to make this trip a success. We were used to travelling away from each other by now, considering it a sign of a healthy relationship, and she was looking at going back to Costa Rica around the same time anyway, staying away until spring.

Images in my head before leaving were of the usual flawless walls breaking down the familiar point, but now I could visualise myself riding them. The best bit about a wave as perfect as J-Bay was that your picture of it would turn out to be the exact visual reality. It *would* break like that if I stayed there long enough and at the right time of year, and I *would* ride it as long as I kept practising regularly and avoided further injury. This was a fantasy that was attainable.

The Durban stage was underway before there was barely time to think, and here I was stepping into the Indian Ocean with this eccentric New Zealander.

Adam turned out to be a pretty good surfer – something I hadn't expected judging from the erratic personality traits he'd shown so far. He'd come across as far too highly-strung and full of random thought patterns to master such a complicated and long-term activity, but these were deceiving first impressions. It would be safe to say he was one of the best Kiwi surfers I'd ever seen. He tore into the playful beach break waves like a man possessed, sending huge chunks of spray into the air each time his board went anywhere near the lip.

He was a lanky guy – even lankier than me – but seemed to have that sixth sense that most great surfers have, being able to control exactly what position his every limb was in at any point during a turn. Nothing was ever out of sync with the flow of the wave, allowing him to look a lot better than some surfers who would have wiped the floor with him technically in a contest. Style goes a long way in surfing, and anyone who tells you otherwise is talking rubbish.

At one point a slightly bigger set rolled through, and Adam managed to pick it off (that sixth sense again), racing high across a sucky wave face before uncoiling and turning abruptly just as I paddled past, smacking me in the face with his aggressive wake. It's so good surfing with people like that, because it pushes you to try harder – a philosophy that has made places like Durban the hotbeds of talent they are.

The session was making me realise how good an idea this Durban-based warm-up camp was going to turn out to be. Yes, unlike Adam, I was going to do this right – when those thick J-Bay south swells knocked in April, guess who would be ready and waiting...

'As long as you don't run out of money, or get killed, you're *definitely*, *one hundred per cent* gonna have surfed there by the time you leave. You bastard!'

The most interesting development of the evening was the New Zealander's change of mood post-surf. He'd calmed down completely – as if having vented some of that frustration and franticness on the waves. 'I'm not usually like that,' he explained. 'I just got a bit pissed off talking about Jeffrey's earlier. I don't wanna go home without what I came for, but shit happens. I'll just have to come back, won't I?'

During the evening, we sat in the bizarre hostel we'd dubbed Alcatraz, having a few dinky-sized bottles of Castle lager while surrounded by violence-proof, prison-type doors and playground-esque drawings of great African animals; lions, buffaloes, giraffes, springboks and zebras. Adam told me about how he too had always wanted to come and score J-Bay. He'd been pretty much everywhere else, but hadn't got round to realising that one wave. The reason he'd tried to surf there so far out of season was apparently work commitments. Ever full of surprises, it turned out he was actually pretty high up in a Colorado construction company.

'The biggest perk of the job, man,' he told me, 'is the fact that winter snow writes off the prospect of work for a couple of months every year. I get to travel at least three months in one go, man. There's a bit of a downside to that, though, too. I have to take all my holidays during the Northern Hemisphere's winter. We work around the fucken clock in the thawed months, and I can't go surfing – *ever*. I might take a few two-day trips down to LA on the plane, but it's not the same, man. You can't surf properly like that. It takes a few days just to remember what to do – getting the feel of your boards again. It sucks. The other problem is that as long as I stay in this job, I'm never going to be able to go to most of the best waves on earth in season, 'cause I can't get the fricken time off. I'll never get J-Bay good, much of Central America too; I'll always have to make do with off-season waves in Indo, the Maldives – and that's only the start. It's a fucker, man. And don't you forget it.

'I give myself a complete personality transplant, man,' he went on. 'I turn into a full-on geek as soon as that plane back to Denver lands. But it's the same going the other way too. I just lose all the tension and overused brain-matter straight away, as soon as I make that first duck-dive. I'm getting bad again now, though. 'Cause I'm going back soon. I fucken hate working. *Sooo* much!'

I was beginning to form a different theory on Adam – this was more than just the normal hatred of work. There was something in the way he twitched pitifully when talking about the 'bum deal' that Colorado winters had given him on holiday time – something that made me realise what was getting Adam's goose right now. It was simple. Here was a surfer, a natural-foot, someone with an interest in style, a guy who had spent a lot of time shaping a life of travelling and looking for surf, driven mad by missing the one wave he wanted most; J-Bay. Most of us knew the feeling from somewhere. Mundaka, for example, was probably one of the best waves on earth when it comes to winding people up. It took me four years of turning up at the place only to discover a millpond, before finally getting the swell conditions right that autumn morning. Seeing that world-famous backdrop, with flat water where the wave should be, was always a grim experience – especially when I knew how much time, money and effort it was going to take to come again.

That wasn't going to happen to me at J-Bay, a place that was less fickle than Mundaka. It was actually one of the more consistent A1-grade waves yet to be discovered – as long as you went *in season*. Like the Kiwi, it would perform a complete metamorphosis – turning almost overnight from the Mediterranean flats found by him, into the J-Bay I intended to find. Once that happened, the constant fury of the Roaring Forties would make sure the place was rideable almost every day of the season.

As Adam went on about his experiences of work and surf, a small audience gathered. Two other surfers staying in Alcatraz, both in their mid-thirties, had overheard us talking and decided to move in.

'You guys surfers?'

'Yeah.'

'Cool, where from?'

'I'm from Wales, and he's from New Zealand.'

'Although I'm actually living and working in Colorado at the moment.'

'Nice.' The two guys duly introduced themselves as Brian and Lenny from California, before going on to quiz me in the usual manner: '*Wales*? Do you guys get surf in *Wales*? It must be only in summer, eh? I wanna go to Ireland some day, or maybe Scotland. That place looks sick!'

Like most people from warmer climes, they found it hard to grapple with the idea of surfing Britain in January, listening wide-eyed to my tales of five-millimetre wetsuits, neoprene hats, boots and gloves, before coming out with the quintessential Californian reaction. '*Fuuuuuuuk*. Sounds in-*sane*, man!'

Lenny and Brian joined us for the rest of the evening, exchanging their stories of surf-travel for ours. We must have covered pretty much everywhere that night – regardless of whether or not any of us had actually been there. Their tales of North Hemi' winter escapes to Puerto Rico and Barbados were consoling to the season-locked Adam, who started to look, at least for a few hours, as if he would succeed in leaving South Africa with J-Bay pushed to the back of his mind.

The two Yanks also praised him for his commitment to work. 'That life's not for me, man,' Lenny remarked. 'I couldn't compromise like that. Fuck, if it wasn't for surfing I'd probably be a damn brain surgeon by now or something. Yeah, it's well and truly fucked up my life. All I've done for the past ten years is either fart around in tropical countries, or hang out in car parks and hostels talking shit!'

They'd also failed to get J-Bay, but remained typically upbeat about it. 'Man, we gotta come back,' Brian smiled. 'Unfinished business, dude!'

Listening to them go on, I wondered how many other conversations exactly like this were going on right now in the rest of the world. People who'd only just met each other getting on like old friends, stoking themselves up with the prospect of how much of the globe there was still left to surf. It always works so much better when you're away from home, because the excitement is already there. We were all sucked in. For the few hours we spent together it wouldn't have mattered if the waves had been flat or ten feet. The feeling would have still been the same. It was enough to send my mind reeling into a list of post-Jeffrey's trips that would have to be taken sooner rather than later. Top of the list, besides Pavones, of course, was now a point break in El Salvador called 'La Libertad'. I'd seen photos before, but the stories told to me that night sent me over the brink.

The need to sleep came eventually, and as I lay looking at the moonlight sliding through the bars of my cell window, it occurred to me again that J-Bay was already playing a hand in the course of the trip. Still a couple of months away, its spirit had begun to get to work. The bug was growing. That insatiable desire to surf every wave on the planet. *La... Libertad... La... Libertad...* The words rolled around my head as I drifted off, followed just seconds before total slumber by something else. *J-Bay's getting nearer... Thou shalt go, soon...*

And then, as if none of it had ever happened, I was woken up by another thought – a slightly more pressing one: the need to find a flat.

★ ★ ★

Looking for flats in Durban wasn't as easy as first expected. Availability within the budget I'd given myself turned out to be pretty limited – not what I'd been told before embarking on this additional leg of my J-Bay pilgrimage. After looking into some adverts and doing a bit of asking around, landing on my feet had begun to look like it was going to be hard. There was, however, one thing that did turn out in my favour: Adam was getting a bit sucked off with living out of the back of his hire car and, having three and a bit weeks left on his ticket before returning to the US, was keen to chip in for an apartment to see those days out in style.

'There's no fucken point at all going back down towards Jeffrey's now,' he said solemnly. 'It's the off-season, plain and simple. Here, though... That's a different story. They're still waiting for the first proper cyclone swell of the year.'

We only passed two more nights in Alcatraz before stumbling upon what was to become our new home. The Pelican Apartments, one half-block back from North Beach, were desperate to attract customers after a fatal shooting in the lobby some months before. The nervous manager, Caucasian sweat beading on his combed-over forehead, offered us a four-bedroom apartment, with breakfast and dinner included at the downstairs cafeteria, for the rand equivalent of about £70 a month.

'A fucken catered apartment for like four dollars a day!' Now it was Adam's turn to look nervous. 'We'd better accept before he realises what he's doing!'

The location of our new palace was, by one hell of a fluke, about as close to ideal as you could ever get for such a ridiculous price. The perennially active beachfront was a stone's throw away – making the three most important activities of surfing, eating and drinking possible with minimal effort.

Our new lodging also had less of the prison feel to it; there was little in the way of cages, extra doors and other such unnerving anti-crime facilities.

'South Africans are all so paranoid,' Adam commented. 'The violence thing is non-existent here, although you'd never know it.'

'Yeah, but you try telling that to Sweat Man down there,' I replied.

Sweat Man, aka Joseph Du Plessis, never did renege on his promise to accommodate us for a price that seemed somehow flawed from his end of the deal. He continued to be pretty good to us too. We were allowed to use his own personal pool table for free and maids were sent to clean our rooms and make our beds on an almost daily basis (for which we couldn't resist giving them a few extra rand, even though 'Meesta Du Plessis said *no*'). Mealtimes were surprisingly formal, which struck us as funny on the occasions we'd sit there wearing flip-flops, blowing water out of our noses and picking sand out of our ears.

The menial jobs were all taken by Zulu staff, who went about their way with remarkable cheeriness considering the pittance they were being paid, exhibiting warm smiles that only seemed common to the darker skinned occupants of the building. Meesta Du Plessis was, despite his apparent kindness to us, far from pleasant to his fellow man in general. As the days moved on, it began to seem as if his offerings of assistance in every aspect of our lives were more motivated by disrespect for the workers than respect for us.

'He's a traditional Durban man,' so Hari the Pakistani receptionist explained to us. 'He has his ways of doing things and nobody is going to make him change that. He's all right in the heart. He could have laid a lot of us off when the Changes happened.'

'The Changes'; in other words the dissolution of the apartheid regime. Durban, like the rest of the country, was heavily caught up in the fallout from the past few decades of hate, terror and politics. The positivity of that moment of ecstasy and human achievement in 1990 could still be seen in the local faces around town – but it had come at a huge price. The rand had lost almost all its value, and opportunities were evaporating for a lot of native Whites – sons and daughters of the old regime who, despite not necessarily being racist themselves, were feeling the pinch of the counter-policies now in place to reverse the damage done by their forefathers. Anyone with the chance to get a foreign passport was doing so.

'It's a big shit sandwich, bru. And we've all had to take a bite, eh,' said Mr Du Plessis's slightly less bigoted son, before going into a diatribe about how good his old man had been to the servants-cum-slaves that he still employed.

'When they brought in a minimum wage for Blacks,' he went on, 'they were forcing all the White employers to make back-payments of years. It wasn't financially possible in most cases, but the Blacks were demanding it anyway. So everybody was going bankrupt, and the stupid kaffas were losing everything. My old man could have done that too, but he didn't. He offered them a deal: no back-payments and a gradual introduction of the wage, in return for being able to keep their jobs. He's not an animal, eh?'

We decided not to contest that one, easy though it may have been. It sounded to us as if they'd basically tried as hard as possible to avoid increasing the wages until they really had to, and neither of us could see the kindness in that. Adam thought the pair of them were full of shit – both

Du Plessis Senior and Junior – and suggested we tried to avoid them from then on. I agreed with him.

That wasn't hard, because the waves had been pumping from the day we'd arrived. Mornings of lukewarm barrels and sucky, open-faced beach break peaks were blending into weeks, and it was safe to say life had never felt better. Downtown Durban had to be one of the most shreddable (easy to surf really well) stretches of coast I'd ever been to. It was like France, only warmer and more consistent. Adam had also been right about the anticipated arrival of cyclone season – as a series of hefty swells began queuing up, waiting eagerly to thrash their way along the New Pier sandbanks. We'd also learned the secret to scoring the peaks almost all to ourselves: don't dawnie! The South Africans are absolutely mad for first-light surfing, most of them liking to log a few waves before going to work. As a result, the most crowded session of the day would be between dawn and 8 a.m. After a little while of learning the hard way (it pays to try and avoid crowds in Durban – just because the surfers are so good that it'll be really hard to get waves off them), we began waiting until after breakfast to begin our daily surf routine. As weeks passed, the Welsh winter stiffness was dropping off me by the day, and we were making friends too.

Those friends were coming from both extremes of Durban life. A ding in Adam's favourite board had led to our meeting with 'J-J', the local surfboard repair man, amongst other trades. J-J was as mad as a March hare, and hilarious to spend time with. He'd show us around the neighbourhoods in which he grew up, losing his directions along the way. 'Oh well, this is where the bus stop *used* to be,' was his favourite line, whenever he wasn't telling us about how he'd done time for a diamond robbery, or introducing us to his even crazier friends, one of whom had lost half his face in a bombing, pre-'Changes'.

Then at the other end of the spectrum were Derek, Stuart and Shaun, all sensible, clean-living family men with stable careers, and friends of the sage-like Durban surfboard-shaper, Spider Murphy. These guys invited us on a weekend surf trip almost the second they met us. We scored some of the less crowded (apparently due to the lack of shark nets!) spots to the north of the city with them, before returning to their house for a well-earned slap-up breakfast. It was then that we realised the reason for their uncannily warm hospitality: 'You guys should come to church with us some time,' Shaun told us, over some coffee.

They were serious about their religious beliefs, but had all the time in the world for anyone else's viewpoint – surfing damn well to boot. These three, along with their other mate Dave (who had to surf with the early dawn crowds because of his job at Spider's factory shop) turned out to be some of the best friends I made during my time at Durban.

Just minutes after dropping Adam off at the airport for a sunrise take-off to Johannesburg and then Denver, where his grim return to a life of hard graft awaited, they were round the apartment insisting I come with them for a surf.

'This morning is gonna be cooking,' Derek explained. 'It's one of the first south swells of the year.'

'South swell... south swell?' There was something in there that I hadn't fully grasped yet. Quick as ever at five in the morning, Derek was a step ahead of me.

'Well, a *sort of* south swell. It's not a *J-Bay* kind of south swell, if that's what you're thinking. Nah, Jeffrey's wouldn't get much surf off this one. But it's still a swell, though, eh?'

We were now dealing with what they called an 'off-season south': it was just a bit of swell, which came from the south – not the sort of raging Antarctic storm that characterised the shift in seasons and the start of J-Bay – no, that was still some weeks away yet.

The new swell direction meant that the downtown Durban beaches were almost flat as we daintily crept away and onto the southern-bound motorway system, everyone thoroughly amped up by the prospect of getting into some 'real waves'.

A little less experienced in what was likely to be their interpretation of 'real waves', I was shitting myself – but bravely trying to conceal it.

Was I going to have a big enough board? Surfers always say that you don't really want to be buying gun-boards over 6'7" (my biggest), unless really intent on paddling out in giant surf. By limiting your quiver thus, you are assured an excuse whenever the waves start breaching the 'very big' mark and start knocking on the door of 'fucking enormous': 'Ah, I'd love to paddle out, you see, except I've only got this 6'7"!'

Even more unsettling was the way in which they had to listen to a taped church sermon along the way. It was Sunday and they were skipping morning obligations to go surfing, so the least they could do was catch up on what they were missing. The only thing was, this was *last* Sunday's sermon – this 'emergency swell' thing was a pretty frequent occurrence. As we passed spot after spot of empty and worryingly big surf, the voice of the preacher didn't flinch. It felt like walking the green mile, or having your last rites read to you. 'Father, we commend into your spirit the soul, and 6'7" semi-gun, of this your humble servant Tom.'

We pulled up at a right-hand point, to the sight of triple-overhead walls. Intimidating surf, and definitely as big as anything I'd ever surfed before, but unfortunately not sizey enough to be able to use the under-gunned argument. The South Africans weren't intimidated, though – there was nobody else out, and a 'fun-sized' swell on the go.

Riding big surf is a completely different act to regular surfing. It's no longer the spirit-cleansing, relaxing walk with nature that we so love to depict. Words like 'glide' and 'mellow' are soon thrown out of the window for a whole new vocabulary, as fun turns to a mixture of fear and desire – or maybe *respect* and desire. You have to want the waves, but at the same time know exactly where your limits lie.

Scientists have looked long and hard at the psychology of high-adrenaline sporting activities, and their findings ring one hundred per cent true for big-wave surfing. Humans are incapable of correctly coordinating their bodies under the pressure of a level of adrenaline they've never experienced before. To draw a parallel, if any of us tried taking a penalty in front of 60,000 screaming football fans we probably wouldn't even be able to kick the ball. In the same way, it is not physically possible to fluently send and interpret all brain signals when taking off on a wave that is too much bigger or heavier than anything you've ever ridden before. Adrenaline is a bit like alcohol, in that you can build up a tolerance (or dependence, as the case may be). With all of this in mind, I was well aware that the only way to get a few good ones that morning would be to stay calm, warm up well and not push the boat out too far where wave selection was concerned. I spent the first hour or so catching some of the 'smaller ones' – just making do with the double-overhead waves instead, odd as it sounds, and watching closely to see how my hosts dealt with the bigger sets.

Familiar with such adrenaline levels, they were all completely at home, swinging around late and toying with the drops. Stuart and Derek were both hitting the lip on waves most Brits would struggle to bottom-turn on, while Shaun concentrated hard on clocking up some serious tube time. All the while they were continually trying to coax me into taking off bigger. When I did eventually take a few of the safer, more shapely big ones, their delighted faces told the story. It was as if, having given up on converting me to their brand of religion, they had decided to settle for the next best thing.

The lack of crowds was probably the reason I'd been able to catch some big waves. In the totally zooed-out breaks where most people come face to face with big surf for the first time, the other surfers in the water are so much more used to the size and power, they leave you only able to catch the scraps or semi-close-outs that they don't want themselves. Here, you really were able to pace yourself and pick your wave. By getting up early and surfing empty breaks like this one, the guys who'd brought me here had rapidly been able to get good at surfing really *big* waves.

On the way back north the subject turned to J-Bay again. 'If you thought that place was intense, wait 'til you see the way Jeffrey's charges down the line,' said Derek. 'Now *that* is intense.'

I was beginning to wonder what I'd let myself in for.

I hoped for a few more big days before the eventual off to J-Bay itself, and did all I could to get as much practice as possible when the opportunities arose.

'There's one thing you're not allowing for,' Dave had reassuringly told me when I visited Spider's shop one last time before leaving Durban for the trek south to Port Elizabeth. 'Even when it's big, J-Bay is so perfect you'll still have a ball. Here the big waves bend and warp, they shift around and the line-up is filled with currents and rips. In J-Bay it's simply a perfect wall of water, that stands up for you. Like I say, man, you'll be all over it. I just wish I was coming with!'

'That's all right. I'll have to make the most of it on your behalf,' I told him.

The bus left at 5.30 a.m. the next morning, and was filled with sleepy traveller types, who looked unfriendly and overly cool. No surfboards in sight, and only one spare seat next to a snoring middle-aged man in an England football shirt. This backpacker spin-off of the Greyhound was called the 'Baz Bus', and seats had been by reservation only. It ran between hostels along the southern Africa circuit, going from Cape Town to Victoria Falls and back on a weekly basis. It was going to take fifteen hours to reach Port Elizabeth, according to the timetable.

As a surfer, 5.30 a.m. is nothing, and I couldn't help feeling a bit of disdain for the various parties on the bus who were moaning about their hangovers and the early departure. Just get on with it, I thought. As the day progressed and people started waking, most conversations shifted from hangovers to that age-old 'anywhere-you've-been-I've-been-better' number. Some guy at the back had done it all, from shitting water in Indian gutters to the gay bars of San Francisco and the mine fields of Cambodia. And at the moment it seemed his main reason for having gone to any of those places was so that he could talk about it. He asked me where I'd been, and almost spat at me when I replied by saying I had just spent several months in Durban.

'You've been in the same place for nearly three months!' he sneered. 'Where are you going now?'

I didn't want to get sucked into this nonsense, so I replied as quickly as I could before looking back out the window. It turned out that the only person I really saw eye to eye with on that journey was the man I'd sat next to. Ian was a member of the revered 'Barmy Army', an English cricket supporters' organisation, the fanaticism of which I kind of admired. These guys went to the ends of the earth pretending to watch cricket matches (the real purpose was sunburn and beer), and I'd met some of them before on a flight to Sri Lanka. Their devotion to the 'mission' was outstanding, and Ian was no different.

As the dirt hills of Kokstad, Mount Frere and then Umtata rolled past, he proceeded to talk to me about anything *except* cricket.

'I love the simplicity of life in these rural parts of South Africa,' he explained. As England's cricketers tour the country often, Ian had been here many, many times. 'You can be in a city like Durban in the morning and by the afternoon people are smiling at you out of mud and straw houses, living off the land, with all they ever need.'

These roads were allegedly dangerous to drive alone, but we saw no evidence of it. The area south of the Drakensberg Mountains was teeming with kids, who would run out at us beaming from ear to ear, waving away as they dropped into the horizon. Apart from the clientele on the bus, we didn't see one frown outside of the window until East London. As we ascended into high ground, a cobalt blue sky threw down a thick palette of land colours, the likes of which send fine-art photographers into a frenzy. The ground looked fertile and varied. I know I'd never be able to live away from the coast, but if I ever had to, then my second choice would be in mountain or hill country.

This had been a very concentrated surf trip so far, I realised. Staying in Durban virtually the whole time, was I missing out on getting to know a vast and fascinating country? Surf travel could be done with different degrees of focus. On one end of the scale lay people like Ed, who loved the journey, saw any waves as a bonus, and needed countries to be as weird and wonderful as possible. Then there were trips like this, where, despite all the other reasons for visiting somewhere, you arrive with tunnel-vision – one purpose alone. I could get excited about both types depending on circumstance, but for now, the latter was the way it had to be.

Ian was starting to discuss plans for the evening. 'My mate lives in PE,' he said. 'He'll put us up for the night and take us for a drink – if you're up for it.'

Why not, I thought.

It was exactly 11 p.m. when we arrived, and his Liverpudlian ex-pat mate, whose name I didn't even catch, was a madman. My stuff was thrown under a bunk-bed (roughly so that I could hear my boards banging inside their bag), and I was pushed straight into a 'dentist's chair' – sitting with your head tilted back while a myriad of potent spirits are poured into your mouth. Next up was a bar about a quarter of a mile down the road, on the edge of a shopping centre, a place where several other cricket fans were drinking and it seemed everybody, male or female, was an acquaintance of either Ian or his mate. A surfer on the piss with the Barmy Army! For a moment I almost thought about jacking the J-Bay idea in and taking up cricket-watching instead.

We had a few drinks there, before Ian began inviting everyone he could find back for a party. By five I was sitting on the bunk, guarding my boards against drunken cricket fans, with proceedings showing no sign of slowing down. I decided that it was my destiny to still get on that bus. My ticket was meant to run right through to Jeffrey's, leaving at six the next morning from a stop half a mile down the road.

Dragging two bags and three boards half a mile at the crack of dawn was hilarious. Blood alcohol levels were at an all-time high, and I kept falling over every few yards. I deserved to get robbed, but it didn't happen. I arrived at the Baz Bus wild-eyed and bruised. The sea of travellers parted down the aisle as people looked up imploring me not to sit by them. I found a seat two rows from the back, lay against the window and proceeded to listen to the idiot from the day before go on about his new hangover and some LSD he'd done in Phuket once.

By now I was too tired and excited to stand any chance of sleeping. This was the final two hours to J-Bay! Because it had been dark by the time we'd done the trip from East London to Port Elizabeth, I hadn't had a chance to see how much the scenery had changed. The road was straight and level, but either side were hillsides covered with aloe plants and dry earth – the defining features of the point at J-Bay.

After an hour or so the hills broke into a stretch of land still laced with the same vegetation, but much flatter. On my right I could see the dunes shown in *The Search* just before the Curren ride, and those over which the crew of *The Endless Summer* dragged their boards towards the mirage almost half a century ago. On the other side a long peninsula stretched out to sea, fringed by a shoreline of black rocks: Jeffrey's Bay.

I was only offered a tantalisingly short view of the point from that angle before it disappeared behind the ever-expanding town outskirts. By now Mr Phuket had fallen asleep, along with his audience, but I felt like bouncing through the roof. As the bus wove its way through the town, every signpost was stickered with surf labels. Eventually a small road came up on our left with a sign that, beneath the surf-brand paraphernalia, clearly read 'Supertubes'. Supertubes was the exact section where the best part of the wave broke.

The driver stopped the bus, called for me to get off, lifted my stuff onto the grass and bade me good day. Here I was. I turned straight round and checked into the place behind me, a large family run dormitory and shared kitchen. The owner, Vanessa, introduced me to my bunk, showed me where to leave my boards and then left me to do what she must have seen people doing every day of the year – run towards the point. It took about ten seconds to go from my new bed to the boardwalks from which all the famous line-up shots of the wave were taken, and I tried to concentrate on nothing but absorbing the view. There in front of me lay the point at J-Bay. Exactly how it had looked in all those posters, films and tales – except for one thing of course: It was *dead flat*. Not a breaking wave in sight!

That was OK, though. Season's start was a few days, or even a week away, I reminded myself. The changeover here was meant to be dramatic, summer sometimes literally dropping into winter overnight. The first of the proper storms would kick off out to sea somewhere way south of Cape Town, before heading up north, spinning off winds that drove the swell in towards J-Bay. The storm was out there, I'd seen it on the Navy charts; it was just a matter of waiting for its payload to arrive.

'Apparently the wind comes up like a million miles an hour offshore, the warm weather stops and then we're only a day away from Supertubes starting to work,' said a guy standing next to me. 'The locals are all getting antsy, 'cause they reckon it's gonna happen anytime soon. You're definitely here at the right time. Anyway, we've been surfing Boneyards at the top over there a little, and there's always a trip going to Seal Point...'

Boneyards was the first section of the wave, right at the beginning of the point. In a swell, it was meant to be a grinding semi-close-out that raced into the start of Supertubes. Now there was a small, knee-high peak trickling along it, with two surfers trying their best to imagine it was a real wave. The guy standing next to me was called Cheyne, from Constantine in Cornwall. Within moments I learned that he had loads of ties with Porthcawl, and that our fathers had been good friends 'back in the day'. Small world? Not when you're at one of the world's best waves, with the start of the season imminent.

By now things were catching me up, and I had to sleep. Cheyne was staying at the same place along with his mate Charlie, and walked with me to the dorm, where I promptly climbed atop a bed in the corner, leaving all my stuff on the bunk below, and passed out within seconds.

When I woke it was into one of those hellish semi-conscious states where you know you need to get up but can't. There were voices in the room – German, I think, and my mind was filled with attempts to analyse the situation. It was obvious now what had happened to me last night. The anticipation of a moment I'd spent too long waiting for had been too much to deal with, and I'd basically resorted to drinking with the Barmy Army to suppress my nerves about arriving at J-Bay. But sod it, I'd missed no waves yet, and the style of my arrival I wouldn't change for the world. My moment had come, I'd stepped out onto the point. Now we just needed a swell.

Cheyne broke my trance.

'Me and my mate Charlie are gonna go ride a few up at Boneyards. Fancy coming?'

I did – this was my motivation to get up, and it took no time at all to roll off the bunk, drink a glass of water and pull out my 6'3".

'You'll need the fullsuit,' Cheyne advised. 'It's not Durban any more.'

It was, in a way, comforting to put a wetsuit on after the past two months in boardshorts. The cold was one element of J-Bay that we Brits could feel accustomed to. It was also probably one of the things that had drawn me here in the first place. While most other famous perfect waves were in warmer waters, this was one that the pros all raved about *despite* the fact that it was friggin' freezing at times, further proving J-Bay really was about the quality of the wave and nothing else.

On the way up the point I was trying to map out where Curren's ride had probably taken place. It was no use. Like Mundaka, you just couldn't say how the wave was going to move until you saw it in real life.

Cheyne was right about the water. My toes went numb at first, finding their feeling after a few minutes. It reminded me of Portugal, where the warm air makes the relative coldness of the ocean really hit you. Cold water also stops you noticing the effects of the sun reflecting off the surface, and after a few small, junky waves, my face was already burnt.

Walking back up the point after the short session, I could feel that the sunshine was of that receding autumn type

– only powerful during the peak of daytime. There was a feeling in the air that it would soon be cold, which only meant one thing: the point would come to life. Supertubes would start working.

Back at the hostel, an older local was milling around, musing how the wave was going to happen soon, while a couple of other foreigners were planning to go out drinking. I was invited, but declined. Bed was calling again.

Sleep came, along with a real sense of achievement. I was here in time for the first swell of the year. Surely the possibilities of something going wrong were limited now.

The next day, my first full one at Jeffrey's, was again sunny with no waves. At breakfast Cheyne said he was going to go to Seal Point with one of the Germans, and that they had room in the car if I wanted to join them.

Seal Point is a more exposed spot about three quarters of an hour south. J-Bay was tucked into the coastline at a ninety-degree angle, so a swell needed to be big in order to wrap into the bay (the reason why it only broke in winter). Seal Point, on the other hand, faced south, straight into the brunt of the Roaring Forties swell window, so when J-Bay was flat, there would usually be a wave there. The only trouble was it wouldn't have quite the same symmetrical perfection.

To tell the truth, that's an understatement. Seal Point is a bloody awful surf spot, or it was that afternoon anyway. There was a rock boil cropping up halfway down the line, making an already desperately uninspiring ride even more frustrating, and what swell the place could muster was weak at best. Cheyne and I ended up surfing the beach break instead, while the German who'd driven us – a pretty good surfer named Tim – stayed unusually excited about the point.

After the session we made ourselves some cheese sandwiches, and sat on the bonnet of Tim's vintage sky-blue VW Beetle, enjoying the small part of the afternoon when the sun got warm enough for you to be able to take your T-shirt off.

'Cool car,' I noted.

'You think? I hired it in Cape Town,' Tim explained. 'It's been nothing but trouble.' His English was perfect.

'Really?'

'Yeah. It was the cheapest one the guy had, and it's broken down three times already.'

'What; between here and Cape Town?'

'No. I've driven it to Vic Falls, Jo-burg, the Kruger and Durban. This is the end of my trip.'

'Tim's worried the wave might not work before his ticket is up,' Cheyne added.

'When's your flight home?'

'Three days.'

'I reckon he should delay it, don't you?' Cheyne looked at me for support.

'Well, if it's the difference between scoring J-Bay and not scoring it, that would be a no-brainer for me. What's wrong? Is there too much of a fee on making changes to the ticket?' I asked.

Tim looked straight at me. 'No. That wouldn't be a problem. It's just the course I'm starting. I have a work placement I need to go to in order to get on my medical degree course this autumn. And it starts next week.'

'Fuck that,' I suggested unsympathetically. 'Tell them you got ill and missed the flight. A few days won't matter, surely!' He was making me feel uncomfortable for some reason.

'No. I've got to do it,' Tim went on. 'I've been travelling for nearly a year. I've been to the Mentawais, all over Indo, I've been to Australia. I've done a lot of surfing, but now I have to do this.'

I chatted to him a bit more. He was probably one of Germany's best surfers, and had just taken a year off from studying to have a real go at it. But now he was totally resigned to the fact that in a week's time he was going to be a serious surfer no longer.

'The course lasts five years, and then I'm going to spend a few more becoming a surgeon. I've had my time of surfing a lot, and it's been great.'

Tim was going to miss J-Bay, and we all knew it.

Driving back through Humansdorp towards Jeffrey's, I felt humbled. The commitment he was showing to become what he wanted was awesome in comparison to the lackadaisical way I'd gone about my own ambitions – and I was probably going to realise mine within the next few weeks. It felt undeserved.

'Horses for courses,' said Cheyne wisely. I decided he was right, and pushed the plight of poor old Tim to the back of my thoughts. He was going to be filthy rich in a decade's time anyway, and then who would be laughing?

If anything, Tim's sense of having fun was bolstered by his imminent return to spirit-crushing normality, although he did have that tension about him that I'd also recognised in Adam the Kiwi. Anyway, the following morning one of the locals invited us on a motorised dinghy-ride up a nearby river, and Tim turned up with a hip flask of straight whisky.

'I'm here for a good time, not for a long time,' he explained, taking a healthy swig.

The surf was still flat, and expected to remain so for another day or two at least, so I headed along, as did Cheyne. There didn't appear to be much purpose to the trip beyond getting drunk, and rolling off some sand dunes we docked by. The madness of waiting for swell was in us all.

We'd rolled the dinghy into the river at a pretty civilised looking boat club, but it didn't take long to be in what felt like the wilds of Africa. The sand dunes were there on our left as we moved upstream, with the bank of bushes and trees hosting all sorts of wildlife – birds, frogs, reptiles, and thousands of insects.

'Just about anything can bite you around here, so watch out,' said Grant, one of the local South Africans who had organised the boat.

'Birds have it good,' replied the now hideously pissed Tim. 'They get to be the most colourful animals, and be able to fly. It's not fair.'

'I have to contest the bit about being most colourful there, bru,' Grant came back at him. 'You oaks haven't met Bruce Gold yet.' His two friends laughed hard at this. I wanted to ask who that was, but suspected they weren't going to give a straight answer to anything right now.

We had started out in some of the hottest sunshine I'd seen since arriving at J-Bay. But by the time we pulled into a small break in the river bank that would let us bring the boat aground and walk into the dunes, shadows had got longer, and the air had developed a nip again. Tim wasn't the only person who'd brought whisky along, and I was grateful for a few swigs from the other member of the party who hadn't yet introduced himself.

As the liquor warmed me from the throat outwards, I asked him his name.

'Uruguay.'

'And where are you from?'

'Uruguay.'

The sand was the first thing to lose its heat, and within a short while it was so cold that nobody wanted to stick around. As we were getting back into the dinghy, someone noted that this was where they'd filmed the scene from *The Endless Summer* when the guys dragged their boards over a dune to land their first sight of South African perfect surf. Just in case it was, we all ran back quickly and rolled down the biggest sand hill within reasonable distance. The South Africans looked at us like we had three heads, but they also understood.

Coming back down the river, we were like sailors who'd lost our bearings, singing sea shanties and picking on anyone who spoke for more than a sentence. Packing up the boat, Grant said that he didn't think *The Endless Summer* had anything to do with the dunes we'd just seen, but that we'd made him laugh anyway. By the time we got home I had a headache and needed some food, as did Cheyne. Tim and Uruguay went out drinking with one of the Aussies. We didn't go for risk of swell in the morning.

They got away with it, though, because it was still flat the next day. The routine of boredom continued for a few more days, punctuated by the odd surf at Boneyards, or even the beach behind it. As planned, Tim left for Germany, pulling out of the little cul-de-sac our hostel was in with a stoic look on his face, but total conviction.

Once the chortling noise of his hired Beetle faded away, Cheyne and I took a walk into the town. It had been funny at first to think that the J-Bay experience went beyond waves, and that there was actually a town that all the photos left out. In the case of Supertubes it was a hamlet of simple condos, guest houses and holiday homes, leading out onto a main road and a small square of shops and restaurants with a mini cinema in the far corner. The main town of Jeffrey's Bay was about a mile south of Supertubes, along the coast.

It too was pretty chock-a-block with newly built homes, along with heaps of discount surf shops and places to eat. It was a blustery place, which felt desolate in the dropping temperatures, even though it was one of the most built-up stretches on the coast. Signs at almost every corner invited you to Billabong and Quiksilver factory outlets, getting bigger the nearer you got. The latter had even paid a couple of youngsters to stand in the streets wearing billboards giving directions. Cheyne was planning to load up with cheap clothing before going back.

'It'll pay for my next trip if I sell it to the right people,' he claimed.

Trawlers Café was high on my priority list because it had a world-famous guest book. It had been signed by almost every high-profile visitor since the sixties. We wanted to put our own doodles in the coveted pages, but couldn't find the poxy place for love nor money.

'Charlie says it's really inconspicuous looking,' Cheyne claimed. 'He reckons it's more like a chip shop than a café or restaurant.'

'Well, it's not going to run away. Let's ask someone back at Supertubes and then come back.' I wanted to wait until I'd surfed the wave before writing in the book anyway.

We returned to the hostel by hitching a lift in the back of a farmer's ute, walking in to find the elder local we'd seen a few days ago in mid-rant: 'Every fuckin' day people saying the same thing – "Where's the swell?", "When's the swell coming?" Hell, I don't fuckin' know. I just live here.' He paused to look at us in the doorway, before getting up and walking outside mumbling to himself.

About a minute of silence elapsed before anyone spoke further.

'Poor guy's been living here all his life,' said a Canadian who was in the middle of watching a surfing video, once we were obviously safe from being overheard.

'And what would be so bad about that?' I enquired.

'Well, all he ever sees is people come here briefly, and then going home having had the times of their lives. Meanwhile, he's not stoked 'cause he knows no different. Perfect waves can get boring too. I bet he ends up wondering how everyone else is stoked apart from him…'

Coming from Britain it is safe to say you'll never see enough perfect surf to get bored of it, and the junk we rode on a day-to-day basis probably helped us appreciate the good stuff more. But searching for perfect surf could become an addiction, and I'd come down with it years ago. Besides making it hard to be happy, it was also an expensive habit. Perhaps Jeffrey's was going to set me free of the bug.

After a few hours the old guy came back, in a much better mood.

'He's probably eaten something at last,' said the Canadian, who'd introduced himself as Patrick.

The three of us – me, Patrick, Cheyne – went for a walk to look at the point again. Still flat. We got chatting to another one of the local crew, whom we knew from the hostel.

'It's coming soon,' he told us. 'If you wake up in the morning and you can hear the sound of water peeling down the point…'

'Then it's on?' I cut him off.

'No. It means it's still not quite happening. If you can hear each individual wave trickling along, then it's still small. If you can just hear a deep sea roar, though… Now *that's* when you know you're about to ride J-Bay.'

A tingle went up my back. It had to be another early night, just in case.

We watched a video after tea – called *Billabong Challenge 2: J-Bay*. Ex-world champ and Aussie legend Wayne 'Rabbit' Bartholomew had organised a speciality event a few years ago at Supertubes; eight world-class surfers hand-picked, a ten-day waiting period for the swell to get to its best, hour-long heats and judging criteria that valued creativity.

At the beginning of the swell another Aussie former world champ, Mark Occhilupo, was filmed noting that the warm-up day was the windiest he'd ever surfed J-Bay. The next morning the contest organisers awoke to find swell had jumped six feet in about an hour, leaving the pros to surf the place as big as it ever got.

'The wind,' I pointed out to Cheyne. 'Remember you said a strong offshore would bring the swell in? That's what must have happened then, when Occy reckoned it was the windiest ever. Windiest equals biggest. Makes sense, doesn't it?'

Cheyne nodded. You had to marvel at the ridiculous range of random factors that had needed to come together to make a place like this possible. A bend in the coastline that contained the right rock and sediment types to erode away at exactly the angle for surfable waves, an approaching seabed with good ocean depths to allow swells to travel fast. Then this had to occur in a place with agreeable storm patterns, while the cherry on the cake was the natural beauty of the place – the aloe plants, pods of dolphins and trippy-coloured birds. The night before, the sea had been covered with phosphorescence too, shingles of fluorescent green on the ocean surface, crackling along the edges of the rocks as the water lapped against the shore.

In the film, Kelly Slater won the event with what the locals were calling one of the best J-Bay performances ever, in surf that was at least triple-overhead. On his last wave after sealing the victory, the video showed Slater with his arm above his head pulling into the section after Supertubes, dubbed 'Impossibles' because the tube there was virtually unmakeable. As the ten-foot wave shut down, swallowing one of the best surfers of all time whole, the camera zoomed out to show the beach and the point.

'Yikes,' said Patrick. 'To think that happened on that stretch of beach there!' He pointed out of the window into the darkness.

Another tingle.

I woke up when it was only just getting light. Was that a trickle, or a roar? – too hard to say. I jumped off the bunk, nudged Cheyne and Patrick, and went to look…

It was a trickle. We should have known. But this morning it was cold and, at long last, there was a wind – the stiffest offshore I'd ever felt. Back in Wales, our prevailing weather patterns meant the only stiff winds we saw were usually south-westerlies – onshores. The idea of a strong offshore wind bringing in swell was unusual to me, but then so was the prospect of hundreds of yards of grinding frontside perfection.

There was a little bit more swell this time too. Enough that the odd two-footer was hitting the debut section of Supertubes and breaking. It wasn't proper J-Bay by any means, but we had to go in.

The waves were faster than they'd looked from land – almost too fast to keep up with at first. Not long later, the number of people in the water had risen to almost twenty. I remembered the crowd dynamics of Pavones, and thought about how this session could give me a chance to get an early look at some of the people we'd be sharing the water with over the coming swell. To tell the truth, I'd never felt so competitive in my life. When it really broke there would be a lot of us, and I was buggered if one of the unfortunate souls who didn't manage a good wave count was going to be me.

As if the powers that be had read my mind, one of the best waves so far showed at the Boneyards reef. I acted fast, paddling like mad towards it. Someone was further up the point than me, therefore having right of way on any wave, but I knew he was too deep to get on this one, and kept monitoring him out of the corner of my eye. He didn't take off, leaving me free to go. The wave walled up well at about waist-high, and I took a high line for a hundred yards of uninhibited speed. A section later, and still on the wave, I realised this was the furthest down the point anything had broken yet, and definitely entering the main racetrack of Supertubes. Still it kept going, tearing down the point and providing little opportunity for any turns at all, until a brief break in pace, which somehow I was ready for, sticking my board on rail and starting a cutback. Almost straight away, though, the wave walled again, and redirecting out of the cutback my fins lost grip, and the board free-fell half a foot back to the bottom of the wave. It was all about instinct now, and I crouched, sticking an arm into the wave face without thinking. The lip came over just enough to give me that circular, twisting tube sound, like a plane going overhead but mixed with the sound of rushing water. As I sped up again it clipped my head, leaving me with cool water running off my fringe. The wave then ran aground, obviously lacking the size to get any further down towards the second half of Supertubes, but already it was a new surfing experience.

Surely that was something like it, I thought, wading in through the rocks to walk back up the beach, stoked beyond belief. This had to be the beginning of the swell.

Something that I'd always struggled with while travelling was being able to concentrate on enjoying the actual moment of being somewhere. I think I read about it in a philosophy book once, and just let it nag at me ever since. People journey thousands of miles to see things they've always dreamt of, and often end up thinking too hard when the moment finally comes, unable to get something else out of their mind – an itch, headache, or pressure to find some sort of nirvana-esque fulfilment from something they've over-hyped. Sometimes expectation is simply not lived up to. That wasn't going to be a problem here, though – the act of surfing a wave for so long in one go clears your mind so completely that you've no time for any of this junk. You are participating in the moment rather than observing.

The wind was hammering off the dunes now, and it was freezing. The crowd was really starting to build too, and I didn't fancy my chances of getting another wave like that again – it would take a fair bit of luck for another to break like it *and* for me to be in position again. After all, in official J-Bay terms, there was still no surf. Wandering back up the point torn between quitting the session while I was ahead or trying for more, the decision was made by another factor altogether.

'Hey, Tom!' Two people were waving at me from the boardwalks. After a moment of squinting, I realised who they were. Derek and Stuart.

'No way! How have you guys ended up here?'

'Stuey's got some work to do in Cape Town, and I had the week off so I've come for the ride,' Derek explained. Stuart had an important administrative role in a big supermarket chain, and was often sent around the country for meetings. He'd seen a chance to try and score J-Bay at the same time as fulfilling his professional obligations. There was a problem, though – his schedule only allowed him one day at Jeffrey's, and he'd picked the wrong one.

'We looked at all the charts we could,' he moaned. 'And our call was for it to come up today. Looks like we've got it wrong – tomorrow's probably going to be the one.'

'Gutted,' I sympathised.

'Yeah, but that's life. We'll get it again.'

'You're in for a good one, though, bru,' said Derek. 'We've been praying for you to have it at its best. You'll really have fun if it breaks four to six foot – that's what we've been asking for you to get.'

'And...? Is that what I'm on for?'

'Well,' he paused dramatically. 'I'd love to say it was, but by the looks of things you're probably in for six to eight!' They were trying to wind me up a bit, though it was probably true. Derek loved the thought of me managing a big swell there, and I knew it. He'd been so stoked for me that morning when we went south and they coaxed me into some huge surf. If I made a good go of serious J-Bay, it would be partly Derek's achievement too. Perhaps it would ease his pain at not being there himself.

'Well, I say bring it on anyway, boys,' I told them. 'I've come this far and I'm not going to shy away when it finally happens.' I hoped I was right.

'That's the attitude.' Derek smiled with pride.

They were going to leave for Cape Town that afternoon – Stuart needed to be present and accounted for by the following morning – so I went for some lunch with them. We sat outside a small restaurant that served simple, healthy dishes, hugging ourselves inside thick coats. Just twenty-four hours ago we'd have been enjoying the sunshine. While we sat and talked, a skinny guy in his forties or fifties came up to us. He had an untended-to beard way down his chest, like a hippie or a Viking, and an old white T-shirt with a crude drawing of a swordfish on it and some Japanese writing. A peak hat with sides was tied around his long, light brown hair, and his sandals clapped against his heels with every step he took.

'Good day, boys,' he cried out. 'The wind is in the air, and soon, soon, soon we'll be…' He stopped to look around him, as if he'd just heard something that no one else could, before dropping into a whisper. 'Soon, my boys, the swell will be here.'

Derek and Stuart seemed to know him. He smiled at us and then walked across the adjacent car park.

'Who was that?' I asked them.

'That was Bruce Gold,' Stuart explained. I remembered Grant joking about this colourful character on our little boat ride. Apparently, he was one of the earliest guys to surf the place, and still rode it with unparalleled style when he could be bothered.

'You'll see a lot more of him if you stick around.'

They dropped me back at Supertubes before making their way south.

'If you see a real thick one hitting the point a bit further down, with a bit of the Impossibles swing in it, take off on it for me,' Derek said as they pulled away.

Heading back out to the boardwalks to check the surf, I noticed the dropping tide had held back the swell from building any more. The wave I'd caught earlier was still about as good as it had got so far, and it didn't look like there was going to be another like it for a while.

It started raining soon after, the thick cloud cover bringing darkness over J-Bay a half-hour earlier than the day before. And still there was the wind. After sharing with Cheyne and Patrick a basic meal of pasta, tuna, chopped tomatoes and cheese, I retired to my bunk to read, stretch and prepare for the morning.

Never far away from being wide awake, I lay there most of the night listening for the sea. At about three in the morning Byron, a South African guy who'd arrived from Cape Town that afternoon, came back from a night out and fell off his bunk giggling. He ended up sleeping on the floor and snoring loudly. An hour or so later I finally made it to sleep. But then Cheyne woke me, while it was still dark.

'I've been to the balcony, and there's no doubt at all this time. It's a roar!'

I was up in seconds and heading out into the half-moonlight to listen. Unmistakable. The Indian Ocean had, in the past few hours, taken on a new character altogether. It was too dark to see much, but we both knew that J-Bay had finally come to life.

'What time is it?' I asked him.

'Shit, it's like four-thirty. It's not gonna get light for ages!'

'No way am I gonna be able to sleep now.'

'Nah, nor me.'

We paced up and down the communal front room and kitchen complex, mugs of cheap tea in our hands, trying desperately to restrain our nervous ambition.

'What time's it light?' Cheyne enquired.

'Dunno. It looks a bit brighter already. Let's take a walk.'

'Good idea.'

We half-ran out of the hostel and up to the end of the cul-de-sac that led onto the boardwalks. Three cars were already parked up. Two were empty with clothes flung wildly across the front seats – their owners clearly in the water. The third had two surfers sitting against the open boot trying to creep into their wetsuits without making any sound at all.

'Is it working?' I asked the obvious, squinting in the direction of the point, along which it was now possible to make out lines of breaking swell.

'Shhhhhhh,' came the whispered reply. 'Keep it down, we don't want people to get up any quicker. Yeah, it's absolutely cooking down there. The swell's come in overnight. It's gonna be a sick day of surfing.'

The sun was still at least half an hour away from rising, but already the land towards Port Elizabeth on our left was starting to glow slightly. These guys were going out into virtual darkness, though – something I wasn't so sure about trying myself.

'Hmm, perhaps we should wait until sunrise,' I suggested to Cheyne.

The other two surfers, now fully suited and waxing up, looked at me. One said, 'Bru, if you wait, you're gonna be the *only* person in town who does!'

He was right, what was I thinking? We ran straight back to get into our suits.

The early glow on the eastern horizon must have been very premature indeed – by the time we got ready, it was still no lighter. Cheyne made two more cups of tea, which we drank in the dark, killing another quarter of an hour or so, before stepping nervously out into the street, across the boardwalks and onto the cold sand.

We could make out a few people in the water, and two more surfers walking back up the point, presumably having already ridden a wave down. Without further fuss I pushed off the rocks and started paddling for my life. The swell was at least head-high, and as clean as you could have hoped for. There were five others in the line-up besides Cheyne.

And then, just like that, my first set of real J-Bay gold feathered on the horizon.

One of the other surfers took the front wave. I could have probably gone myself, but was eager to see someone else do it first. The takeoff looked easy enough, but from there it was still not quite light enough to see the rest of the ride. The only way to do that would be through first-hand experience.

Cheyne went on the next one, a beautiful looking wave with not a drop of water out of place. I had to be next.

Mine looked identical to Cheyne's, lining up seamlessly across the entire point, with an orangey dawn glow stirring across the face as it moved through the glassy surface. *Keep calm, now paddle*, I muttered under my breath, and then *pop*, up and riding. The speed made it all easy, and I held onto the longest bottom turn I'd ever done. You didn't need to see the wave properly at all – it had its own way of communicating with you. As if there was an afterburner under my back fin, the board accelerated out of the bottom turn and into the next section with barely the need to move. On any other wave the obvious thing to do when travelling that fast would be to blast the lip as hard as you ever had in your life, but already the next twenty yards of water had stacked up and begun to pitch too top-to-bottom for that to be possible. I revved across it, staying about a foot from the curl, before setting my outside rail slightly in order to drop back down the face, avoiding the next pitching section by millimetres. I could have tried to pull into it, but where was the rush? J-Bay was good enough like this for now.

Hitting the flats at the bottom of the wave, I had momentum to burn. My next bottom turn could be delayed as long as I wanted, or so I thought. But already the next section was standing up. The drive back up the face had to be cut short, because my board could barely hold the speed. After two or three more attempts to joust with the lip, the wave was running away from me, the water in front draining off the rock bottom like river rapids. I kicked out – way out, getting launched six feet into the air and landing safely in the deep water behind. Buzzing all over, I started paddling back up the point. There was no sign of Cheyne, and I didn't know where to come in across the rocks in order to walk it like the other guys. It didn't matter, though – a good paddle could wind me down again anyway.

The sets were coming constantly now, and every one of them was being ridden. Sunrise had broken just moments after the end of my first ride, bringing the full jaw-dropping spectacle into sight. It was awesome. The wave was marching down the Supertubes section, the pitching lip chugging flawlessly the whole way. Cold water has a higher density than warm, and this further intensified the power. Like me, a lot of other people were just about managing to stay ahead of it, only fitting in the odd turn in places where the wave was definitely going to allow it. In *The Search*, Tom Curren had got tubed and done several big carves on his first ride here, although how he managed that level of control in such intense circumstances was a mystery, and too much to think about for the moment.

The only way to cope, I realised, was going to be to catch another one – that would stop me thinking too much.

It didn't take that long to paddle back towards the start of the wave. Once I reached one section away from the end of Boneyards and the beginning of Supertubes, the next chance came almost immediately.

A goofy-footer went for one, but was too far back to make it onto the face. He knew he was going to get no further, and jumped off. I was next in line and spun around to go.

It was the same format of ride all over again. All I could do was try to get used to the speed. Bottom turns were no longer necessary in the way I'd always used them, needing to be much more drawn out, and quite how to successfully hit a lip that was changing shape so rapidly without getting flipped head over heels was a mystery to me. Primary objective was to keep making the sections, bleeding off the speed when necessary to hold the perfect J-Bay line. More often than not that required you to take the highest track on the wave face that you could get your board into. This was like surfing's equivalent to off-piste downhill. A totally new wave-riding feeling and approach.

This was it. One very important part of a lifelong goal had just been completed. I was surfing J-Bay; now all that was left to do was to try to surf it well.

Ride, paddle up the point, ride, paddle up the point, and still all I could do was work at keeping up with the wave. Some of the other surfers in there knew exactly what they were doing though. An hour into the session, while getting washed around by a bigger set, I recognised a guy from Durban up and riding. He was driving high across the first section into a big barrel, escaping just before it pinched shut. Racing ahead of the lip, he gently faded his way back down, killing off most of his speed with a hard bottom turn, and setting up for a second tube. This time the wave stayed open, getting hollower and faster. The guy flew out of it a few seconds later, and careered past me into another sucking wall. As I pushed my board away and dived deep under the whitewater, there was just enough time to see the lip pour over him a third time. Ten minutes later I saw him paddling back up the point in a state of utter delirium.

After a while I noticed Patrick in the line-up, and Byron, the Cape Towner who'd stumbled in drunk a few hours ago.

'Your head must be feeling sore,' I suggested.

'Nah, bru. Just a few beers to get to sleep properly, eh!' He coughed a hard, tar-filled clearout, spat yellow phlegm into the water and then changed the subject. 'Surf looks good.'

'Yeah. It's pumping.' The dropping tide was making the waves really dredge out now, and some were frighteningly hollow. 'You surfed here before?' I asked.

'Jeez, yeah. We try to come several times a year.' As Byron spoke, someone up the point blew out of a bomb set, leaving him next in line. A little sleepy perhaps, he accidentally left it too late, paddling dazed into a double-overhead wave. As it pitched, he was hanging under the lip, but this didn't faze him at all. He simply jumped to his feet and swooped into an airborne take-off, connecting the edge of his board to the water at the last possible minute, and only just in time to lock into a desperate bottom turn as the wave broke on his head. A violent shower of spray hammered down on us, lifted off the back of the wave by the strengthening wind, and when it cleared I looked to see if Byron had managed to stay on his feet. He had, as demonstrated by the huge chunk of water that his pivoting board slapped out of the next breaking section.

'That guy fuckin' rips, eh?' said a young Australian face I recognised from the hostel next door to us. Just about every person in the entire area was in the water by now.

This made the idea of breakfast very enticing – we early birds had secured our fix by now. One more wave, I decided, and it was time to have a go at finding the way in. It wasn't as difficult as expected. There was an eccentric, half-triangle-shaped house in the dunes a few hundred yards down from the boardwalks, and another tailor-made gap in the reef lay just in front of it – exactly like the one that let you into the line-up at the top of the point. As I let some waning whitewater push me gently through the keyhole, Cheyne was already on the sand.

We evaluated our first session favourably: no major wipe-outs, no aggression attracted from anyone, but plenty of waves and a feeling that we hadn't been overly cautious. I'd spent years surfing my way up to this, and was here to make the most of the opportunity. Over the next few weeks, my goal was to start learning how to *surf* J-Bay, as opposed to merely riding it.

An hour later, we were sipping at post-breakfast coffee in a café just up the road, feeling pleased with ourselves and thinking about when to hit the water again. Byron came in from his session and sat down to order some food for himself.

'What a wave, eh, boys!' he remarked, brimming with national pride, just as anyone would be.

'Incredible,' I replied. 'How good was that by J-Bay standards?'

'Oh, it's hitting about sixty per cent at the moment. In a few days the sand in the point will move around a bit, and then it'll get better. Mind you, it'll be harder to catch waves once they start peeling longer, because people won't be getting shut down as often – there'll just be one long, perfect section from start to finish. You boys will be all over it, though. For sure.'

I was taking a liking to this Byron character. He was big and loud, with a brashness that entertained those in his company, but which might have seemed cocky or attention-seeking to others.

'Hey, waiter!' he called. 'Do you want to come and play tennis with these eggs? What else d'you expect me to do with this – eat it? Don't make me laugh, bru. You oaks must know what "over-easy" means. Jeez!'

★ ★ ★

J-Bay's contribution to the way we ride waves today is immeasurable; its place in the story of the glide cannot be overstated. I'd just paddled out and surfed one of the defining surf spots of an age, and it was hard not to be overwhelmed by the occasion.

Two hundred yards behind us was where Terry Fitzgerald had performed his timeless, soul-arching, hyper-extended bottom turn (the epitome of 'grace under pressure'), Mark Occhilupo his ballistic backhand attack in the 1984 Billabong Country Feeling Classic contest and Tom Curren his flawless first ride there at the beginning of the nineties. We had just surfed the same break in which Kelly Slater pushed the outermost limits of gravity on his way to breaking every record competitive surfing has, and where Derek Hynd had conducted his well-known experiments with a range of obscure surfboard designs. Jeffrey's Bay brings the best elements of style and creativity out of a surfer, and I was now hoping it could do the same for me.

I remembered those young Durban surfers who followed the trail taken by the crew of Bruce Brown's *The Endless Summer* – the original tale of surf exploration that had led to the discovery of the nearby point at Cape St Francis, now known as 'Bruce's Beauties'. Lacking in the exploration infrastructure of the large and meticulously planned American film crew that had preceded them, these young South Africans soon got lost and ended up in what was then a small fishing village just beyond Humansdorp, an inconspicuous cluster of buildings named Jeffrey's Bay. At the end of that village was a point break that looked ten times better than the *Endless Summer* one, and that was that.

Since then, J-Bay has become a wave of dreams – those thick, fast speed walls the stuff of fantasy. Better than snowboarding, skateboarding, wakeboarding; any of the impostors that have sprung up to try and eliminate the need to paddle out. It is a water luge, an oceanic freight train. Power and symmetry beyond belief. It's Indo without coral cuts, the Philippines or Mentawais without malaria.

Thou shalt go, I'd told myself, once I'd been surfing long enough to know what a good wave was. And here I had come. For once, it was time to stop looking forward to other surf trips, stop reminiscing about ones past. This moment needed to be taken for what it was, absorbed to last forever. These waves I had to keep, and take with me for the rest of my surfing days.

'To tell the truth, though, bru, nobody's yet managed to ride it better than the dolphins do,' said Byron. 'That food was bloody awful,' he added. 'Let's get out of here and hit the water again.'

En route to go-out number two, Byron told me a little more about the older days of J-Bay. About how during the early years, the right-wing white supremacists had hated the laid-back, tolerant attitude of the camping surfers.

'Mind you, they probably had a point. My old man and his buddies reckoned oaks used to hang out in the dunes whacking up on heroin and then surfing high as kites. Imagine six- to eight-foot J-Bay off your face with just two or three others in the water!'

He told us how they'd felt on learning Tom Curren was on his way just after the fall of apartheid and the lifting of sanctions; and then a bit about Bruce Gold and the other pioneering surfers from his generation – guys who'd turned up with nothing and spent their whole lives just riding J-Bay.

'And most of them have still got nothing,' he explained. 'But they've led lives some of us would kill for, eh?'

We suited up and headed for the jump-off spot in the rocks. On the boardwalks we saw Bruce himself, just coming out, his greying beard dripping with seawater. He still had a hat on, which he'd worn during the session.

'Hey, Welshie!' He smiled at me. 'You boys getting some good ones?'

'Yeah, awesome,' I replied. Good surf robs you of vocabulary – this must have been the twentieth time I'd given that answer so far today.

'Well, make sure you go into town and sign the book...'
He presumably meant the Trawlers Café guest book we'd so
far failed to find.

'OK, you'll have to tell us where it is.'

'I will. You're staying a while, right?'

'Yeah.'

'First things first, eh; enjoy your surf.'

'I will. Thank you.'

'Goooood.' Bruce smiled at the three of us. He had one
of those highly animated South African accents – highly
animated and highly contagious.

A few minutes later, I was in the line-up and stalking for
waves once more. Staying alert, it wasn't long before I was
again plunging into another J-Bay magic carpet ride.

At the end of a long one, many surfers were choosing to
walk back up the point, rather than paddle. But this early into
my time here, the novelty of watching the wave as I made
my way back up the line-up had not begun to wear off. J-
Bay thunders down the point like nothing you've ever seen
before. When you've just kicked off the ride of your life, and
are a long way down towards Impossibles, the sight of four
or five mechanically formed tubes grinding along in uniform
succession is like a mirage, only as you paddle further towards
it, nothing changes – it's real. During those paddles I kept
resorting to a tried-and-tested mind technique: *Right, now
look around, here you are. J-Bay [breathe]. Look around [breathe],
take it in, feel this moment, 'cause you'll be gone soon.*

This wasn't so easy to do while actually up and surfing
waves. One of the things I'd looked forward to here was the
prospect of rides so long you had time to think – to construct
ideas *as you rode*. How naive that had been! At this stage J-
Bay required far too much concentration to think anything
more than that which came instinctively. Rides there were
like a form of advanced meditation, and incredibly draining
on both mind and body.

After another two surfs that day, I slept like a baby come nightfall. A sleep so deep you could have a thousand dreams, or maybe more – one for every good wave ridden in my life to date.

I rode J-Bay during the best part of all available daylight hours for the next week and a day. During that time, all waves began rolling into one, and my entire body and mind began aching from constantly paddling and riding waves. It was a relief when the swell finally dropped to waist-high, allowing for a few beers and the prospect of a day's rest.

In one of the town's late-opening bars, Cheyne, Patrick, Byron and I bumped into Bruce Gold. Once again he'd made his mind up that we unequivocally had to 'sign the book as soon as possible'.

'Bru, I've been watching you throughout the swell. D'you know, you can read a guy's personality from watching him surf, and the one thing I know about you is that your mission won't be complete here unless you go and sign that book!'

There was now nothing I was more up for than a half-cut conversation with Bruce about the intricacies of putting together a truly perfect Jeffrey's ride. Over several more beers we talked about Curren's end-of-apartheid wave, Occy's backhand, Slater's cavalier lip-dance, the Fitzgerald soul-arch, the local rippers and much more. I told him my story about deciding to come here a decade before, and he was visibly moved.

We talked about peoples' learning curves at J-Bay – how some surfers were faster than others at working the place out – and we talked about the speed line, board design and the future for the wave (he was pessimistic about the potential overdevelopment of the town, and even claimed buildings on the dunes were stopping sand blowing into the reef like it used to, gradually altering the shape of the wave).

As the night moved on, the conversation ended with a descent into what was either deep surf philosophy ('philo*surfy*', as Bruce called it), or total gibberish. I have a drink-blurred memory of commenting on drawing the perfect speed-arc, implying I had either thought far too hard about one bloody wave, or otherwise hit on some form of absolute truth. But the response I recall clearly. A long, understanding stare and then: 'Welshie. Sign that book!'

A pat on the shoulder, a slight tipping forward of his beer bottle and Bruce was off, in search of somewhere to dance. We let him go.

Two days later, most of which were spent sleeping and eating, the second swell arrived.

I felt like a veteran by now, the two days off from surfing really clearing my mind, and focusing me on the job.

'It can take a lifetime to find and ride the perfect wave here,' Grant had told us one morning, as he stared out to sea and waxed up a 6'7" round-pin. I hoped to be getting closer, now starting to put turns into my rides, opening up for myself another dimension of J-Bay surfing.

It struck me as funny – once the quest for the perfect wave was complete, you still had the much tougher ambition of finding the perfect *ride* to keep you occupied – or perhaps that was what made it the perfect wave: the fact you could never master it.

That said, some of the older locals surely weren't far off. They rode boards somewhere in the 7'0" to 8'0" range, with pin-tails built for straight-line speed. One man in his fifties was paddling into waves from way back up at Boneyards, sticking himself right in the crux of the breaking curl and racing all the way through to Impossibles on every one. He'd then get out and walk back up the beach, wearing a face of total concentration, before paddling out at the top of the point and doing it all over again. His sessions lasted hours – longer than guys who were half his age.

And then there were the dolphins – the most hard-core locals of all. Byron had been right. Sometimes up to ten times a day the line-up would get invaded by pods of them, hooking into the wave at the start of Supertubes, and surfing all the way down. Sometimes they'd pop out into the air, using the swell's momentum to turbo boost higher than they normally would in open ocean, while other times they'd zigzag mid face, pulling out the back just as Impossibles shut down, and blowing air out of the deep water behind, before swimming back up the point to do it all over again. They'd ride single waves in packs, or they'd hog them to themselves. Sometimes they'd even join a lucky surfer along the way. They had the added virtue of scaring away sharks too.

'If there're lots of dolphins around then you've no chance of getting chaa'd by a shark,' Byron claimed. J-Bay's shark-attack record was much lower than most other spots in South Africa – which, given the numbers that surf there, must add weight to this theory.

It was inspiring to see the dolphins ride waves, but the most exciting interaction with them for me was when they swam past you in the line-up, occasionally taking air right next to you. These animals had been surfing J-Bay for hundreds and thousands of years before humans, and their presence seemed to confirm all that felt inherently right about my quest to ride there.

A few more swells came and went, and each time I was getting more in sync with how to surf Supertubes. My turns were getting progressively tighter, and I was learning the wave and its moods. I'd ridden it mellow and clean-faced, wild and windy, thick and angry. But my visa was running out, along with cash resources. As I always knew it would, my time in South Africa was coming to an end. Before leaving I had to sign 'the book', and by now it was safe to say I could think of enough to write about J-Bay.

Grant dropped me into the town centre during my penultimate afternoon in the country, and gave me directions to Trawlers Café. A tiny fish 'n' chip bar – extremely modest in comparison to some of the other eateries in town, but a place that had been here since the beginning. A black woman with a warm expression was sitting behind the counter listening to a dusty, pocket-sized radio. You had to ask for the book, as it was safely kept behind the till – there weren't a lot of pages left empty, which is one reason why Bruce had been so emotional about it. I flicked through for a while, tracking down the names and comments of all sorts of pros and legends – all raving about some of the best waves they'd ever seen in their lives, and vowing to come back again and again. Some of these people had been all over the world, discovered and pioneered spots everywhere, but still maintained J-Bay had no equal. This little artefact contained decades of international stoke.

Arriving at the current date and the next free page, I scrawled something about how the place had brought me to a new level of surfing experience, about the pushing of boundaries and the sight of a perfect wall coming at you as you paddled back up the point, all the while trying not to think too hard so that it would still read like a natural response to the wonder of J-Bay. Before signing, I took a moment to look back over my comments – these three thoughts were obviously the main components of my J-Bay story, and the essence of what I was going to take away with me. Not wanting to get too sentimental, or to embarrass myself by having too much of a moment in this discreet shack, I went ahead with a signature, adding *Cymru am byth* – 'Wales forever' in Welsh – for good measure, then closed the book and handed it back over the counter.

I bought some chips, and walked back in the direction of the main road to Supertubes, looking for someone to hitch a lift with.

There were waves that afternoon at the point, although it was getting smaller again, and I surfed. I didn't want to know what the conditions would be like tomorrow, afraid to think that it could be my last session. I knew it was likely, given past swell patterns, that it would decrease further, probably prompting a lay-day.

The ending was just as I'd hoped it would be; insignificant enough to be open-ended, with a return to J-Bay one day in the future inevitable.

A woman who was a friend of Grant took me to my flight for a small fee, after a lazy, swell-starved morning. She advertised herself as running a regular airport taxi, and she may well have been telling the truth. She had a tiny, two-door car which barely held my board and luggage, and took her toddler son, complete with his entire toy collection, along for the ride.

The surf wasn't up to much the morning we left for Port Elizabeth airport, and it was a sunny day. Summer was making a sporadic return – a bad sign for surfing.

'It won't last long; maybe even a matter of hours,' my 'taxi' driver informed me. 'There's another front coming soon, and another swell.'

'When I get home summer will be in full swing, just about,' I told her.

'Do you guys get a summer?'

I left J-Bay, as had been my goal, with no regrets. The plan, from my point of view, was executed perfectly – plenty of prior experience of travel and foreign waves and a good idea of how to do it right, all resulting in a high wave count, and a successful journey to the surf spot of my dreams. I was on a high, and almost relieved to finally get some bad luck.

That came in the form of a jobsworth check-in supervisor, who told me there was a charge for the surfboard. I knew this not to be the case.

'Sir, there is a charge, and if you don't pay it you'll have to leave that board here.'

'I checked with the airline when I phoned to confirm last week. There's an optional insurance charge, but no mandatory fee.'

'Whoever gave you your information was not straight with you. It's going to cost...'

I decided to spin a little story. 'Look. I've got no money left. That's why I'm shipping out. I'm a pro surfer. I've won nothing here, and have got a really important contest to fly to, and can't borrow boards off someone there, because they won't work right for me. I need those boards to make *this* flight...' Who was I trying to kid? Did I really just say that?

It didn't work anyway.

'Board-s?' The guy's lips began to form an evil grin. He'd got me.

'No. I meant *board*. Just the one.'

'Let me take a look.'

Shit!

Surfers had brought all this on themselves. The way it used to go was you broke your board on a trip, then put it in your boardbag to fly home. When you arrived the other end you opened the bag at the airport to check everything was OK, and then claimed the baggage handlers had snapped it and promptly demanded compensation. Because so many had done it, airlines were now wising up to the trick and charging for board-carriage – to cover the compensation costs being paid out. Either that or they were asking you to sign disclaimers before they checked boards in.

Anyway, the guy found three boards in my bag – not one – as I knew he would, and decided to treble the charge. I really did have no money, so it wasn't funny. But the pro surfer nonsense ended up saving me in a way.

'If it's true you really do need these boards tomorrow in England...'

'Wales.'

'Wales. If you really do need them, the only way you can do it is to take two, and leave one as a deposit. When you pay our London office the fee, we'll ship your other board over.'

'Done.' I pulled out the most battered of the three, and left it at the desk, never to be reclaimed. Its value was probably less than the excess charge anyway. I boarded the short internal hop to Johannesburg with a vision that the next person to ride it would be some stoked kid, just learning and in need of a handout – like the little chap at Pavones. Either way, my dearly beloved Luke Young 6'2" was soon to be hundreds of miles behind me, and thousands of feet below. Oh well, I couldn't stay, but the board could. Lucky for some.

International departure lounges are funny places. I find that people wander around coldly frowning at each other, as if to imply that their purpose and destination is far superior to anyone else's. Either that or you meet really friendly travellers perhaps nervous of flying and keen to talk. Standing in the queue at Jo'burg to board the flight to London, most of the other passengers didn't want to come near me. My clothes looked old and cheap, and I had the wild-eyed look of someone who'd been up to no good – or at least that's how it felt. I bought some sweets and an overpriced copy of *Surfer Magazine* on a credit card, and decided not to open it until in the air.

When I did start reading, the magazine turned out to be a special travel issue. It wasn't long before I was buzzing with excitement again. I pressed my forehead to the cold window and stared from above the clouds at the blood-red African sunset.

J-Bay had fulfilled everything asked of it. I'd realised it would some time ago, but still it surprised me – usually things you wait so long for are anticlimactic. Perhaps it was the fear of a life with this ambition ended or killed off that had led me to postpone it so many times. I needed to get comfortable with the idea of completing the quest that had given me an excuse for such fulfilment along the way, before being ready to bring it to an end. And anyhow, my enjoyment of it would have surely been less if I'd gone immediately after leaving school. Lack of experience, no knowledge of how to ride waves like it – these had to have been dealt with first.

Pavones was in the magazine. Would that be the next trip? I did have unfinished business there, for sure. I wanted to shout out, or to leap and run up and down the cabin. There was still so much more of the planet left to surf. The beauty of surf travel was the never-ending variety of the destinations; developed or virgin, cold or warm, dark or light water. You could alternate languages and cultures, and all the time the waves would change. And of course, there were going to be more waves like Jeffrey's out there too – spots so awesome that they'd give you that feeling of total absorption, and live up to everything expected of them...

France was in the magazine too, and Australia – all the usuals. There was a little section about surfing Japan, and stories about people going to China and Iceland. Another crew had been to Pacific Russia. It looked cold, but exotic. The next pages concerned the tropics: the Caribbean, more wild islands in Indo, a barrelling Mexican right-hander with red-rock backdrop, the La Libertad wave in El Salvador and another somewhere in the South Seas. Then there was South America – Peru and Ecuador looked intriguing, and I remembered some friends saying they'd surfed a world-class left in Chile. The photos of the Maldives looked inviting too – small, fun waves, a bit like Lazy Lanka.

The next page showed that although likely to be the best, J-Bay was certainly not the only good wave in Africa. One Moroccan point break was doing a pretty good imitation of it. The island of Reunion, just off Madagascar, looked like a serene set-up overleaf, and then I needed to put the magazine down to stop myself overloading again. Deep breaths, calm down...

I began to sleep a little, my mind flicking through the various places I could plan another surf trip to. *La... Libertad... La... Libertad...* Had the life I'd chosen now chosen me? I remembered Tim from Germany – was he missing surfing at the moment? I compared him to Adam the Kiwi, and Lenny from California – the guy we met at Alcatraz who said he'd be a brain surgeon if it wasn't for surfing, but who smiled with total contentment when he said that all he'd done for the past ten years was either wait around in tropical countries or hang out in car parks and hostels talking shit. I was drifting off further into that sleep-cum-limbo that comes with thousands of feet of altitude and an artificially pressurised cabin.

Hours of the same routine passed by, occasionally punctuated by the odd *ping!* telling sleeping passengers in vain to re-fasten their seatbelts for turbulence. Eventually it was getting lighter outside, then there was another *ping!* and breakfast was served. I wondered what the waves were like in Porthcawl at the moment. It was going to be good to get home, but only for so long.

'Ladies and gentlemen, we are now beginning our descent into London Heathrow.' Was this the end of something? I asked myself.

And then the realisation:

'No, it's the beginning of something; it's a start.'

Glossary

6'2"/6'3": The surfboard length – surfboards are usually named after the shaper, followed by the length. For example: 'In the shop they had a nice Al Merrick 6'4", but an even nicer Luke Young 6'2".'

A-frame: See **Peak**.

Beach break: A wave **set-up** that occurs at a beach, and over a sand bottom.

Backhand/backside: Surfing with your back to the breaking wave.

Barrel: See **Tube**.

Boardies: Boardshorts – the one piece of clothing that epitomises the freedom of surf culture. Most boardies are just below knee length, and hang low on the waist. Naturally, they need to be durable, and made of water-resistant material.

Bottom turn: The basis of all good surfing, and the source of speed and good positioning; a bottom turn is the act of turning back up the face of a wave after having **dropped in**.

Burned: When another surfer 'cuts you up' and wrecks your ride, usually either by stealing your wave at the point of **take-off**, or deliberately **taking off** on a wave you are already riding.

Circus: A nickname sometimes given to the ASP World Tour.

Close-out: When a wave does not peel along in a manner suited to surfing. A wave that closes out will simply **shut down** too quickly to be ridden. Most beach breaks and reefs can be prone to closing out at lower stages of the tide, as the shallower water makes them break sooner. See also **semi-close-out**.

Corduroy: When long, straight swell lines travel across blue water in clearly visible succession the sight is often likened to the uniform grooves in corduroy material. It's not known who coined this term, but 'corduroy lines' has become a surf term in its own right – representing an ideal of the perfect surfing swell.

Dawnie: Short for 'dawn patrol'. The act of getting up at first light to surf. Some love it; some hate it – most of us feel both sentiments at the same time.

Deep: Describes a surfer's position when he/she is very close to, or even behind, the place where a wave will begin to break. If you get stuck too deep, then you may have to take a wave on the head instead of being able to catch it, unless of course you are adept enough to attempt taking-off **late**.

Dropping in: The act of descending a wave. The term can also refer specifically to catching somebody else's wave in order to make a statement of some kind. A 'drop-in' will usually be inflicted on a surfer who has been disrespectful or overly greedy. The distinction lies in the preposition attached. You drop in *to* a wave, but in the second sense you would drop in *on* a person.

Duck-dive: A technique used to dive under breaking waves while paddling out, so as to avoid getting pulled back to shore by them. Duck-diving involves deliberately sinking your board, and then pushing yourself down before it resurfaces. It's not easy!

FCS: An acronym for Fin Control System – a detachable skeg mechanism that allows surfers to chop and change fin sizes and shapes as conditions change. See also **K-Fin.**

Flats: The flat area of water in front of a wave, scientifically called the 'trough'. The 'flats' are not really part of the wave, and only the best of surfers can ride through them without losing all their speed.

Freesurfing: A term used by competition surfers to denote surfing whilst not in a contest. The number one cure for losing in Round One is usually going for a freesurf away from the contest area (closely followed by a beer or ten!).

Fronthand/frontside: Surfing face-on to the breaking wave.

Glass-off, evening: At dusk, winds often drop, making the water surface appear still and glass-like. If this happens during a swell the resultant favourable surfing conditions are known as an 'evening glass-off'.

Glissexpo: An 'extreme sports' trade show held in Anglet, south-west France every September. *La glisse* (meaning 'the slide' in English) is an umbrella term used in France to describe all sports that involve an element of sliding, such as surfing and snowboarding.

Grommet (grom): A young surfer, usually under the age of eighteen, although it can also be defined by size or age in relation to others. For example, a twenty year old on a trip with two thirty-five year olds can probably expect to still be called 'grom'.

Gun: A board designed specifically for catching and riding big waves. A 'gun', to the average challenger, is usually at least 6'7" long (they have been known to go up to 12' at elite big-wave spots), and has a more streamlined shape with a sharpened **pin-tail** so as to hold in the water when travelling at speed. One thing you do not want to be when tackling bigger waves is **under-gunned**! See also **semi-gun**.

Junky: Poor waves, but not quite poor enough to refuse surfing them. 'Junky' can sometimes be fun, if you're in the mood.

Keyhole: A gap in rocks, through which surfers can enter and exit the water at reef and point breaks.

K-Fin(s): A brand of **FCS** fins that are the signature model of multiple world champ Kelly Slater.

Late: A late take-off, or late drop, is when a surfer catches a wave from a much steeper position than common sense may normally advise – they have left it 'late' to **drop in**, taking a great risk, although late take-offs are often the trademark of very good, adventurous surfers.

Leash: A cord that runs from the surfboard and is strapped to the ankle in order to prevent losing your board when surfing.

Left-/right-hander: Describes which way a wave is peeling. A 'left-hander' will break from left to right when viewed from the beach, and vice versa.

Lip: The pitching crest of a wave or the critical section of water that is just about to tumble.

Longboard: A surfboard with a rounded nose, that is either over nine feet in length or three feet taller than its owner. Longboards paddle faster than **shortboards**, are more buoyant and need less wave power to start moving. They are less manoeuvrable, though.

Line-up: The place to sit for catching an oncoming wave. The term comes from the way surfers usually 'line up' one or more prominent landmarks (such as rocks or buildings) in order to maintain position while surfing.

Mechanical: Adjective used to describe a surf spot where most waves break with almost identical form, in the same place, every time. This usually only occurs at the best **reef breaks** and **point breaks**.

Offshore/onshore: The direction of the wind. Onshore winds blow from the sea to the land and wreck surfing conditions, while offshore winds blow the other way and cause waves to break cleanly, suiting surfers much more.

Off-the-lip/off-the-top: A basic surfing manoeuvre, for which you turn to the pitching lip and glance off it to ride back down the wave. This is sometimes also called a **re-entry**, as it involves 're-entering' the wave.

Peak: A wave that peels off in both directions (right and left) at the same time. A particularly good peak will be called an **A-frame**, as it resembles the shape of a letter 'A'.

Pin-tail: The tail end of a surfboard if it has been shaped into a pointy template that almost resembles the nose of the board. A pin-tail is designed to cope with speed, and will usually only be used on a **gun**, although some high-performance shortboards now sport 'rounded pins', the use of which is subject to much debate within the board **shaping** industry.

Point: A piece of land that protrudes out to sea. Points are always good places to start looking for waves, as they have usually formed as a result of wave impact, duly assuming shapes that deflect waves in a manner that makes them peel perfectly for surfing.

Point break: A wave that breaks along a point. Many of the world's most famous waves are point breaks, as a point usually makes waves form with uniform repetition, eliminating a lot of the hard paddling work that can go into catching waves at **beach breaks**.

Quiver: A collection of surfboards belonging to an individual surfer, all of which form an active part of his/her regularly used equipment. Pros can travel with quivers of over ten boards, while most serious travellers will have up to three – one for small waves, one for good waves, and one for big waves.

Rail: The smoothly curved side edge of a surfboard, which engages with the water during turns. Well-made rails are an essential part of a good board.

Reef break: A wave **set-up** that has a reef below its surface. Like **point breaks**, reef breaks are often more **mechanical** in behaviour than **beach breaks**.

Right/left-hander: Describes which way a wave is peeling. A 'right-hander' will break from right to left when viewed from the beach, and vice-versa.

Rip: This word has two meanings in surfing. The noun 'rip' describes a current of moving water. However, the verb 'to rip' means to surf extremely well. The origin of the latter probably comes from the way good surfers are often described as 'ripping a wave to shreds' – hence the term **shred**.

Re-entry: See **Off-the-lip**.

Roaring Forties: A storm pattern located around the 40-degree mark in the Southern Hemisphere. A typical Roaring Forties storm will spin off the south-east coasts of Africa and Madagascar, supplying Indonesia, South Africa, Western Australia and numerous other Indian Ocean surf zones with good waves.

Rock boil: When a single protruding rock lies just below the surface and causes the clean wave face to bubble like a cauldron. A big enough rock boil can cause a wave to break completely, and rarely are they considered a good thing.

Search, The: A famous film and hugely successful marketing campaign by Rip Curl Wetsuits, which began in the early nineties with a film sequence of Jeffrey's Bay set in post-apartheid South Africa and now encompasses a ten-year-plus poster series, numerous more films and a range of travel accessories and clothing.

Section: A single stretch or unit of breaking wave. The verb can also describe a wave that stops peeling and momentarily **closes out**. For example: 'I couldn't make it to the end of that wave, because it sectioned horribly.' See also **Shut down**.

Semi-close-out: A wave that is peeling very, very fast – almost closing out – but which is still just about surfable.

Semi-gun: A board that is starting to take on a **gun** template, but which is still relatively close to the length you'd normally use in fun-sized surf. 'Semi-guns' usually have **pin-tails**, but are not quite as narrow as proper big-wave boards, and rarely exceed 7' in length.

Set/s: A group of waves arriving in succession, all of which are going to be of use to surfers – unless it's a **close-out** set, that is, in which case it's time to paddle for the horizon!

Set waves: The biggest/best waves coming through that day.

Set-up: A coastal feature that looks like it may produce a surf spot, be it a finger of rock, a point or a sandbar.

Shape: A word sometimes used for a surfboard: 'Hey, that's a nice shape you're carrying there.' The verb 'to shape' denotes the act of making a surfboard by hand. A wave can also be described as having a good shape, meaning the wave is suited to surfing, but in that sense the word is self-explanatory.

Shaping/shaper: As stated above, shaping is the art of surfboard making. Most surfboards are handmade by experienced 'shapers' using a planer and sandpaper. Machines have been used to mass-produce boards in recent years, but it's not the same. How can you tell a machine that a particular **shape** goes like a magic carpet?

Shortboard: A board not usually more than a foot taller than the surfer, with a pointed nose. Unless otherwise stated, all the surfers in this book are shortboarders.

Shred: See **Rip**.

Shut down: When a wave runs away from you, leaving you locked behind a **section** with no hope of making it back onto the wave face. At some long point breaks, surfers wait for others to get 'shut down' before taking off on the next **section** themselves. See also **Close-out**.

Spit: The spray that flies out of the end of a **tube**. 'Spit' is a result of compressed air and water leaving a wave's chamber, and only really occurs in the hollowest conditions imaginable. Spit can often have another function, as the rush of air can carry 'tubed' surfers to safety.

Snake: A snake is somebody who does not wait his or her turn when surfing, but rather poaches waves of others by sneaking into the **take-off** zone ahead of them. While 'snaking' is completely legal in a surfing contest, trying it while **freesurfing** will almost certainly make you the recipient of a **drop-in**.

Stick: Surfboard. See also **Shape**.

Stinking/sick: Terms used by surfers to mean 'incredible' or 'amazing'.

Stoked: Very happy, ecstatic. In the noun form, 'stoke' refers to a state of happiness or ecstasy.

Sucky: Adjective used to describe a wave that is changing shape very quickly, pulling a lot of water out of the **flats** and pitching forward aggressively. In small conditions and with a sand bottom, 'sucky' waves are usually a good thing, but in large, **reef break** conditions... well, watch out!

Surfari: A way of describing a surf trip.

Take-off: The take-off is the specific part of the wave at which you jump to your feet and drop in. For beginners, finding a wave with an easy take-off is essential. See also **Deep** and **Late**.

Top to bottom: A wave is described as breaking 'top to bottom' when it is very hollow, heavy or powerful. The term refers to the lip of the wave pitching unhindered from the top (or crest) of the wave, to the bottom (or trough).

Tube: When a wave pitches hollow enough to ride underneath or behind the breaking lip.

Under-gunned: Arriving in a big-wave situation but not having a sufficiently long or streamlined surfboard to cope with the conditions. A horrible predicament that has led to some of the worst and best moments in surfing history.

Zooed-out: Jam-packed, crowded, difficult to catch waves. Miki Dora once described a crowded day at Malibu saying, 'It's a zoo out there', and the term has stuck ever since.

Acknowledgements

Thanks to all of the following for invaluable help in some part of the completion of this project, and the trips it describes:

Chelsey Fox at the Fox & Howard Literary Agency; Jennifer Barclay and Carol Baker at Summersdale; Rob Middlehurst, Prof Meic Stephens and others at the University of Glamorgan; all at Realm Europe and Double Overhead, especially Brad and Julie Hockeridge, Mark Schofield, Rhino Thomas and Jem Evans; the Welsh Coast Surf Club and Welsh Surfing Federation, not least Huw John, Linda Sharp and Lynda Keyward; Luke Young Shapes; Simon and Melanie Tucker at Surf Academy; Stuart 'Ed' Butler; Greg Owen and No Limit Wetsuits; Andrew, Mike and Jean Cockel; Peter Britton Photography; Val, Mike and Richard Grove; Alex Lewis at Taith Photography; Peter Price at A-frame Photography; Rhyd Lewis and Fiona Carroll; Math Hapgood; Martin John and Laura Morgan; Steve and Nicola Horn; Sinead Lawrence; Tristan, Janet and Geoff Davies; Chris Noble and Scott Maine; Christian Enns; Isaac Drought; Marc Evans and Joele Rumbelow; Anne Gallagher; Roz Marron for checking the accuracy of the drunken Scot talk; Stella Levy; Jason Hazael; Yannick, Ram, Sugath, Akalanka and Jai and Sumana in Midigama; Huw Williams; Hugo Moore; Matt Way; Tom Brown; Paul Bambridge; Pauline and Keith Lawrence; Paul Anderson, grandparents Pat and John Anderson MBE and Jane and Peter Wilson; my mother Cathy Hutcheon and her husband Dave; and my late, great aunt Dorothy Anderson for the desk and everything else.

Tom Anderson was born in Watford in 1980, but only lived there briefly before moving nearer the coast. He grew up and learned to surf in Porthcawl, South Wales, representing the country as a junior. He was educated at the University of Glamorgan, and has written for several surfing magazines, basing virtually every major life decision upon riding waves.

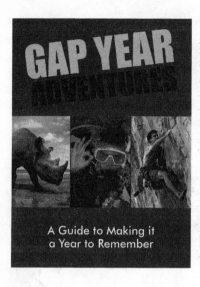

GAP YEAR ADVENTURES

A Guide to Making it a Year to Remember

Travel Guides

£3.99 Pb

ISBN: 1 84024 486 0

ISBN 13: 978 1 84024 486 1

Your gap year stretches ahead of you, begging to be filled with sun-drenched beaches, treks through exotic landscapes and thrilling exploits. How can you plan the adventures to make the most of your time out?

This essential guide is crammed with exciting ideas from around the world, from abseiling to zorbing, diving with sharks to learning yoga from the masters. Discover how to make your gap year truly unforgettable.

'practical common sense advice for anyone going travelling'

HUSH, **Cambridge University**

**BACKPACKING
SAFETY TIPS**

**A Guide to Enjoying
Any Trip Safely**

Travel Guides

£3.99 Pb

ISBN: 1 84024 492 5

ISBN 13: 978 1 84024 492 2

Backpacking adventures are all too often cut short by a stolen wallet or 'Delhi belly'. Instead, you can be aware and be prepared.

These essential tips will put your mind at rest, leaving you to concentrate on making your travels the stuff of dreams.

www.summersdale.com